SOUTH ASIAN ECONOMIC DEVELOPMENT IN THE ERA OF GLOBAL TURBULENCE

South Asia's developing nations have been enjoying moderate to high growth over the past decade before the global pandemic of 2020 began. This new edition provides an up-to-date guide to the growing markets in South Asia in the post-COVID-19 period. It offers an analysis of the changes and consequences of high sustainable growth, investigating what has been achieved in the region over the last 2001–2023 from a macroeconomic viewpoint, identifying new challenges to 2030, and the end of the UNSDGs period.

Part I of the textbook presents an analysis of how South Asia is rated against Southeast and East Asia in recent decades in economic and social terms.

Part II focuses on South Asia's economic development over 2000 and the early 2020s. It demonstrates that globalization enhanced global trade and that trade further increased the region's prosperity up to 2020.

Part III identifies major governance issues that were responsible for South Asia's social and economic underperformance due to the COVID-19 pandemic. This new edition includes a new chapter about AI and South Asia in the future. The textbook advocates for a shift in focus from policy reform *per se* to the more challenging task of implementing institutional reform that will invigorate the capability of the political leadership to bring about rapid, sustained, and poverty-reducing growth in South Asia in the post-COVID-19 era. The book also considers climate change and the environment, and it analyses the impact of these changes and developments on the economic, health, and social conditions in South Asia. The concluding chapter demonstrates current political unrest in three South Asian nations, Sri Lanka, Pakistan, and Bangladesh, termed the South Asian Spring.

Offering an analysis of the changes and consequences of high sustainable growth in South Asia, this textbook will be useful for students and researchers in Development Economics, Business Economics, Development Studies, and Asian Studies.

Moazzem Hossain currently is an adjunct Associate Professor in the Department of Business Strategy and Innovation (BSI) under Griffith Business School at Griffith University, Australia, and a former SMR professorial fellow at the University of Hull, United Kingdom. He is also the founder chairman of the University of Skill Enrichment and Technology, Bangladesh.

Eliyathamby A. Selvanathan is a professor of econometrics in the Department of Accounting, Finance, and Economics at Griffith University, Australia. He is also the director of the Economic Policy Analysis Program (EPAP) of the Griffith Business School.

Maneka Jayasinghe is a professor in economics and dean of School of Business at the Faculty of Arts and Society at Charles Darwin University, Australia.

Saroja Selvanathan is a professor of econometrics in the Department of Accounting, Finance, and Economics at Griffith University, Australia, and co-editor-in-chief of the *Journal of the Asia Pacific Economy*.

Rajat Kathuria is a professor at the Shiv Nadar Institution of Eminence, New Delhi, India.

SOUTH ASIAN ECONOMIC DEVELOPMENT IN THE ERA OF GLOBAL TURBULENCE

3rd Edition

Moazzem Hossain, Eliyathamby A. Selvanathan, Maneka Jayasinghe, Saroja Selvanathan and Rajat Kathuria

Routledge
Taylor & Francis Group
LONDON AND NEW YORK

Cover image: ©Mamunur Rashid

First published 2025
by Routledge
4 Park Square, Milton Park, Abingdon, Oxon OX14 4RN

and by Routledge
605 Third Avenue, New York, NY 10158

Routledge is an imprint of the Taylor & Francis Group, an informa business

British Library Cataloguing-in-Publication Data
A catalogue record for this book is available from the British Library

ISBN: 978-1-032-71613-8 (hbk)
ISBN: 978-1-032-71611-4 (pbk)
ISBN: 978-1-032-71624-4 (ebk)

DOI: 10.4324/9781032716244

Typeset in Times New Roman
by Apex CoVantage, LLC

CONTENTS

TABLES

FIGURES

MAPS

BRIEF BIO OF AUTHORS

Mamun Ahmed is an investment banker and entrepreneur in Dhaka, Bangladesh. Currently, he is pursuing a PhD in Data Science/Artificial Intelligence. He owns and operates top-tier financial institutions, including a leading investment bank and brokerage house. His expertise spans fundraising, issue management, underwriting, portfolio management, and full-spectrum merchant banking activities in Bangladesh's capital market. His articles and blogs appear in various social media platforms, news outlets, and online publications, covering diverse domains and genres.

Moazzem Hossain is an adjunct Associate Professor at Griffith University's Business School, Australia. He has had a long association with Routledge Publishing since 1999. He published in the first and second editions of this volume in 1999 and 2010, respectively. The third edition has now been a challenging one in post-pandemic times. In the past, Moazzem was nominated by Griffith University as the reviewer of the IPCC's two projects implemented between 2018 and 2021. His contributions at a global level with climate change issues over the last 20 years have been recognized through these appointments as one of the reviewers of the UN IPCC documents used for the preparation of the Assessment Report 6 (AR6). Moazzem is the Founder Chairman of a private university in Bangladesh called University of Skill Enrichment and Technology (USET) since 2019. He is currently holding the position of Editorship of the *Business and Economics Journal* of Springer Nature.

Paul Howard was previously the programme director for the Bachelor of Asian Studies and is a lecturer within the Department of Business Strategy and Innovation at Griffith University, Australia. He is a member of the Griffith Asia Institute. His research broadly focuses on policy and development in Asia. More specifically, his current research focuses on the political economy of sanitation in Asia with specific focus on India and Cambodia and other regional countries. The interplay between formal policy and actual outcomes for citizens is an area of his interest. He also has research interests in specific aspects of political economy and development in the region, like China's climate policy, the development of renewable energy in the region, and worker migration and development in the Mekong sub-region.

Maneka Jayasinghe is Dean of Business School and Professor in Economics at the Faculty of Arts and Society at Charles Darwin University, Australia. She has also taught previously at Griffith University (Australia). She completed her PhD at Griffith University (Australia), a Master of Economics at the National University of Singapore and B.Ec. degree at the University of Colombo (Sri Lanka). She is an Applied Economist, and her research interests include Poverty and Wellbeing, Consumer Demand Analysis, Energy Economics and Tourism Analysis. She has published two research monographs and numerous articles in leading international journals, such as *Energy Economics, Journal of Travel Research, Empirical Economics, Applied Economics, Social Science and Medicine,* and *Social Indicators Research.*

Rajat Kathuria is the dean of the School of Humanities and Social Sciences and the professor of economics at Shiv Nadar Institution of Eminence. He is the former director and chief executive of the Indian Council for Research on International Economic Relations (ICRIER), India. He worked with the Telecom Regulatory Authority of India during its initial years. He was the co-chair of the T20 Digital Task Force under India's G20 presidency. Rajat has over 20 years of experience in teaching and 25 years of experience in economic policy, besides research interests on a range of issues relating to digital markets regulation, trade, and industrial policy. He has worked with the World Bank in Washington DC, and carried out research assignments for several international organizations, including ILO, UNCTAD, Japan Economic Foundation (JEF), and ADB. He has published in international and national journals, besides in popular magazines and newspapers. He has also edited several books, including for Routledge and Springer-Verlag.

Govand Khalid is a lecturer at the School of Social Science, Macquarie University, Australia. His research interests include political philosophy, the history of ideas and theories of subjectivity, and the political economy and history of technology in the context of novel and unprecedented technological systems and power structures such as artificial intelligence, big data analytics, and biotech.

Vishal Rana is an assistant professor of management at the University of Doha for Science and Technology, Qatar, and an adjunct lecturer in the Department of Business Strategy and Innovation at Griffith Business School, Griffith University, Australia. He is an early career researcher. His research interests focus on ethical AI, work design, and innovation and entrepreneurship. He has published in esteemed blogs such as *Business & Society, the London School of Economics Impact Blog, The Qualitative Report,* and *Thunderbird International Business Review.*

Eliyathamby A. Selvanathan is the director of the Economics Policy Analysis Program (EPAP) and the professor of econometrics at Griffith University, Australia. He has also taught previously at the University of Jaffna (Sri Lanka), Murdoch University (Australia), and the University of Western Australia. He was educated with a B.Ec. (Hons) at the University of Jaffna, MSc in Operations at the University of Bucharest (Romania), and PhD in Quantitative Economics at Murdoch University and the University of Western Australia. His research interests include applied econometrics, tourism economics, consumer demand models, and stochastic index numbers. He has published ten research monographs and well over 100 articles in leading journals such as *Review of Economic Studies*, *Journal of Econometrics*, *Journal of Business and Economic Statistics*, *Review of Economics and Statistics*, *Energy Economics*, *Journal of Travel Research*, and *Tourism Economics*. Selva has held several senior management positions, including Deputy Dean (Staffing), Discipline Head, Higher Degree Research Director and Deputy Head of Department, and Deputy Director of GU Statistics and Research Design Support Unit. He was the recipient of the PVC's Research Excellence Award—HDR Supervision. He has also supervised more than 24 PhD candidates.

Saroja Selvanathan is Professor of Econometrics at Griffith University, Queensland, Australia, and the Co-Editor-in-chief of the *Journal of the Asia Pacific Economy*. She has held a number of senior management positions, including Director of Statistics and Research Design Support (STARDS) Unit, Deputy Dean (Research and Postgraduate Studies), Head of the Economics, and Business Statistics Discipline and Deputy Head of Department. Saroja is a member of the Griffith University Health and Safety Committee, Griffith Business School Promotions Committee and Griffith Business School Group Board. She has also taught previously at the University of Jaffna (Sri Lanka), Murdoch University (Australia) and The University of Western Australia. She completed her BSc (Honours) specializing in Statistics with First Class at the University of Jaffna, MPhil in Harmonic Analysis at Murdoch University, and PhD in Quantitative Economics at The University of Western Australia. Her research interests include consumer demand, time series analysis, tourism economics and applied econometrics. She has published seven research monographs and over 100 journal articles. She has received several awards in research and teaching, including *Vice Chancellor's Excellence in Research Award—Research Supervision* and *Vice Chancellor's Excellence in Teaching Award—Innovation Across the Institution*.

PREFACE

The developing South Asian nations had been enjoying moderate to high growth over the decades immediately before the pandemic COVID-19 hit almost all the economies of the globe in 2020. Living conditions improved in all nations of the region before 2008. What made this prosperity possible? It is now widely recognized that globalization enhanced global trade, and more and more trade enabled this region to further prosper. For example, commodity trade, trade with services, and expatriate workers employed in the Middle East and Southeast Asia (remittances) made a breakthrough on the growth front. While South Asia has been making strong progress, new challenges have also emerged in recent years. The most important among them is climate change, which has a devastating impact on the economic and social aspects of the region. The present global economic slowdown will not help either due to living cost crises experienced by almost all nations on earth. Like globalization, the effects of climate change and global food, fuel, and financial crises have no bounds. Thus, while the present version of South Asian Economic Development updates the economic and trade data between 2001 and 2022, the new issues of climate change, information economy, and local governance are addressed as well. As in the first and second editions, the study focuses on the four populous economies of South Asia: Bangladesh, India, Pakistan, and Sri Lanka.

One may recall that in the 1950s and early 1960s, countries such as Sri Lanka and India were predicted by prominent economists to have a bright future. It causes considerable surprise in retrospect to note that, in 1950, Sri Lanka was considerably richer than some East Asian economies, such as Korea (in terms of per capita gross domestic product (GDP) as measured in purchasing power parity (PPP) dollars). Pakistan (then East Pakistan, now Bangladesh) also had a higher per capita income than Korea. Indian industrialization started in the mid-19th century. Korean industrialization lagged by at least 50 years. Yet, Korea is now a 'high-income country' (a member of the Organization for Economic Cooperation and Development (OECD), the club of the more developed nations). It has been a member of the OECD since 1996. However, Korea suffered from the fallout of the 1997 Asian currency crisis but recovered sharply (within only three years, by 2000). The South Asian economies, on the other hand, continued to languish as 'low-income' economies until the mid-1990s. These economies, however, have been growing moderately after embracing economic reforms in the early 1990s, and subsequently the information revolution has been supporting an unprecedented telecommunications (mobile in particular) infrastructure in recent years, which has helped advance growth. It is this optimistic tale of two Asias that prompted the authors to take a renewed look at a group of South Asian economies in the present edition. Having said that, as global economies have been suffering from COVID-19 since 2020, South Asia too did not escape the slowdown and is continuing.

With the economic reforms taking place from the early 1990s, the question is: are the outcomes any better? Several studies of the World Bank in the post-reform era articulate that significant changes have taken place in at least the areas of poverty reduction and education in recent years (until 2019). Particularly in the case of Bangladesh and India, the Bank has been painting optimistic pictures. According to the Vice President of the South Asia Region of the World Bank, in 1991, 57 per cent of Bangladesh's population was living below the poverty line. By 2000, this number came down to 49 per cent. Over the period 2000 to 2005, the poverty rate further declined to 40 per cent, with around six million people lifted out of poverty (www.worldbank.org).

As far as the extreme poverty goes, the proportion of households living under a straw roof—a highly sensitive indicator of extreme poverty—fell from 18 per cent of the population in 2000 to 7 per cent in 2005. While this is certainly a phenomenal achievement for Bangladesh, the World Bank recognizes that the achievements of the East Asian and Southeast Asian nations, like China, Thailand, and Vietnam, simply cannot be matched. For example, the poverty rate in Vietnam fell from 58 per cent in 1992 to 20 per cent in 2005. In other words, the Bank insists that although the proportion of the poor in Vietnam was like that in Bangladesh in the early 1990s, it is now around less than half that in Bangladesh. The main reason Vietnam overtook Bangladesh is that Vietnam's annual rate of growth was on average 2.5 percentage points higher than Bangladesh's annual rate of growth during this period. One can make similar parallels between China and India. While India's rate of growth has been impressive since the early 1990s, it is also lagging behind China's growth by almost 2.5 percentage points annually over the decade of 1995–2005.

With such a comparative environment existing in two Asias, Part I of the present edition very closely analyses how South Asia rated against Southeast and East Asia in recent decades in economic and social terms. Part II generally deals with South Asia's economic development over 2001 and 2022. Part III identifies the major governance issues that were responsible for South Asia's social and economic relative underperformance after the COVID19 pandemic and the South Asia Spring.

This study accepts the standard refrain that the policy regime is the primary and proximate influence on growth performance. However, we believe that the ideas and ideology that drive the convictions of political leaders are important in understanding why particular notions about appropriate policies are assimilated and others are rejected. Moreover, once a given policy regime takes hold, the disengagement from failed policies of the past can easily become a slow and faltering process, largely because political influences reinforce initial policy choices. This in turn condemns economies to protracted periods of modest performance and even stagnation. Such a sympathetic and nuanced interpretation is important in understanding why the South Asian economies were unable to reach a phase of rapid, broad-based growth in the 1970s despite optimistic predictions about their future in the 1960s and even the 1950s.

This study also accepts the standard refrain that policy reform entailing macroeconomic stability, trade liberalization (including a hospitable climate for foreign investment), privatization, and deregulation and determined public action in the areas of basic education and health are the key ingredients of national economic success. This may be construed as a mere reaffirmation of current orthodoxy, but it is difficult to ignore the robust edifice of theory and evidence that has built up over decades.

This study embraces the view that economists can no longer regard themselves as technocratic guardians of neutral policy advice. This means focus must shift from policy reform per se to the more challenging task of implementing institutional reform that will invigorate the capability of the political leadership to bring about rapid, sustained, and poverty-reducing growth in South Asia given the pandemic years of 2020–2022 and now recovering. However, the present wars between Russia and Ukraine and Israel and Hamas (Palestine) made the post-pandemic recovery largely reversed. The central task now is to redirect the focus of governments in South Asia to ensure that the core functions of the state (i.e. a stable, non-distortionary policy climate; a secure foundation of law; investment in basic education, health, and infrastructure; protection of the vulnerable; and protection of the environment) are efficiently provided. At the same time, the reform agenda must be sensitive to the goal of ensuring that durable democratic institutions, traditions, and values have been preserved and corruption has been made punishable. This is a fundamental challenge, but one that must be met to secure the emergence of a prosperous South Asia in the second quarter of the 21st century.

This edition is the product of the collective efforts of five authors and a few colleagues of Griffith University, particularly in terms of planning, designing, and collecting research materials. Any remaining errors and omissions are the collective responsibility of the authors.

Brisbane 2024

ACKNOWLEDGEMENTS

Eliyathamby A. Selvanathan and Saroja Selvanathan would like to acknowledge the support provided by the Department of Accounting, Finance and Economics and Griffith Asia Institute, Griffith Business School, Griffith University, Australia. Moazzem Hossain paid a few visits to India over 2015 and 2023 too. He collaborated with Professor Rajat Kathuria of the New Delhi-based International Management Institute (IMI). Hossain also benefitted from attending several conferences of the National Association of Software and Services Companies (NASSCOM), based in New Delhi, about India's information and communications revolution since the mid-1990s.

Kathuria gratefully acknowledges the support of the Indian Council for Research on International Economic Relations (ICRIER), based in New Delhi. Maneka Jayasinghe acknowledges various research grants received from the Faculty of Arts and Society, Charles Darwin University, Australia to facilitate this project.

The works of Paul Howard and Vishal Rana of Griffith Business School were crucial in launching three new chapters: Chapters 13, 14, and 15. Govand Khalid from Macquarie University, Sydney, Australia, and Mamun Ahmed from the University of Skill Enrichment and Technology (USET), Narayanganj, Bangladesh, have contributed towards the new chapter on 'Artificial Intelligence (AI)' in this edition. We once again acknowledge their support and co-operation.

Moazzem Hossain
Eliyathamby A. Selvanathan
Maneka Jayasinghe
Saroja Selvanathan
Rajat Kathuria

PART I

Introduction

1

SOUTH ASIAN ECONOMIC DEVELOPMENT

First quarter of the 21st century

Moazzem Hossain

Introduction

The story of the four South Asian economies can be described as a case of a promising beginning that never quite consolidated into sustained economic success. They were—or at least some of them were—endowed with initial conditions that were, in many ways, better than those faced by some of the East Asian miracle economies. This is a conspicuous fact because many of the economies of East Asia—the Northeast Asian industrial giants of Taiwan (Province of China), South Korea, and mainland China; the vibrant city-states of Hong Kong and Singapore; and the dynamic Southeast Asian economies of Indonesia, Malaysia, Vietnam, and Thailand—have worldwide attention as rare exemplars of rapid, sustained, shared, and poverty-reducing growth. Admittedly, some of these success stories (such as Thailand, Malaysia, and Indonesia) have gone through a period of turbulence since the 1997 financial crisis, but one cannot be but impressed by the enduring results of the 'East Asian Miracle.' Today, South Asia is often exhorted to learn from success by 'looking east.' Yet, as Hicks (1989) notes, there was a time when prominent economists predicted that countries such as India and Sri Lanka would be the economic success stories of the post-Second World War period.

The above discussion has alluded to the type of methodology that is best suited to the analysis of national economic success or failures. One can—as this study does—adopt an explicitly comparative perspective. Alternatively, one can undertake an in-depth examination of individual countries. Both approaches have their merits, but the literature on South Asian economic development seems to be dominated by country-specific expertise (especially on India) rather than scholarship that seeks regional generalizations. In this edition we tried to include the relevant contributions in this field during the post-2000s era. Hence, one can claim it remains to be seen whether this third edition will or will not be overwhelmed by a crowded field. Having said that, in this volume the authors tried to present a story painted by how once in a century pandemic (COVID-19) affected the South Asian region since 2020 economically and the climate change making the region like other regions of the world, the economic growth suffered over the last 50 years and continues to do so to 2050 if the ambitious global objective of keeping emissions of CO_2 to zero.

DOI: 10.4324/9781032716244-2

Focus of this chapter is on initial conditions, but it also reflects on some of the reasons behind the rather gradual and hesitant disengagement from inappropriate policies of the past that lie behind the protracted period of modest performance of the economies of the region over a period of more than half a century. One hopes that such an analysis will provide a pertinent background for appreciating the agenda of reform that will occupy South Asia as it embraces the present millennium.

Initial conditions

This section develops the following themes:

- The South Asian economies were, in some respects, better off than some East Asian economies in the 1950s and 1960s—a point that was noted earlier.
- The legacy of British colonial rule that South Asia inherited was, in some respects, a boon rather than a burden when one considers the tradition of fiscal conservatism, the development of a modern civil service, and the advanced nature of industrialization, in colonial India relative to world norms.
- Having said that, one must remember that Britain left South Asia after almost 200 years of colonization in 1947, except Sri Lanka. It is civil service in the South Asian nations even now, after 77 years since colonization ended. These nations failed to make any changes; rather, many observe that bureaucracy has been more of a barrier than a boon in economic development in the South Asian region. It would sound too strong to many in the civil service in the sub-continent; unfortunately, this is what the reality was in the early period of the 21st century. The coalition of civil service together with armed forces and permanent existence of political clouts over a long time makes some parts of South Asia almost ungovernable. Most importantly, population density and some parts of South Asia for being densely populated, an effective governance becomes impossible in recent years.

Reflecting on a case of failed potential: South Asia in the 1950s and 1960s

In the 1960s, it appears that South Asian countries were seen as better performers than that of Korea.

Consider Table 1.1. It compares GDP per capita (expressed in PPP terms: US$) and basic human development indicators of Bangladesh, India, Pakistan, and Sri Lanka with South

TABLE 1.1 Initial conditions: per capita GDP and human development indicators, 1960–2023, South Asia versus Korea

Country	*GDP per capita ($PPP)*			*Adult literacy*			*Life expectancy (years)*		
	1960	*1995*	*2022*	*1970*	*1995*	*2015*	*1960*	*1995*	*2023*
Bangladesh	621	1,380	6,263	24	37	62	39.6	56	74
India	617	1,400	7,112	34	51	72	44.0	61	72
Pakistan	820	2,230	5,377	21	36	56	43.1	62	67
Sri Lanka	1,389	3,250	12,200	77	90	93	62	72	77
Korea	690	11,450	45,560 (2022)	88	95+	98	53.9	72	84

Sources: UNDP (1996, 2020), World Bank (1997, 2020), World Bank (2023–2024).

Korea (henceforth Korea)—an archetypal East Asian economy—in 1960 and 1995. The striking fact is that in 1960 Korea was poorer than Pakistan and Sri Lanka and was only marginally richer than Bangladesh and India. Yet, by 1995, Korea graduated to a 'high-income' economy (as classified by the World Bank). It became a member of the OECD in 1996 and is poised to reach the rank of 'Group of 7' (G7) nations by 2020 (Korea Development Institute 1995). The South Asian economies, on the other hand, remain laden with the dubious label of 'low-income' economies.

Another issue worth emphasizing is that in 1960 India had already achieved one of the so-called golden rules of growth as proposed by Lewis (1955), namely, that self-sustained growth requires a national saving ratio of 12–15 per cent. The saving ratio for India in 1960 was well within the Lewisian benchmark and never fell below it in subsequent years. In contrast, the national saving ratio for Korea in 1960 was apparently a mere 1 per cent (James et al. 1989: 64)!

The recent performances shown in Table 1.1 on three indicators are certainly encouraging in terms of GDP per capita ($PPP) and life expectancy for 2022–2023. All the nations had steady increases from 1995 to 2022–2023 in income and in improvements in life expectancy.

Table 1.2 extends the notion of initial conditions by focusing on the notion of 'convergence' over the 1950–1995 period—that is, the extent to which the economies being considered have, over the designated period, converged to US living standards (also measured in per capita $PPP dollars). The basic notion behind convergence is that poorer economies grow faster than richer nations (using the United States as a benchmark) and—as a result—catch up with their affluent counterparts (Helliwell 1994). As expected, there is rapid convergence in the case of Korea, but hardly any such evidence for South Asia. This simply reflects the rather different growth rates that were achieved—particularly after the 1960s. Per capita real income growth rates in the 1960–1970 period for South Asia were 1.8 per cent *vis-à-vis* 2.0 per cent—hardly a difference worth noticing. After the 1960s, the divergence became overwhelming: East Asia grew at rates (in per capita terms) that were overwhelmingly faster than Southern norms (UNDP 1996, 2020).

The case of Sri Lanka is particularly striking. Even as far back as 1950, Sri Lanka's average income was almost twice the level of that of Korea, and its life expectancy in 1960 was significantly above the developing country standard. Not surprisingly, Sri Lanka attracted the epithet of the 'best bet in Asia' (Jigging 1976). Yet, the best bet in the region simply fell behind in recent years.

TABLE 1.2 Per capita GDP of South Asian economies and Korea as a percentage of US GDP (PPP: US$ per capita) 2022, $64,623

Country	*1950*	*1960*	*1970*	*1980*	*1995*	*2022*
Bangladesh	–	8.3	7.0	6.5	5.1	9.72
India	7.1	7.5	6.5	5.7	5.2	11.0
Pakistan	9.0	7.8	8.4	7.6	8.3	8.3
Sri Lanka	11.4	10.2	9.4	9.4	12.1	18.9
Korea	7.6	8.2	11.8	24.8	42.4	70.5

Sources: Pre-1995 figures: Kravis and Lipsey (1982, Table 1.4); Helliwell (1994: 24); 1995 and 2022 figures: (World Bank 1997, 2020; World Bank 2023)

Note: Bangladesh was part of Pakistan until December 1971.

One could argue, of course, that relative income levels tell a misleading story. School enrolment rates in Korea in 1950 and 1960 were well above the norms achieved by Bangladesh, India, and Pakistan so that by 1970 the gaps in adult literacy among this group widened very sharply (see Table 1.1). Some observers highlight this difference to explain the emergence of the Korean economic miracle. Thus, Birdsall et al. (1995) calculate that if Korea had Pakistan's enrolment rate of 1960, its 1985 level of per capita GDP would have been 40 per cent lower than what was attained. Yet, there are nagging puzzles. Athukorela and Jayasuriya (1994: 29) note that in 1950, Sri Lanka's school enrolment rate was markedly higher than Korea's (54 per cent vs. 43 per cent). Why did Sri Lanka languish and fail to capitalize on its initial endowments while Korea flourished? One could invoke the incidence of internal political strife in Sri Lanka, but this really emerged in the 1980s, 20 years after the presence of growth-promoting initial circumstances!

Yet another possible explanation lies in the perennial issue of the reliability of data. The cynic could note that one is dealing with dubious statistics: Sri Lanka was simply not as well off in the 1950s and 1960s as the income figures and human development indicators suggest. While such doubts are well-founded, they are invariably difficult to resolve. It is beyond the competence of this book to offer firm judgements on the reliability of key statistics in Sri Lanka (and South Asia in general) vis-à-vis Korea (and East Asia in general). In the absence of pertinent expertise, this study seeks refuge in an agnostic assumption: while the overall quality of data varies over time, there are no systematic region-specific biases so that key statistics on country A are as good (or as bad) as those on country B.

One needs to move away from a mere emphasis on relative income levels (or even human development indicators) and provide a more complex interpretation of initial conditions by emphasizing historical legacies and institutions. It is at this juncture that one can emphasize common traditions that bind the economies of the region together—despite frequently highlighted differences in religion and ethnicity.

Evolution of South Asian economies: the role of ideas and ideology

Identifying initial and post-independence conditions represents an important and fundamental step in understanding the evolution of national economies. Such an investigation has in turn generated a central question: why has South Asia failed to capitalize on its initial endowments? Some tentative suggestions were offered in the previous discussion, but the issue needs to be re-visited in greater depth.

From the perspective of an economist, the policies that are adopted ultimately influence growth performance. The theme of this section is that ideas and ideology that drive the conviction of political leaders are important in understanding why particular notions about appropriate policies are assimilated and others are rejected. Moreover, once a given policy regime takes hold, the disengagement of failed policies of the past can easily become a slow and faltering process, largely because political influences reinforce initial policy choices. This in turn condemns economies to protracted periods of modest performance and even stagnation. Such a sympathetic and nuanced interpretation is important in understanding why the South Asian economies were unable to reach a phase of rapid, broad-based growth in the 1970s despite optimistic predictions about their future in the 1960s.

From the dirigiste doctrine to issues in governance: an overview

Soon after gaining independence from British colonial rule, South Asia—in common with many countries in the developing world—embraced a development strategy whose key components formed the substance of the so-called 'dirigiste doctrine.' This may be construed as an expression with pejorative overtones, but it is used here as a shorthand reference for a set of interrelated elements that form part of an overall policy approach. Elements include the following:

- Import-substituting industrialization (ISI)
- Extensive state intervention in financial and labour markets
- A significant reliance on state-owned enterprises (SOEs)
- A general predilection for detailed planning and regulation

It should be emphasized that the precise timing of the onset of dirigisme in South Asia varied from country to country. India moved in a resolute manner from the eve of independence. In the case of Sri Lanka, import controls really started in earnest around 1956.

The case of Bangladesh also deserves to be highlighted. It was part of Pakistan until 1971, when it emerged as an independent nation after the termination of a bitter civil war that exacted a heavy toll in terms of human lives and destruction of property and infrastructure in Bangladesh (former East Pakistan). The adoption of the dirigiste doctrine in Bangladesh owes more to the circumstances of its history than to a conscious intellectual predilection among its politicians and policymakers.

The process, as Turner and Hulme (1997: 178) demonstrate, drawing on Chowdhury (1992: 57–70), started in an innocuous fashion. The political leaders, who found themselves in power in an independent Bangladesh, traditionally espoused centrist economic philosophies. They really did not have the ideological conviction or the organizational capacity to oversee an economy that was centrally controlled. Things changed inadvertently after the nine months of bloody civil war that preceded the acquisition of independence in December 1971. The government found itself picking up the ownership and management of 725 industrial units—representing 45 per cent of the country's fixed assets in the industrial sector—because they were abandoned by their non-local owners, who (from West Pakistan) left the country. Within a few months, the government decided to embark on a programme of nationalization of jute, sugar, and textile industries owned by non-Bengalis. This pushed the state ownership of modern industry from 34 per cent in 1971 to 92 per cent by mid-1972. Furthermore, all banks were nationalized and reconstituted into six banks. The ideological basis for this development was subsequently provided by the inclusion of socialism as one of the pillars of the Constitution. A detailed analysis of the causes behind this ambitious and sudden expansion of state ownership in Bangladesh is beyond the scope of this study, but the strategic context in which Bangladesh found itself matters. Both India and the former Soviet Union were the key allies of Bangladesh during the nine-month liberation war in 1971. They supported the political leadership militarily and financially in its fight to carve out a new nation. It does not seem too far-fetched to suggest that a grateful group of politicians and policymakers felt obliged to embrace the dirigiste ideals of India and the former USSR.

With the benefit of hindsight, one can argue that the dirigiste doctrine in South Asia and elsewhere was misguided. Its inherent weaknesses have been exposed by the turbulent era of the 1970s and 1980s as issues in macroeconomic stabilization and structural adjustment became the global agenda for coping with traumatic change. Its decline has been precipitated by the dismantling of the Soviet Union and Eastern European bloc.

At the risk of some degree of overstatement, one can maintain that dirigisme lies at the root of the key problems that afflict the contemporary South Asian economies: low to moderate saving and investment (although India seems to have fared better than the regional average), low human development (with the exception of Sri Lanka), weak fiscal position of the government, SOEs, and insufficient engagement with international markets. The policy prescriptions for coping with these problems are, by now, well known. Thus, there is the need for a credible commitment to fiscal prudence as a core element of macroeconomic stability, determined public action in the areas of basic education and health, privatization and deregulation of both product and factor markets, a resolute move towards trade liberalization, the creation of a conducive climate for the acquisition of foreign capital, human development and technology, and the pursuit of regional co-operation within a multilateral framework.

A focus on comprehensive policy reform in South Asia (and elsewhere) has gradually led to the realization that economists can no longer be technocratic guardians of neutral policy advice. Considerable research efforts are being invested by scholars and practitioners in trying to identify the elusive institutional variables that underpin the policy-making capacities of governments. This evolving intellectual tradition is typically subsumed under the rubric of 'governance,' a term that tries to capture studies that focus on the ability of governments to promulgate and credibly implement appropriate economic and social policies as a means of understanding why some economies flourish and others falter.

The issue of governability has clearly infected current thinking on development policy (World Bank 1997, 2020), but one can detect antecedents of this in the 1970s and earlier (back to Adam Smith!). Bauer (1971: 27), for example, admonishes developing countries for their 'preoccupation with central planning (that) has, paradoxically, contributed to serious neglect of essential government tasks.' These early reflections have proven to be remarkably prophetic. Issues of governability occupied the 2000s and the early part of this millennium.

The intellectual roots of the dirigiste doctrine

Why were the first-generation politicians and practitioners attracted to state-led development that entailed detailed planning and regulation and a focus on domestic markets? One must understand the power of economic ideas and the way such ideas get assimilated in the political process. As Krueger (1993a: 353) acknowledges: 'There is ample reason to believe that, in many developing countries, the initial choice of an import-substitution development strategy was made by well-intentioned individuals behaving as benevolent social guardians.'

The intellectual underpinnings of dirigisme can be traced to the work of a few 'first-generation' development economists, such as Rosenstein-Rodan, Nurkse, Singer, Prebisch, and Myrdal (see Arndt 1987: Ch. 3). Bhagwati (1984) has re-interpreted this strand of scholarship as encompassing the twin notions of export pessimism and market failure. The export prospects of the primary products of developing economies were seen to be limited. In addition, international trade was seen as a mechanism of international inequality, enriching the rich nations and impoverishing the poor—a view that developed into 'dependency theory' (e.g. Furtado 1973; Sunkel 1969). The typical developing economy was also characterized by endemic market failure expressed specifically as the failure of private producers to internalize external economies (Rosenstein-Rodan 1943). Mainstream economics was belittled as a 'special case' reared in the cultural, social, and political context of Western market economies (Seers 1962). These concerns evolved to a stage where they entailed a focus on state-led, 'big-push' industrialization that relied primarily on domestic markets.

It is in such a prevailing intellectual milieu that the first-generation policymakers in South Asia and elsewhere put dirigisme into practice. The notion of autarkic industrial development was particularly influential in India through the role of Mahalanobis, 'physicist turned planner' (Arndt 1987: 76). India was one of the first—if not the first—countries in the developing world to produce a meticulously detailed development plan (it ran to 671 pages!) in 1952 (Turner and Hulme 1997: 136). It causes considerable surprise in retrospect to realize that the author of this plan—the Indian Planning Commission that was set up in 1950—became the precedent for the creation of the Economic Planning Board in Korea in 1961, but with rather different results (Haggard 1990).

The demise of the dirigiste doctrine: the early literature

It is often suggested that the tide against dirigisme turned with a landmark report on a comprehensive evaluation of ISI in seven developing economies (which included some South Asian countries) by Little et al. (1970), but one can detect dissenting voices well before the publication of this report (Rodrik 1992). To take one prominent example, Raúl Prebisch, regarded as one of the prime intellectual architects of ISI, apparently raised concerns about the viability of ISI in his later writings (Arndt 1987: 78–81). Power (1963) was one of the first applied studies of the impact of ISI. He regards Pakistan as a case of 'frustrated take-off' and pins the blame on ISI—although the prevailing perception was that Pakistan was a successful case of ISI (Papanek 1967).

Despite such examples of dissent, it would be fair to say that Little et al.'s (1970) report provided the primary intellectual ammunition against ISI. In retrospect, one is struck by the potency of its observations:

> The studies on the seven countries indicate that . . . policies that are followed to promote import substitution are harmful for the economic development of these countries. Industrialization sheltered by high levels of protection had led to the creation of high-cost industries. . . . With high industrial prices, maintained behind high tariffs, industrialization has been carried out at a high cost to agriculture. . . . Ponderous administrative control has held up decisions and has led to excessive stocks and the creation of a multitude of firms operating below capacity. . . . The most serious result of these policies, however, is that the nascent industries have come to depend on their profits on government decisions, and so have formed the habit of devoting their efforts to obtain privileges by pressure on the government rather than by cutting costs.
>
> *(Little et al. 1970: xviiiff)*

The emerging critique of ISI at the beginning of the 1970s was given a major boost by subsequent contributions (see, e.g., Bhagwati 1978). One must also note the seminal contributions of McKinnon (1973) and Shaw (1973) on the deleterious effects of interventions in financial markets that broadened the attack on dirigisme. These studies argue that such policy measures as selective credit allocation and general controls on interest rates led to 'financial repression.' This in turn had 'real sector' effects: both the volume and efficiency of saving and investment were adversely affected. The net result was a drag on growth.

Debates on interventions in financial markets continue to occupy current debates in development policy. It appears that the early enthusiasm that greeted the thesis of 'financial repression' with its clear message of the need to liberalize financial markets is being replaced by a more cautious view. There is a greater sensitivity to the complexity of the reform of financial markets and appreciation of the fact that it cannot be seen as the panacea to the economic problems that plague many developing countries, including South Asia.

The issue of interventions in labour markets, and the way they formed part of a comprehensive critique of dirigisme, appears to have received less attention in the early 1970s. In the 1980s, a contribution by Fields (1984) drew attention to the thesis that variations in labour market interventions could partly explain variations in growth performance in the seven economies that he studied. The analysis of the relationship between interventions in labour markets and economic performance subsequently became embroiled in contentious interpretations of coercive labour legislation as the necessary price to pay for rapid growth (Deyo et al. 1987).

Current debates on the role of the labour market in economic development seem to be shifting in a different direction. One detects the emergence of a more circumspect view that is questioning earlier, strident versions that labour market interventions *per se* are inimical to growth (see details in Part II).

The rise and decline of dirigisme in South Asia

South Asian policymakers were not completely unresponsive to the early warning signs of a range of problems affecting ISI. In fact, attempts at trade liberalization were made in 1964 in Sri Lanka (Athukorela and Jayasuriya 1994) and in 1966 in India (Lal 1995)—a timing that was quite close to the much-vaunted policy reforms that were implemented in East Asia. Sri Lanka also followed this up with a more comprehensive programme of liberalization after 1977. The programme was eventually undermined by an unsustainable public sector investment boom and the rise of ethnic hostility (Athukorela and Jayasuriya 1994). A study in 1967 even lists Pakistan among a group of countries that were successfully making the transition to export-oriented industrialization (Keesing 1967).

Despite such examples of episodic trade liberalization in the 1960s and 1970s, the fact remains that the South Asian economies were still less open than their Southeast and East Asian counterparts at the beginning of the 1980s. Thus, the average tariff rate varied from 6.5 per cent in Singapore to 33 per cent in Indonesia; the corresponding rates ranged from 75 per cent in Bangladesh to 44 per cent in Sri Lanka (James et al. 1989: 33). The picture has changed for the better since the early 1990s thanks to the economic reform measures taken in almost all the nations (see more in Part II).

Why has there been such a slow dismantling of dirigisme in South Asia? Why is the region still some way behind—perhaps by a decade—than even Southeast Asia in terms of a vigorous adoption of economic reform? What are the forces that are at work in propelling the economies of the region towards further change?

The answers to these compelling and complex questions are by no means simple and obvious, but some suggestions can be made. Some authors such as Lal (1989, 1995) and Bhagwati (1993) find cultural antecedents. Thus, in India, 'Brahmin' bureaucrats with an entrenched disdain for business and an ingrained attachment to Fabian socialism remained wedded to the policies of the past. This was reinforced by a prickly nationalism that was manifested in a predilection to shun foreign markets and external expertise.

Attitudes displaying prickly nationalism can, of course, be encountered in many parts of the world and are not the preserve of Indians. Despite this, an antibusiness, Brahmin bureaucrat model (reflecting India's caste-ridden society) cannot be easily generalized to the rest of South Asia. In Pakistan, for example, one has always detected a coy alliance between the military, bureaucrats, and big business (the so-called 22 families in the 1960s), an alliance that supported dirigisme, condoned the unequal distribution of economic benefits between East (presently Bangladesh) and West Pakistan, and contributed to the tragedy of 1971 (Adams and Iqbal 1983). Bangladesh had to fight a liberation war against Pakistan from March to December 1971 for nine months. In the case of Sri Lanka, the model of the Brahmin bureaucrat clinging tenaciously to the tenets of regulation and control is also difficult to uphold, given that Sri Lanka made moves towards trade liberalization in the 1970s on a more significant scale than India did. Inter-ethnic hostility and the political difficulty of dismantling welfare subsidies probably played a role in slowing down the reform efforts. In Bangladesh, the emergence of a highly successful export-oriented garments industry in the early 1980s bears testimony to the ability of private enterprise to circumvent the limits posed by inward-oriented industrialization. The fact that an overall policy thrust towards much greater openness has not emerged reflects entrenched political forces rather than a culturally driven, anti-business ethic of the state.

While country-specific factors are at work in restraining the capacity of the economies of South Asia to make a comprehensive and credible commitment to policy reform, there are common forces at work that suggest that the momentum for change will not go away. One of the common forces is represented by external actors—most notably multilateral and other international agencies that act as conduits for the transmission of new ideas and ideology pertaining to policy management.

Studies on East Asia have consistently drawn attention to the fact that US aid advisers played a significant role in facilitating the policy change in Korea and Taiwan (Haggard 1988, 1990, 1994). It is worth remembering too that the intellectual onslaught against dirigisme was ushered under the tutelage of the OECD (the sponsor of the work by Little et al. 1970), the Asian Development Bank (the sponsor of the work on ISI in Southeast Asia), and the US-based National Bureau of Economic Research (sponsor of the comprehensive studies by Bhagwati, Krueger, and others). The World Bank took up this mission at a later stage with a great deal of zeal and vigour and ushered in an era of 'structural adjustment lending' (SAL) in the 1980s.

The antecedents of SAL may be seen in the well-established approach that the International Monetary Fund (IMF) has used extensively in dealing with countries undergoing balance of payments (BOP) crises (Killick and Bird 1984). SAL, however, has tried to deliberately differentiate itself from the IMF approach by emphasizing medium-term and long-term issues in policy reform rather than limiting itself to short-run stabilization issues (which is seen as the preserve of the IMF). SAL may be interpreted as an attempt to formalize the role that donors and foreign experts in developing countries play as catalytic agents for change. Thus, concessional loans are granted to developing countries in exchange for 'conditionalities' that must be met. Inevitably, such conditionalities have meant a demonstrated commitment to a reduced level of government intervention in the economy. They have also included institutional and administrative reform as part of the conditionalities.

Despite the long-standing relationship with the World Bank and frequent contact with the IMF, the general verdict is that a donor-driven policy reform agenda has had modest success in South Asia. This is consistent with the view of critics who—drawing on the experience of SAL in other parts of the world—argue that a SAL-type approach has been quite modest in terms of influencing long-term economic growth as governments have worked out ingenious strategies for neutralizing or diluting the policy reform agenda of donors (Mosley et al. 1991). The implication is that external actors face inherent limits when they take on the ambitious task of using financial leverage for shaping economic changes in sovereign nations. It can work in some cases, as it apparently did in parts of East Asia. External actors seem to be particularly productive in the more general area of advocacy of new ideas in policy management and institutional reform. Ultimately, the conviction and commitment of the national leadership crucially matter. Such convictions and commitments are partly a response to paradigm shifts in the domain of development policy that typically occur under the tutelage of international organizations; they are also a recognition of the long-term problems created by dirigisme.

One of the long-term problems of dirigisme that is sowing the seeds of change is a continuing 'fiscal crisis.' This view is clearly seen in the work of Lal (see Lal and Wolf 1986; Lal and Myint 1995; Lal 1987, 1989, 1995). It can also be detected in the work of Fishlow (1990) on Latin America and Krueger (1993b), although the latter is couched in a more general framework. The thesis of the fiscal crisis may be briefly summarized as follows.

Once an initial policy choice in favour of dirigisme is made, it creates a group of beneficiaries who in turn support further state control and deregulation, thus 'politically reinforcing initial policy choices' (Krueger 1993a: 352). Over time, the vicious combination of entrenchment of politically determined benefits to favoured groups and the consolidation of an informal economy (or 'black economy') that emerges in response to pervasive regulation and slow economic growth erodes the government's revenue base in the face of inflexible expenditure commitments. This creates a fiscal crisis. Governments try to cope with them through a combination of inflation tax and internal and external borrowing. Such attempts are usually reflected in more acute BOP and political crises. The response generates reform cycles. An initial effort to cope with an impending crisis typically occurs with a package of stabilization-cum-liberalization policies; once the crisis is over, there is a tendency to revert to politics as usual. However, because the underlying economic performance does not improve on a sustainable basis and because the political forces retarding change in a dirigiste regime remain largely intact, the fiscal crisis re-emerges to generate yet another announced (but unsustainable) reform programme.

One can detect features of the reform cycle in South Asia. One only must recall short-lived episodes of liberalization in the 1960s and 1970s and modest progress in the 1980s in implementing donor-driven initiatives. Whether the economies of the region will break out of these oscillations between reform and retrenchment into a sustained phase of radically changed policies is a central question that remains unanswered even after substantial efforts and major reforms that have advanced since the early 1990s.

Objectives of the immediate past volume

The second edition of the volume was published in 2009 and took the view that—articulated at some length in the final chapter—the promise lies in moving away from policy reform *per se* to the more challenging task of implementing institutional reform that will invigorate the capability of the political leadership to bring about rapid, sustained, and poverty-reducing growth in South Asia. The major objective and the theme of the second edition captured the following observations. The central task is to re-direct the focus of governments in South Asia to ensure that the core functions of the state are efficiently provided. At the same time, a further reform agenda for the 2000s and beyond must be sensitive to the goal of ensuring that durable democratic institutions and sustainability in the newly found information economy are preserved. This is a fundamental challenge, but one that must be met to secure the emergence of a prosperous South Asia in the 21st century.

South Asian nations and a brief political history

South Asian nations are Bangladesh, Bhutan, India, the Maldives, Nepal, Pakistan, and Sri Lanka. The major religions in South Asia are Hinduism, Buddhism, and Islam. The region is packed with people with numerous ethnic backgrounds. Class and caste are ancient problems in South Asia (see Uppal 1977: 120–151). There are problems of occasional religious intolerance on two fronts: Hindu-dominated India and Muslim-dominated Pakistan and Bangladesh. However, at present, these are not as acute as they were in the past except in India. Since 11 September 2001, this region has changed drastically due to several terrorist attacks carried out in India and Bangladesh. Pakistan has been seen as the home of terrorism and has been the victim of major attacks, with the assassination of its leader, Ms. Benazir Bhutto, in 2008. In Sri Lanka, the civil war over the initial 25 years reached a climax, with government forces taking over territories captured earlier by the Tamil Tigers. In the next section, a brief political profile of the four countries is presented, and some of their unique features are highlighted up to the COVID-19 pandemic in 2022. The major sources of information presented in the next section are daily newspapers of individual countries and weekly publications such as *Asiaweek* and *The Economist*.

India

The profile of pre-1990 India has been summarized by Sen (1990) in the following manner:

> India's reputation as a land of riches is as ancient as the history of its poverty. The mixed reputation has changed in recent centuries, and India is seen these days primarily as a land of poverty, famines, diseases, squalor, caste, untouchability, separatism, and chaos. This reputation is not altogether undeserved.
>
> *(Sen 1990: 7)*

Is modern-day India as pessimistic as Sen, a world-famous Indian-born economist and Nobel Laureate in economics, sees it? Who is to blame Sen? The 76 years of independence brought India a good deal of reputation worldwide. These include the world's largest democracy, the largest populous nation, the third largest economy (GDP in PPP terms), and, finally, the largest movie maker (Hollywood being the second largest). Such reputation was offset by tragic images of human indignity, poverty, and suffering until the beginning of the new millennium. Today's India has 30 per cent (almost 300 million) of its people living in abject poverty compared to more than 40 per cent in the 1990s. This is a breakthrough after a long and sustained period of low growth and high poverty. However, more than 300 million in abject poverty in the 21st century is indeed a very high number by any standard.

Politically, India has shown great stability since independence in 1947. India has had a Westminster style of government since independence. The Indian Congress party, which brought independence from the British, has ruled for all but about 25 years. Out of Congress' more than 40 years in government, Nehru, India's hero for independence, his daughter, Indira Gandhi, and his grandson, Rajiv Gandhi, ruled the country as prime ministers for more than 35 years. This party once again led a coalition government between 2004 and 2009 under the premiership of a former World Bank official, Dr. Manmohan Singh, who initiated the economic reform process in the 1980s and early 1990s as the then finance minister of India. In the general election held in May 2009, the government of Dr. Manmohan Singh returned. It has governed India for another five years, until 2014. The present government of Indian Prime Minister Modi was elected to office almost ten years to this day. In a general election held in the middle of 2024, Narendra Modi has won and formed the government to 2029.

Bangladesh

Bangladesh currently has more than 117 million people compared to 75 million at the time of its independence in 1971. During the last 53 years, the population has increased by more than 1.5 million a year. Bangladesh's overwhelming problem is control of population. This vast population has created all sorts of problems for Bangladesh on all fronts: economic, political, and/or social. Almost 70 per cent of the total population lives in more than 100,000 villages. More than half of them have no land resources for generating income for livelihoods. For this huge number of people, the main sources of income are daily wage labour in agriculture. However, this nation, over almost the last 53 years after independence since 1971, has established some world-class industries too. Most importantly, the readymade garments and associated industries have grown remarkably. Having said that most recently, on 5 August 2024, the government of Sheikh Hasina, former Prime Minister, was overthrown by the student-peoples movement. She ruled the nation since 2009. In the meantime, the PM, Sheikh Hasina, fled to India on 5 August 2024 and is seeking temporary asylum in India. At the time of writing this chapter in August 2024, she has been residing in Delhi. Immediately after she left for India, the angry mob in Dhaka, capital of Bangladesh, ransacked her official residence called *Ganah Bhaban* (Peoples' Place) at midday on 5 August 2024. However, this sudden uprising remains significant too for political stability for years to come. The student-people-led uprising against the government is almost the same as 'Arab Spring' in the Middle Eastern Muslim nations in 2011. Politically, Bangladesh has shown great instability since independence in 1971. The father of independent Bangladesh, Sheikh Mujibur Rahman, was assassinated by some disgruntled soldiers on 15 August 1975. The army and quasi-army ruled the nation from 1975 to 1990. The democratic governments were established in 1991 when Khaleda Zia was elected Prime Minister until 1996. Sheikh Hasina, the daughter of the father of the nation, was elected as Prime Minister in 1996–2001. Khaleda Zia returned to power once again in 2001–2006 as Prime Minister. There was a caretaker government backed by armed forces that ran the nation for two years from 2006. Sheikh Hasina came back as Prime Minister in the 2008 election and was elected for another four consecutive terms to 2029 but lost her position over a revolution that took place on 5 August 2024.

Since 8 August 2024, Bangladesh has had an interim government backed by the Bangladesh Army and revolutionary leaders, led by Professor Dr. Muhammad Yunus, a Nobel Laureate and the founder and chief of an NGO called *Grameen Bank*. The interim government has been committed to bringing back democratic government in Bangladesh after bringing some changes to the present constitution. A full picture of the revolution can be found in Chapter 17, the last chapter of this volume about the South Asia spring involving three states of South Asia in the 2020s.

Pakistan

The word 'Pakistan' first surfaced in the later part of the British rule of the Indian sub-continent. Poet-philosopher Muhammad Iqbal articulated the concept in 1931 when he proposed a separate state for Muslim-majority provinces in northwestern India. The word 'Pakistan' was borrowed later by the All-India Muslim League to name the new nation of Pakistan. It emerged as an independent state in 1947, without satisfying the wish of Iqbal but within the framework of Jinnah and his followers. Pakistan was formed in two wings, east and west, separated by a hostile independent India for more than 1,500 kilometres. Ultimately, the east wing (now Bangladesh) became independent after fighting a liberation war for nine months in 1971. The west wing finally became Pakistan, the geographical location of which has partly satisfied the dream of poet Iqbal.

Pakistan has a turbulent political history that has continued to the present. The first casualty of political assassination in Pakistan was former Prime Minister Liaquat Ali Khan in 1952. In 1956, it proclaimed an Islamic Republic. Under chaotic civilian governments in the centre as well as in the east and west wings over 1956–1958, the military intervened in the central government and took power in 1958. General Ayub Khan proclaimed martial law throughout Pakistan and ruled until 1969, when he was deposed by General Yahya Khan during a civil disobedience movement. General Yahya promised to hold a general election immediately after assuming power. He kept his promise. A general election was held in 1970. In the Parliament of Pakistan, 56 per cent of the Members of Parliament came from the east wing and the rest came from the west wing. All the east wing's members won the Awami League under the leadership of Sheikh Mujibur Rahman. In the west wing, Zulfikar Ali Bhutto's Pakistan People's Party (PPP) won all members.

However, in an absolute sense, the Awami League was elected as the majority party in the 300-member Parliament with 56 per cent of members. General Yahya declined to relinquish power to the majority party (in this case the Awami League), and Bhutto declined to sit in the opposition. This resulted in the deadlock of the 1970 general election results. The people of the east wing demanded that General Yahya keep his promise to transfer power to the hands of the elected government. The demand was denied. Instead, Yahya's military attacked the civil and security (police and paramilitary) installations in Dhaka to quell the civil unrest on the night of 25 March 1971. The independence of Bangladesh was declared on 26 March 1971 by east wing leader Sheikh Mujibur Rahman, who was arrested and taken to the prison in Rawalpindi on the night of 26 March 1971. A civil war broke out in Pakistan, and finally, with military support from India, Bangladesh gained liberation from Pakistan. Pakistan's 93,000 troops surrendered to the joint forces of Bangladesh and India in Dhaka on 16 December 1971.

After the civil war, Bhutto assumed power in the new Pakistan within the boundary of former West Pakistan. General Zia-ul-Haq deposed Bhutto in July 1977 and tried him for a political murder instigated by Bhutto. He was hanged in 1979. General Zia-ul-Haq was killed in a mysterious air crash in August 1988 after ruling Pakistan for almost a decade. Bhutto's daughter, Benazir, became Prime Minister in 1988 but was dismissed by the President on a corruption count in 1990. Nawaz Sharif was voted to power in the next election but was also dismissed by the President in 1993 due to charges of electoral fraud and massive corruption. The Supreme Court restored the government of Nawaz, but he resigned. In the 1993 election, Benazir was swept back into power and was Prime Minister of Pakistan until November 1996, when she was sacked by the President on corruption and incompetency grounds. A general election was held in February 1997 and won by the Muslim League headed by Nawaz Sharif, who once again became Prime Minister of Pakistan. In 2000, Pakistan reverted to military rule by General Pervez Musharraf, who ruled until a general election in 2008, when he was thrown out of power. The PPP of the late Benazir Bhutto won the election, and her husband, Asif Ali Zardari, became President (for five years). Since early 2009, President Zardari has become embroiled in a deadly tribal war against Taliban insurgents in Swat Valley, the northwestern province of Pakistan. Benazir Bhutto was assassinated by a Taliban insurgent. Pakistan is once again under military rule for some time. Finally, there was an election held in 2018, and Imran Khan was elected as Prime Minister until 2024. There was an election held in 2024, and Imran Khan was barred from running in the 2024 election due to corruption charges. The 2024 election results have just been finalized. A coalition government came into power in a controversial outcome of the general election in 2024. The Pakistan Muslim League (PML) of Nawaz Sharif and the PPP formed the government, having the Prime Minister from the PML and Asif Ali Zardari from the PPP appointed as the President in March 2024.

Sri Lanka

The Sri Lankan political profile, since its independence from the British on 4 February 1948, is a mixed bag of stability and political adventurism. Among the four countries of this study, it is Sri Lanka that the British left in a sound state in both economic and political terms. Being an island state, Sri Lanka—the British called it Ceylon—was a jewel in the British Indian crown. Sri Lanka was a home of scenic beauty and paradise in the Indian Ocean. In modern days, however, the paradise is lost due to political adventurism by Sri Lankans. Over the last 25 years, the country has become a land of separatism and ethnic violence.

D.S. Senanayake was the first Prime Minister of then Ceylon. After gaining independence, Senanayake ruled the country until 1953. Solomon Bandaranaike formed a strong government in 1956 after a short transition period between 1953 and 1956. However, he was assassinated by a Buddhist monk because of a religious disagreement in 1959. The country was then led by Sirimavo Bandaranaike, the wife of Solomon Bandaranaike, until 1965. From 1965 to 1970 the country was governed by Dudley Senanayake, the son of the first Prime Minister. Sirimavo regained power in 1970 and renamed the country the Republic of Sri Lanka—an expression with an ancient connotation—in May 1972. The long reign of Sirimavo came to an end in 1977 when she lost the general election to a veteran campaigner of Sri Lankan politics, J.R. Jayewardene. Jayewardene replaced the 1972 Constitution and assumed power as executive President of the country. During Jayewardene's regime, the Tamil separatist movement erupted in northern and eastern provinces in 1983. Ranasinghe Premadasa, the former Prime Minister under Jayewardene's regime, was elected President in late 1988. The 1987–1989 JVP (Janatha Vimukthi Peramuna) insurrection was an armed revolt in Sri Lanka by the Sinhalese youth movement led by the Marxist-Leninist JVP against the Government of Sri Lanka. The insurrection, like the previous one in 1971, was unsuccessful. The main phase of the insurrection was a low-intensity conflict that lasted from April 1987 to December 1989. In the meantime, the Tamil insurgency movement intensified in the northern and eastern provinces. There was an attempt by India in 1987 to mediate the Tamil conflict. India sent its troops to northern Jaffna to put down the Tamil uprising. Indian forces were withdrawn in early 1990. The fighting between Tamil separatists and the security forces, including the army, reached a climax in the mid-1991. Since

1992, military engagements have been withdrawn by both sides, and attempts are being made to reach a peaceful political solution.

The country was put into a great crisis again on May Day in 1993 when a suicide bomber killed President Premadasa in an election rally. In the 1994 election, Chandrika Bandaranaike Kumaratunga, the younger daughter of Solomon and Sirimavo Bandaranaike, swept to power. Chandrika assumed the position of President and made her mother, Sirimavo, Prime Minister. Under the present constitution, the President is both head of state and head of government. Sri Lanka, despite fighting a civil war for the last quarter of a century, has enjoyed democratically elected governments over the last 60 years, unlike Pakistan and Bangladesh. In June 2009, the Sri Lankan government finally won the 26-year civil war against the Tamil Tigers. The separatist movement by the Tamil minority comes to a halt with the Tigers thrown out by the Sri Lankan army from their last stronghold.

A summary of the political history of the four countries since their independence suggests one common feature. In all four countries, since independence, the government was changed through military intervention or political assassination at least once. This problem destabilized the various governments in Pakistan and Bangladesh several times until the presently democratically elected governments came into place in both countries. India and Sri Lanka have enjoyed relative calm and stability in government, except both countries suffer from an acute problem of terrorism, regional insurgency, and separatist movements.

The other common feature of South Asia is poverty. As can be seen in Part II, substantial progress has been made on poverty elimination and implementing UN Millennium Development Goals (MDGs) agenda (2001–2015) over the one and a half decades. However, this progress has been reversed in the last two years due to the global food and fuel price crisis and global economic slowdown, the like of which has not been seen since the Great Depression in the 1930s, observed by a recent UN study. Since the COVID-19 years, the number of people in poverty has increased by 100 million in South Asia, and the total number of people in poverty has once again reached 400 million and above. This figure is the region's highest in four decades. The UN further observes that presently three-quarters of the region's population survive on less than US$2 a day. Indeed, this is quite alarming considering that almost all the nations in the region have had so much success before the COVID-19 pandemic struck in 2000.

Readers' guide

This study spans 17 chapters that are grouped into four broad clusters or parts. Part I contains four chapters, including this introductory chapter, which also includes a synoptic political history of the economies under study. There are also three empirically driven chapters that review various aspects of economic growth, human development, and demographic dynamics, primarily over the immediate last two decades to 2023. The range of performance indicators for South Asia is linked with Southeast and East Asian benchmarks in some chapters.

Part II forms the bulk of this book. It encompasses eight chapters that cover a diverse range of key themes in South Asian economic development. The chapters cover a new chapter on artificial intelligence (AI) and the future of South Asia, labour market institutions, the MDGs, macroeconomic management, economic reform, trade and economic integration, agriculture and rural development, climate change, poverty alleviation, and information technology issues. The chapters highlight both achievements and deficiencies. Moreover, each chapter introduces the major debates. The issues are discussed in the context of received theories, including a critical assessment of them.

Part III considers three topics: whether there are replicable lessons of success, focusing on the recent experience of AI and its development in South Asian economies (Chapter 13), and what success with covering sanitation facilities over the last two decades in South Asia compared with Southeast Asia (Chapter 14). India's presidency of G20 in 2023 and the inter-regional cooperations around SDGs achievements presented in Chapter 15. Chapter 16 examines South Asia in the first quarter of the 21st century and what next? The final and concluding Chapter 17 concerns South Asia Spring taking Sri Lanka, Pakistan, and Bangladesh.

Bibliography

Adams, J. and Iqbal, S. (1983) *Exports, Politics and Economic Development of Pakistan 1970–1982*, Boulder, CO: Westview Press.

Arndt, H. W. (1987) *Economic Development: The History of an Idea*, Chicago: University of Chicago Press.

Athukorela, P. and Jayasuriya, S. (1994) *Macroeconomic Policies, Crises and Growth in Sri Lanka, 1969–90*, Washington, DC: World Bank.

Bauer, P. T. (1971) "Economic history as theory", *Economica*, 38: 163–179.

Bhagwati, J. N. (1978) *The Foreign Trade Regimes and Economic Development: Anatomy and Consequences of Exchange Control Regimes, National Bureau of Economic Research (NBER)*.

Bhagwati, J. N. (1984) "Why are services cheaper in the poor countries?" *The Economic Journal*, 94.

Bhagwati, J. N. (1993) *India in Transition: Freeing the Economy*, Oxford: Clarendon.

Bhagwati, J. (1994) "Regional and multilateralism: An overview", in R. Garnaut and P. Drysdale (eds.), *Asia Pacific Regionalism: Readings in International Economics*, Sydney: Harper Collins.

Birdsall, N., Ross, D. and Sabot, N. (1995) "Inequality and growth reconsidered lessons from Asia", *World Bank Economic Review*, 9, 3: 477–508.

Chowdhury, T. E. (1992) "Privatization of state enterprises in Bangladesh, 1975–84", in G. Lamb and R. Weaving (eds.), *Managing Policy Reform in the Real World*, EDI series, Washington, DC: World Bank.

Deyo, F. (ed.) (1987) "State and labour: Modes of political exclusion in East Asian development", in F. Deyo (ed.), *The Political Economy of the New Asian Industrialism*, Ithaca and London: Cornell University Press.

Fields, G. (1984) "Employment, income distribution and economic growth in seven small economies", *Economic Journal*, 94, 1: 74–83.

Fishlow, A. (1990) "The Latin American state", *The Journal of Economic Perspectives*, 4, 2: 61–74.

Furtado, C. (1973) "The concept of external dependence in the study of under development", in C. K. Wilber (ed.), *The Political Economy of Development and Underdevelopment*, New York: Random House.

Haggard, S. (1988) "The politics of industrialization in the Republic of Korea and Taiwan", in H. Hughes (ed.), *Achieving Industrialization in Asia*, Cambridge: Cambridge University Press.

Haggard, S. (1990) *Pathways from the Periphery: Politics of Growth in the Newly Industrializing Countries*, Ithaca, NY: Cornell University Press.

Haggard, S. (1994) "Conclusion", in A. J. MacIntyre (ed.), *Government and Business in Industrialsing Asia*, Ithaca, NY: Cornell University Press.

Helliwell, D. (1994) "Empirical linkages between democracy and economic growth", *British Journal of Political Science*, 24.

Hicks, G. (1989) "The four little dragons: An enthusiast's reading guide", *Asian-Pacific Economic Literature*, 4, 2: 35–49.

James, W. E., Naya, S. and Meier, G. M. (1989) *Asian Development: Economic Success and Policy Lessons*, Madison: University of Wisconsin Press.

Jigging, J. (1976) "Dismantling welfarism in Sri Lanka", *Overseas Development Review*, 2.

Keesing, D. B. (1967) "Outward looking policies and economic development", *Economic Journal*, 77: 306–320.

Killick, A. and Bird, G. (1984) *The IMF and Stabilization: Developing Country Experiences*, New York: St Martin's Press.

Korean Development Institute (1995) Seoul.

Kravis, I. B. and Lipsey, R. E. (1982) "The location of overseas production and production of US multinational firms", *Journal of International Economics*, 12: 201–223.

Krueger, A. O. (1993a) *Political Economy of Policy Reform in Developing Countries*, Cambridge, MA: MIT Press.

Krueger, A. O. (1993b) "Free trade agreement as protectionist devices: Rules and origin", Working Paper No. 4352, National Bureau of Economic Research (NBER), April.

Lal, A. (1994) *Impact of Uruguay Round Agreements on Less Developed Countries' Exports: An Initial Assessment*, Washington, DC: World Bank, International Economic Department.

Lal, A. (1995) "India and China: Contrast in economic liberalisation", *World Development*, 23, 9: 1475–1494.

Lal, D. (1987) "The political economy of economic liberalisation", *World Bank Economic Review*, 1: 2.

Lal, D. and Myint, H. (1995) *The Political Economy of Poverty, Equity and Growth: A Comparative Study*, Oxford: Clarendon Press.

Lal, D. and Wolf, M. (eds.) (1986) *Stagflation, Savings and the State, Perspective on the Global Economy*, New York: Oxford University Press.

Lewis, W. A. (1955) "Economic development with unlimited supplies of labour", Paper presented at The Manchester School (pp. 139–191), May.

Little, I., Scitovsky, T. and Scott, M. (1970) *Industry and Trade in Some Developing Countries: A Comparative Study*, London: Oxford University Press.

McKinnon, R. (1973) *Money and Capital in Economic Development*, Washington, DC: Brooking Institution.

Mosley, P., Harrigan, J. and Toy, J. (1991) *Aid and Power: The World Bank and Policy-Based Lending, Vol. 1: Analysis and Policy Proposals*, London: Routledge.

Papanek, G. (1967) *Pakistan's Development: Social Goals and Private Incentives*, Cambridge, MA: Harvard University Press.

Power, J. H. (1963) "Industrialization in Pakistan: A case of frustrated take-off", *Pakistan Development Review*, Summer.

Rodrik. D. (1992) "The limits of trade policy reform in developing countries", *Journal of Economic Perspectives*, 6, 1: 87–105.

Rosenstein-Rodan, P. (1943) "Problems of industrialization of Easter and Southeaster Europe", *Economic Journal*, 53, 210–211. Reprinted in Agarwal, A. N. and Singh, S. P. (1963) *The Economic Underdevelopment*, New York: Oxford University Press.

Seers, D. (1962) "The limitations of the special case", reprinted in Mere, G. M. (1984) *Leading Issues of Economic Development*, 4th Edition, New York: Oxford University Press.

Sen, A. K. (1990) "How is India doing?" in *The Indian Economy and Its Performance since Independence*, Delhi: Oxford University Press.

Shaw, L. (1973) *Financial Deepening in Economic Development*, New York: OUP.

Sunkel, R. (1969) "National development policy and external development in Latin America", *Journal of Development Studies*, 6: 1.

Turner, M. and Hulme, D. (1997) *Governance, Administration, and Development: Making the State Work*, London: Macmillan.

UNDP (1996, 2020) *Human Development Report 1996, and 2020*, United Nations Development Programme, Oxford: Oxford University Press.

Uppal, J. S. (1977) *Economic Development in South Asia*, New Delhi: Tata McGraw Hill Publishing Company.

World Bank (1997, 2020) *World Development Report 1997: The State in a Changing World*, Oxford: Oxford University Press.

World Bank (2023–2024) "Human development report, HDR", in *Breaking the Gridlock, Reimagining Cooperation in a Polarized World*, Oxford: Oxford University Press.

World Development Report (2023) *Migrant, Refuges, and Societies*, Oxford: Oxford University Press.

2

BENCHMARKING SOUTH ASIAN ECONOMIC PERFORMANCE

Eliyathamby A. Selvanathan, Maneka Jayasinghe, and Saroja Selvanathan

South Asian economies witnessed a substantial economic transformation during the last three decades. However, not all the nations in the region experienced uniform growth. In particular, India and Bangladesh demonstrated remarkable economic performance owing to the economic reforms brought to these nations since the early part of the 1990s. The noteworthy economic growth in the region has contributed to a significant reduction in poverty in the region. This chapter attempts to capture the overall economic performance of four countries in the South Asian region, namely Bangladesh, India, Pakistan, and Sri Lanka. A comparative analysis of the four nations under study (Bangladesh, India, Pakistan, and Sri Lanka) will be carried out with that of four nations of Southeast Asia (Malaysia, Thailand, the Philippines, and Vietnam) in terms of economic factors such as overall growth rate as well as sectoral growth rates, savings, investment, exports, and imports during the last three decades. Southeast Asia made a major breakthrough on the economic development front in the 1990s and early 2000s. This analysis will at least partly help to answer the frequently asked question in the literature: is South Asia catching up Southeast Asia? In the analysis below, the economic performances between the periods 1990 and 2022 are discussed with a special emphasis on COVID-19 impact as well as prospects for the future.

An overview of economic performance

The overall performances of the economic indicators of countries in South and Southeast Asia are captured in Tables 2.1 to 2.9.

Growth performance

Figure 2.1 presents the historical growth performance of four South Asian countries. Since the early 1990s, the GDP growth rate in Bangladesh has been relatively stable with occasional fluctuations compared to its other South Asian neighbours and has shown an upward trajectory till the COVID-19 downturn. Bangladesh's economic growth has rebounded in the post-pandemic years. Bangladesh has not reported a negative growth rate since 1972, and more specifically, it

DOI: 10.4324/9781032716244-3

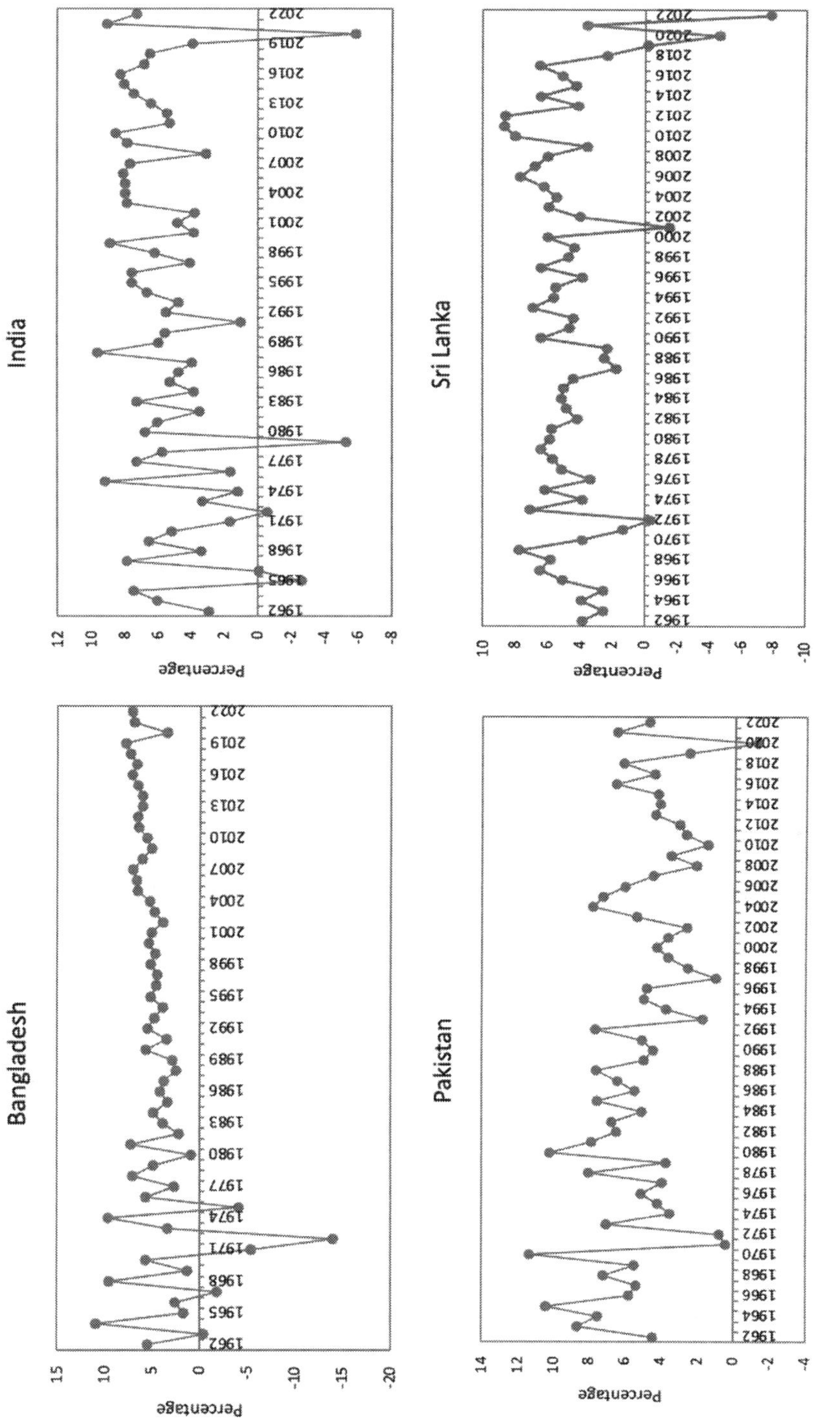

FIGURE 2.1 Growth performance in South Asian countries 1962–2022

Source: World Development Indicators, World Bank (2023)

TABLE 2.1 GDP growth rates in South Asia and Southeast Asia 1990–2022 (%)

Country	*GDP growth rate*						*GDP per capita growth rate*					
	1990	*2000*	*2010*	*2019*	*2020*	*2022*	*1990*	*2000*	*2010*	*2019*	*2020*	*2022*
South Asia												
Bangladesh	5.6	5.3	5.6	7.9	3.5	7.1	3.4	3.3	4.4	6.7	2.3	6.0
India	5.5	3.8	8.5	3.9	−5.8	7.2	3.3	2.0	7.0	2.8	−6.7	6.5
Pakistan	4.5	4.3	1.5	2.5	−1.3	4.7	1.1	1.1	−0.8	0.9	−3.0	2.7
Sri Lanka	6.4	6.0	8.0	−0.2	−4.6	−7.8	5.1	5.4	7.0	−0.8	−5.1	−7.9
Mean	5.5	4.9	5.9	3.5	−2.1	2.8	3.2	3.0	4.4	2.4	−3.1	1.8
SD	0.8	1.0	3.2	3.4	4.2	7.2	1.6	1.9	3.7	3.2	3.9	6.7
CV	14	20	54	96	203	256	51	63	84	134	125	367
Southeast Asia												
Malaysia	9.0	8.9	7.4	4.4	−5.5	8.8	5.9	6.1	5.6	3.1	−6.6	7.5
The Philippines	3.1	4.4	7.3	6.1	−9.5	7.6	0.7	2.1	5.4	4.4	−11.0	6.0
Thailand	11.2	4.5	7.5	2.1	−6.1	2.6	9.4	3.4	6.8	1.9	−6.3	2.5
Vietnam	5.1	6.8	6.4	7.4	2.9	8.0	2.8	5.6	5.3	6.4	1.9	7.2
Mean	7.1	6.2	7.2	5.0	−4.6	6.8	4.7	4.3	5.8	4.0	−5.5	5.8
SD	3.7	2.1	0.5	2.3	5.3	2.8	3.8	1.9	0.7	1.9	5.4	2.3
CV	52	35	7	46	116	42	81	44	12	49	98	40

Source: World Development Indicators, World Bank (2023)

Note: SD—standard deviation; CV—coefficient of variation.

is the only country in South Asia that maintained a positive growth rate during the pandemic year. India demonstrates an upward trend, however, with substantial fluctuations. India reported a negative growth rate twice in its history, in 1979–1980, due to a severe drought that affected most parts of the country and oil supply disruptions, and in 2020 due to the pandemic. However, India has been able to bounce back notably during the post-pandemic period. Economic growth performance in Pakistan has also seen substantial fluctuations over time, although a negative growth rate was only reported during the post-pandemic period. Sri Lanka managed to maintain a GDP growth rate above 3 per cent throughout its history, despite occasional drops and negative growth rates reported in 1972, 1987–1989, and 2010 due to political instability linked with the JVP insurrection and civil war. However, after the pandemic-induced economic downturn in Sri Lanka in 2020, unlike its South Asian neighbours, the country's economy did not bounce back due to the economic crisis.

Table 2.1 presents information on the overall growth performance of the selected eight Asian countries during 1990–2022. This table also presents the summary measures across the four South and Southeast Asian countries, separately, in the form of mean, standard deviation, and the coefficient of variation (CV) where appropriate. During 1990–2010, all countries in South Asia recorded a positive growth rate (on average, with the mean growth rate across countries varying between 5 and 6 per cent), with India showing the highest growth rate (8.5 per cent) in

2010, followed by Sri Lanka (8 per cent). Bangladesh grew moderately, between a 5.3 and 5.6 per cent growth rate, whereas Pakistan showed a drastic decline from 4.5 per cent in 1990 to 1.5 per cent in 2010. The political chaos and the terrorist threats over the last three decades were behind the low growth in Pakistan. However, by 2019, economic growth in India and Sri Lanka slowed substantially, with Sri Lanka reporting a negative growth rate. While India's fall in the GDP growth rate was a result of contracted manufacturing activity, weakened investment, and a decline in overall consumption demand, that of Sri Lanka was particularly due to the disrupted economic activities, such as tourism, foreign investment, and overall business activities, followed by the 2019 Easter Sunday bombings. Leading up to 2019, Bangladesh emerged as a fast-growing economy, outpacing Asian peers, such as India and Sri Lanka. This was mainly driven by increased domestic demand, foreign investment, and sound growth-oriented macroeconomic reforms. In 2019, Bangladesh recorded a 7.9 per cent GDP growth rate. The year 2020 was an exceptional year with COVID-19-induced economic downturn across the globe. All countries in South Asia except for Bangladesh (which had a reduced growth from 7.9 to 3.5 per cent) experienced a negative growth rate, with India recording the highest (–5.8 per cent), followed by Sri Lanka (–4.6 per cent).

Interestingly, all South Asian countries under consideration except Sri Lanka bounced back and showed an even stronger economic growth rate in 2022. India and Bangladesh reported a 7.2 and 7.1 per cent GDP growth rate, respectively. Pakistan also recorded a moderate growth rate of 4.7 per cent in 2022. In 2022, the Sri Lankan economy recorded its deepest economic contraction in seven decades (−7.8 per cent GDP growth rate), mainly owing to the ripple effects of the unprecedented economic crisis amidst the domestic and global headwinds that impeded the post-pandemic recovery. During the same period, apart from the COVID-19-induced economic slowdown in 2019 and 2020, Malaysia, Vietnam, and the Philippines demonstrated strong growth performance in 2022. While the economic performance of Malaysia and Vietnam appeared to rebound quickly from the 1997 currency crisis, the Philippines and Thailand continued to have a notable economic slowdown during the 2000s before gaining momentum in the late 2000s. As can be seen in GDP growth figures in Table 2.1, while the Philippines has emerged as a strong economy after COVID-19, the growth rate in Thailand is the slowest in the region, mainly due to the contraction in exports and ongoing fiscal consolidation. The uncertainty in the economic growth rate in South and Southeast Asian countries due to COVID-19 is well reflected by the higher variability measured by the CV in 2020. However, the uncertainty settled well in Southeast Asia while it continued in South Asia, particularly in Sri Lanka, due to the economic and political uncertainty from 2019.

In terms of per capita growth rate between the countries of these regions in 2022 (keeping population growth rate in mind), Malaysia and Vietnam have experienced the highest rate (above 7 per cent), followed by India, Bangladesh, and the Philippines (above 6 per cent). The lowest rates, however, were experienced by Sri Lanka (−7.9 per cent), followed by Thailand and Pakistan (below 3 per cent).

Table 2.2 presents comparative sectoral (agricultural, industrial, and service) growth performance during 2000–2022. As can be seen, overall, the agriculture sector has shown moderate growth in South Asian countries during the period of concern, except Sri Lanka, which registered a negative growth rate in 2020 and 2022, mainly owing to the newly introduced organic farming policy that banned the use of agrochemicals in farming. Against the widespread

TABLE 2.2 Sectoral growth rates in South Asia and Southeast Asia 2000–2022 (%)

Country	*Agriculture*					*Industry*					*Service*				
	2000	*2010*	*2019*	*2020*	*2022*	*2000*	*2010*	*2019*	*2020*	*2022*	*2000*	*2010*	*2019*	*2020*	*2022*
South Asia															
Bangladesh	7.4	6.2	3.3	3.4	3.1	6.3	7	11.6	3.6	9.9	14.4	0.9	11.5	−17.5	29.4
India	−0.01	8.8	6.2	4.1	4.0	5.8	7.9	−1.4	−0.9	4.4	18.2	19.5	−3.4	−9.1	13.6
Pakistan	6.1	0.3	0.9	3.9	4.3	1.3	4.0	0.3	−5.7	6.8	16.0	7.6	13.2	1.5	5.9
Sri Lanka	1.5	7.0	0.5	−0.9	−4.6	7.3	8.4	−4.1	−5.3	−16.0	18.0	−12.3	1.7	−29.6	10.2
Mean	3.7	5.6	2.7	2.6	1.7	5.2	6.8	1.6	−2.1	1.3	16.7	3.9	5.8	−13.7	14.8
SD	3.6	3.7	2.6	2.4	4.2	2.7	2.0	6.9	4.4	11.7	1.8	13.3	7.9	13.2	10.2
CV	95	66	96	90	249	51	29	432	210	920	11	338	138	96	69
Southeast Asia															
Malaysia	6.1	14.4	1.9	−2.4	0.1	10.7	4.9	2.6	−6.1	6.5	16.1	10.4	−1.0	−8.6	14.5
The Philippines	3.4	1.3	1.2	−0.2	0.5	6.6	9.8	5.5	−13.1	6.5	13.7	20.3	2.6	−16.1	10.9
Thailand	6.8	−0.5	−1.0	−3.3	2.4	2.6	10.4	0.02	−5.4	−0.7	15.8	14.2	−3.0	−19.7	6.8
Vietnam	4.6	0.5	2.7	3.0	3.4	10.1	−9.9	8.2	4.4	7.8	21.0	8.5	6.2	4.1	5.7
Mean	5.2	3.9	1.2	−0.7	1.6	7.5	3.8	4.1	−5.1	5.0	16.7	13.4	1.2	−10.1	9.5
SD	1.5	7.0	1.6	2.8	1.6	3.7	9.5	3.5	7.2	3.9	3.1	5.2	4.1	10.5	4.0
CV	5.2	3.9	1.2	−0.7	1.6	7.5	3.8	4.1	−5.1	5.0	16.7	13.4	1.2	−10.1	9.5

Source: World Development Indicators, World Bank (2023)

claims that organic methods can produce comparable agricultural yield, domestic rice production declined by about 20 per cent, and tea production fell by 18 per cent, adversely affecting Sri Lanka's foreign exchange earnings. Overall, from the late 2000s to 2022, the Southeast Asian region showed a lower agricultural sector growth rate than its South Asian neighbours, with the most notable fall seen in Malaysia (from 14.4 per cent in 2010 to 0.1 per cent in 2022). However, Thailand and Vietnam appeared to be picking up the agricultural sector growth in 2022, with registered growth of 2.4 and 3.4 per cent, respectively.

Apart from the pandemic-related slowdown, Bangladesh continued with a strong performance in the industry and service sectors in the South Asian region, followed by India. While Pakistan showed a low to moderate industry and services growth rate during the same period, the industry sector demonstrated a negative growth rate in Sri Lanka since 2019. The exceptionally broad import ban introduced in Sri Lanka in 2019 to ease the balance of payment (BOP) crisis in the country significantly disrupted the manufacturing industry.

Table 2.3 provides information on the sectoral share of GDP in the two regions of Asia, taking three periods into consideration: 2005, 2015, and 2022. The information highlights further structural changes that have occurred in these economies over the last 17 years. In 2005, agriculture's contribution to GDP in the South Asian region varied between 17 per cent (Sri Lanka) and 22 per cent (Pakistan), while the contribution of the agriculture sector in the Southeast Asian region was moderate, varying between 9 per cent (Malaysia) and 21 per cent (Vietnam). The shares in Malaysia, Thailand, and the Philippines were below 15 per cent. This structure has dramatically changed for South Asia; for Bangladesh (11 per cent) and Sri Lanka (9 per cent), while Pakistan and India have retained the 22 and 17 per cent, respectively, contribution to GDP from the agricultural sector by 2022. Among Southeast Asia, only in Vietnam and the

TABLE 2.3 Sectoral share of GDP in South Asia and Southeast Asia 2005–2022 (%)

Country	*Agriculture*			*Industry*			*Services*		
	2005	*2015*	*2022*	*2005*	*2015*	*2022*	*2005*	*2015*	*2022*
South Asia									
Bangladesh	20	15	11	27	27	34	49	54	55
India	18	16	17	27	27	26	54	48	57
Pakistan	22	23	22	25	20	20	53	53	58
Sri Lanka	17	8	9	26	30	30	57	54	61
Mean	19	16	15	26	26	28	53	52	58
SD	2	6	6	1	4	6	3	3	3
CV	12	40	40	4	17	22	6	6	4
Southeast Asia									
Malaysia	9	8	9	52	38	39	40	52	52
The Philippines	14	11	10	32	31	29	53	59	61
Thailand	10	9	9	44	36	35	46	55	56
Vietnam	21	15	12	41	34	38	38	42	46
Mean	14	11	10	42	35	35	44	52	54
SD	5	3	1	8	3	5	7	7	6
CV	40	26	14	20	10	13	15	13	12

Source: World Development Indicators, World Bank (2023)

Philippines has the percentage fallen sharply from 21 to 12 per cent and from 14 to 10 per cent, respectively. Malaysia and Thailand maintained the same level of around 9 per cent. Between 2005 and 2022, in South Asia, the industry sector's contribution to GDP increased in Bangladesh and Sri Lanka while it declined in India and Pakistan. Bangladesh's increase has been 7 per cent, and Sri Lanka's by 4 per cent.

On the other hand, in Southeast Asia, the industry sector's contribution to GDP has fallen across all four countries. The most significant fall in the contribution to GDP by the industry sector is seen in Malaysia (13 per cent), followed by Thailand by 9 per cent. The services sector's contribution to GDP in South and Southeast Asia has experienced an extraordinary expansion over the last three decades. It is evident from the figures in Table 2.3 that the services sector's share of GDP has increased in all countries under consideration in the Asian region between 2005 and 2022, with the largest growth seen in Malaysia (12 per cent). Overall, the services sector's contribution to GDP in South and Southeast Asian countries exceeds 50 per cent, except in Vietnam, which is about 46 per cent.

Domestic savings and investment

Table 2.4 provides comparable information on savings and capital formation (formerly known as domestic investment) as a percentage of the GDP of South and Southeast Asian countries between 1990 and 2022. Until 2019, all the South Asian nations experienced growth in domestic savings, except Pakistan, before experiencing a slight decline or stagnation in 2022, potentially owing to the pandemic-related economic slowdown. In Southeast Asia, all the nations experienced a slight reduction in savings except Malaysia. Regarding capital formation (investment), all the nations except Pakistan in South Asia and Malaysia and Thailand in Southeast Asia experienced growth over this period. While the most notable decline in capital formation was seen in Thailand (13 per cent), the most remarkable growth was seen in Vietnam (20 per cent), followed by Bangladesh (16 per cent).

The information presented in Tables 2.1–2.4 also demonstrates that the COVID-19 pandemic had substantial adverse implications on most of the South and Southeast Asian economies.

TABLE 2.4 Domestic savings and capital formation ratios in South Asia and Southeast Asia (% of GDP)

Country	*Gross domestic saving*				*Gross capital formation*			
	1990	*2005*	*2019*	*2022*	*1990*	*2005*	*2019*	*2022*
South Asia								
Bangladesh	23	32	36	34	16	17	32	32
India	21	34	30	30	27	37	30	31
Pakistan	18	16	11	11	19	16	15	16
Sri Lanka	24	25	32	33	22	27	34	34
Southeast Asia								
Malaysia	30	37	25	27	32	22	21	24
The Philippines	22	38	32	22	23	19	26	25
Thailand	33	28	32	27	41	30	24	28
Vietnam	34	33	31	33	13	34	32	33

Source: World Development Indicators, World Bank (2023)

Export growth and expansion

Export growth and expansions are necessary conditions for achieving a high economic growth rate in any country. Over the last 30 years, the Southeast Asian economies experienced substantial growth in exports. Table 2.5 presents South and Southeast Asian performance with external trading between 1990 and 2022.

South Asia's country-specific analysis suggests that among the four countries studied, all the countries except Sri Lanka showed strong export growth during 1990–2005. In Southeast Asian countries, the Philippines and Vietnam experienced a growth in exports, while Malaysia and Thailand showed a reduction during the same period. All countries under consideration experienced a notable drop in exports in 2019, with India, Malaysia, and Thailand experiencing even negative growth. Nevertheless, by 2022, exports appeared to have rebounded in all countries in South Asian economies except for Pakistan.

All South Asian countries, except for Sri Lanka, experienced a notable growth in imports in 2005 and 2022 despite the sizeable slowdown during 2019. While the imports increased substantially in 2022 in almost all countries except Sri Lanka, import growth in Southeast Asian countries (Thailand and Vietnam) is moderate in 2022. Sri Lanka continued to experience double-digit negative growth in imports in 2022, potentially owing to the import ban on a broad range of products to save the depleting foreign exchange reserves during the economic crisis.

Table 2.6 provides information about the expansion and contraction in merchandise trade over the last three decades, between 1990 and 2022. In all South Asian countries, the BOP slightly deteriorated during the 1990–2005 period, and it continued to deteriorate drastically towards 2019 and 2022. Of all the Asian countries under consideration, Malaysia was the only country that managed to maintain a BOP (declining) surplus since 2005. While Thailand and Vietnam reported a BOP surplus in 2019, by 2022, both countries showed a BOP deficit.

As can be seen in Table 2.6, among South Asian countries, Bangladesh and India showed a notable improvement in foreign reserves during 1990–2022. Pakistan and Sri Lanka demonstrate growth in foreign reserves until 2019 and a substantial fall during the post-pandemic period. Overall, among all countries under consideration, Sri Lanka shows the lowest level

TABLE 2.5 External trade annual change in South Asia and Southeast Asia (%)

Country	*Exports*				*Imports*			
	1990	*2005*	*2019*	*2022*	*1990*	*2005*	*2019*	*2022*
South Asia								
Bangladesh	17.8	43.0	11.5	29.4	9.3	38.1	0.5	31.2
India	11.1	26.1	−3.4	13.6	3.4	32.3	−0.8	17.1
Pakistan	1.1	17.6	13.2	5.9	−3.5	35.1	7.6	11.0
Sri Lanka	6.7	6.7	1.7	10.2	7.9	2.7	−3.5	−19.9
Southeast Asia								
Malaysia	17.8	8.3	−1.0	14.5	26.3	8.9	−2.4	15.9
The Philippines	2.3	12.5	2.6	10.9	9.9	3.7	2.3	13.9
Thailand	13.4	7.8	−3.0	6.8	23.7	16.2	−5.2	4.1
Vietnam	12.9	17.8	6.2	5.7	−4.5	14.2	4.9	3.7

Sources: World Development Indicators, World Bank (2023)

TABLE 2.6 Current account 1990–2022 in South Asia and Southeast Asia (balance of payment in US$ million)

Country	*Current account balance*				*Total reserves*			
	1990	*2005*	*2019*	*2022*	*1990*	*2005*	*2019*	*2022*
South Asia								
Bangladesh	−397	−173	−2,948	−14,369	628	2,767	32,012	32,929
India	−7,036	−10,283	−29,762	−79,050	1,520	13,192	43,237	52,141
Pakistan	−1,661	−3,606	−8,557	−11,997	295	10,032	13,421	6,159
Sri Lanka	−298	−650	−1,843	−1,452	422	2,649	6,689	2,962
Southeast Asia								
Malaysia	−869	19,979	12,795	12,271	9,754	69,857	10,172	11,329
The Philippines	−2,695	1,990	−3,046	−18,115	924	15,925	79,823	86,850
Thailand	−7,281	−7,641	38,256	−15,742	13,305	50,690	21,681	20,227
Vietnam	–	−560	13,101	−1,074	–	9,050	78,334	86,539

Sources: World Development Indicators, World Bank (2023)

of foreign reserves. Among Southeast Asian countries, foreign reserves in the Philippines and Vietnam have seen dramatic growth of more than $80 billion. Although in 2005, Malaysia and Thailand had substantially higher levels of foreign reserves ($70 billion and $51 billion, respectively), foreign reserves fell drastically thereafter and are currently sitting at $11 billion and $20 billion, respectively. Overall, the figures show that the COVID-19 pandemic had a notable adverse impact on BOP and foreign reserves in most South and Southeast Asian countries.

Integration with the global economy

South and Southeast Asia require significant financing to meet ambitious development goals, including to achieve clean energy transition goals. Although development aid has been regarded as an important means of financing development needs in developing countries, traditional grant-based development aid will no longer be sufficient to meet the development needs in Asia. Therefore, external funds through foreign direct investment (FDI) and integration of these economies with global trade will continue to play a substantial role in sourcing external funds to meet development needs in Asia.

Table 2.7 presents some information about the integration of all the economies with global trade in terms of improvement in merchandise trade, trade in services, and attracting net FDI over 1990 and 2022.

During 1990–2005, merchandise trade, as a percentage of GDP, clearly improved for all South Asian countries (except Pakistan) and Southeast Asia. Bangladesh and Pakistan have picked up merchandise trade in 2022 after a slowdown in 2019. When considering the trade in services, India has consistently improved during 1990–2022, whereas all the other countries have seen some fluctuations. The most significant drop in trade in services (as a % of GDP) is seen in Vietnam, Pakistan, and Sri Lanka. Net FDI growth has been moderate in South Asia, while for Southeast Asia, it has been strong for Vietnam. Net FDI accounted for about 4 per cent of Vietnam's GDP, and this has not been that much adversely affected by the pandemic. On the

TABLE 2.7 Integration with the global economy in South Asia and Southeast Asia

Country	*Merchandise trade (% of GDP)*				*Trade in services (% of GDP)*				*Net foreign direct investment (% of GDP, net inflows)*			
	1990	*2005*	*2019*	*2022*	*1990*	*2005*	*2019*	*2022*	*1990*	*2005*	*2019*	*2022*
South Asia												
Bangladesh	16.7	33.4	28.0	31.1	3.5	5.6	4.5	4.4	0.01	1.2	0.5	0.3
India	12.9	29.6	28.6	34.4	3.3	12.1	12.2	14.2	0.07	0.9	1.8	1.5
Pakistan	32.4	28.5	23.0	27.2	8.8	7.8	5.0	4.9	0.6	1.5	0.7	0.4
Sri Lanka	57.2	62.2	35.8	42.2	13.4	14.9	13.6	5.4	0.5	1.1	0.8	1.2
Southeast Asia												
Malaysia	133.4	178.3	121.4	158.9	21.2	29.1	23.2	18.7	5.3	2.7	2.5	3.6
The Philippines	41.8	84.5	48.6	55.6	9.9	14.0	18.4	16.4	1.1	1.6	2.3	2.3
Thailand	65.7	121.0	88.7	119.1	14.9	24.7	25.4	20.5	1.1	4.3	1.0	2.1
Vietnam	79.7	120.0	154.8	178.7	–	15.0	10.7	9.4	2.8	3.4	4.8	4.4

Source: World Development Indicators, World Bank (2023)

TABLE 2.8 Regression estimation results: GDP versus FDI

	Log (GDP)	*Standard error*	*P-value*	*t-value*	R^2
Bangladesh	2.618	0.277	0.000	9.466	0.72
India	2.211	0.155	0.000	14.24	0.85
Pakistan	1.503	0.093	0.000	16.143	0.85
Sri Lanka	1.205	0.082	0.000	14.648	0.83

other hand, figures for Bangladesh, Pakistan, Sri Lanka, and Thailand were disappointing since net FDI declined for these nations, particularly during 2005–2019.

Table 2.8 presents the regression model estimation results for the relationship between GDP and FDI. The results reveal a statistically significant positive relationship between GDP growth and FDI inflows in all countries under consideration. Figure 2.2 graphically demonstrates the same relationship.

Indebtedness

External indebtedness is one of the major indicators of a country's performance in economic development and indicates the direction the economy is heading in the future. Over the last three decades, in South and Southeast Asia, the burden of external debt as a percentage of gross national income (GNI) from various bilateral and multilateral sources has been declining in Bangladesh, India, Pakistan, and the Philippines while it is on the increase for Sri Lanka from 2019. In the Southeast Asian countries, the external debt as a percentage of GNI has stayed somewhat stable in Thailand and Vietnam during the last three decades. The sources of major multilateral debt are the World Bank, the International Monetary Fund (IMF), and the Asian Development Bank. To measure the consequences of external debt and its future trend in an economy, three major indicators are generally used. These are external debt as a

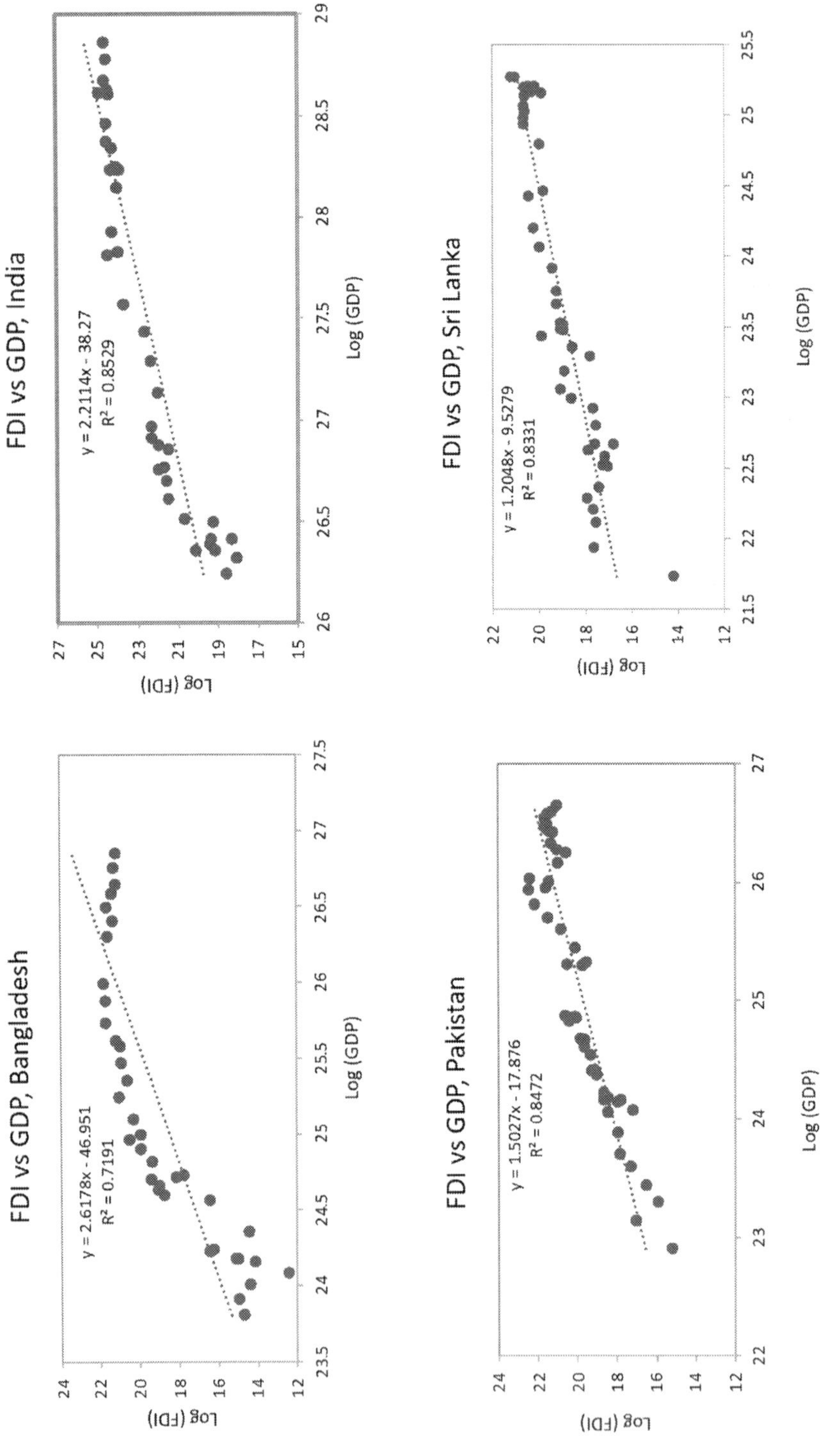

FIGURE 2.2 Relationship between GDP and FDI inflows in South Asian countries 1976–2022

percentage of GNI, external debt as a percentage of exports, and debt-service ratio. The debt-service ratio is an expression of total debt service (interest and part payment of the principal) as a percentage of exports. Table 2.9 presents this information for all the nations studied. By any standard, these figures are a matter of concern for Pakistan and Sri Lanka in South Asia. The rest of the nations in both regions demonstrate a comfortable zone in recent years (less than 6 per cent).

Table 2.10 compares South and Southeast Asian countries in terms of their outstanding debt as a percentage of GNI between 2005 and 2022. As noted earlier, the statistics relating to Sri Lanka are very concerning, with outstanding debt accounting for over 50 per cent of GNI in 2022. Bangladesh and Pakistan in the South Asia region and the Philippines and Vietnam in the Southeast Asian region have a double-digit outstanding debt as a percentage of GNI.

TABLE 2.9 External indebtedness 1990–2022

Country	*2005*	*2022*
South Asia		
Bangladesh	22	11
India	16	6
Pakistan	30	20
Sri Lanka	48	52
Southeast Asia		
Malaysia	46	–
The Philippines	67	13
Thailand	32	7
Vietnam	38	10

Source: World Development Indicators, World Bank (2023)

TABLE 2.10 Outstanding debt in South Asia and Southeast Asia (% of GNI)

Country	*Total external debt ($ million)*				*External debt as % of GNI*				*Debt service as % of exports of goods and services*			
	1990	*2005*	*2019*	*2022*	*1990*	*2005*	*2019*	*2022*	*1990*	*2005*	*2019*	*2022*
South Asia												
Bangladesh	11,510	17,439	57,317	75,501	38.1	25.5	17.1	20.3	33.7	10.3	4.5	5.9
India	12,156	111,406	448,737	465,673	26.4	14.9	20.0	18.6	27.2	15.4	2.9	2.2
Pakistan	16,643	31,613	92,845	106,652	52.9	29.4	35.0	34.2	22.7	21.1	31.4	37.8
Sri Lanka	5,053	10,045	45,812	47,795	73.6	42.5	64.8	81.0	14.8	10.9	25.4	13.3
Southeast Asia												
Malaysia	15,328	50,981	–	–	–	–	–	–	–	–	–	–
The Philippines	25,241	51,733	65,277	90,877	61.5	49.8	20.2	26.0	25.6	14.6	6.0	5.0
Thailand	19,842	42,389	116,747	108,081	33.5	32.4	34.0	39.9	11.4	5.8	0.6	0.5
Vietnam	21,378	16,282	97,621	106,545	38.4	32.9	38.6	37.7	–	7.2	1.6	1.1

Source: World Development Indicators, World Bank (2023)

Major indicators of macroeconomic balance

Three major macroeconomic indicators and their performances in recent years will be analysed in the conclusion of this chapter. These indicators are the fiscal balance, movements in the exchange rate under a more flexible regime, and the inflation rate.

The estimates on fiscal deficit show how healthy the economy is in terms of lending and borrowing. The exchange rate figures show whether the rate is behaving in such a manner that it will not be detrimental to the export-led policies of the government. The inflation rate shows the economy's stability in terms of aggregate demand during a high-growth period.

With respect to the above macroeconomic indicators, Table 2.11 provides a mixed picture during the period of 1990–2022. Among the South Asian countries, the fiscal balance worsened in Bangladesh, Pakistan, and India, especially after 2005, while that of Sri Lanka improved gradually since the 1990s. Among the Southeast Asian countries, Malaysia demonstrated a substantial improvement by moving from a deficit to a surplus during the 1990–2022 period, while the other three countries, the Philippines, Thailand, and Vietnam, reflected the adverse impact of the COVID-19 pandemic on fiscal balance in 2022. The currencies of all countries in South and Southeast Asia have experienced further depreciation in terms of a year-to-year fluctuation between 2005 and 2022. Among these nations, Malaysia (since 2005) and Sri Lanka (in various periods) have been practicing a managed float exchange rate regime by pegging their currency against the US$. Sri Lanka moved to a fully floating exchange rate regime in 2023 to address the current economic crisis and safeguard its depleting foreign reserves. This has resulted in the country's currency depreciating almost ten times compared to 1990. Inflation has seen some fluctuations in all South and Southeast Asian countries. Most countries under consideration have experienced a rise in inflation by 2022 compared to 2005, except in Vietnam. The pandemic-induced supply and demand shocks, the effect of the Russian-Ukrainian war on the oil market, and global food inflation explain this unprecedented hike in inflation rates in the Asian region, particularly in Sri Lanka. The prices of consumer goods have skyrocketed in Sri Lanka since 2019 due to restrictions on imports and a short supply of locally produced agricultural

TABLE 2.11 Major macroeconomic indicators in South Asia and Southeast Asia 1990–2022

Country	*Fiscal deficit/surplus (% of GDP)*				*Exchange rate, US$1 = LCL (annual average)*				*Inflation (% per year)*			
	1990	*2005*	*2019*	*2022*	*1990*	*2005*	*2019*	*2022*	*1990*	*2005*	*2019*	*2022*
South Asia												
Bangladesh	−1.3	−0.3	−0.8	−3.1	34.6	64.3	84.5	91.7	6.1	7.0	5.6	7.7
India	−2.2	−1.3	−1.0	−2.3	17.5	44.1	70.4	78.6	9.0	4.3	3.7	6.7
Pakistan	−4.2	−2.5	−2.7	−3.2	21.7	59.5	150	204.9	9.1	9.1	10.6	19.9
Sri Lanka	−3.7	−2.7	−2.1	−2.0	40.1	100.5	178.7	367	21.5	11.6	3.5	49.7
Southeast Asia												
Malaysia	−2.0	13.9	3.5	3.0	2.7	3.8	4.1	4.4	2.6	3.0	0.7	3.4
The Philippines	−5.3	1.9	−0.8	−4.5	24.3	55.1	51.8	54.5	12.2	6.5	2.4	5.8
Thailand	−8.5	−4.0	7.0	−3.2	25.6	40.2	31	35.1	5.9	4.5	0.7	6.1
Vietnam	–	−1.0	3.9	−0.3	6,538	15,859	23,050	23,271	–	8.3	2.8	3.2

Sources: World Development Indicators, World Bank (2023)

goods due to import restrictions on fertilizer. It remains to be seen how severely the oil shock impacts the overall inflation of the nations studied in the years to come.

From the above analysis, it appears that all the countries studied are still experiencing difficulties in overcoming pandemic-related economic slowdowns. Among all the countries studied, Sri Lanka, followed by Pakistan, are the most struggling countries, with highly depreciated currencies, increased debt burdens, and problematic macroeconomic indicators. While other countries studied have appeared to have somewhat rebounded the economic performance to the pre-pandemic level, one must be cautious about the future developments in macroeconomic terms of these regions since the present global economic slowdown and global inflations have the capacity to wipe out almost all the gains achieved over the last decade or two by these developing countries.

Clearly, the pandemic-induced global economic slowdown has severely hit South and Southeast Asia and will have a lasting impact for many years. For example, although robust growth in South and Southeast Asian countries has resulted in a notable increase in health, education, and living standards with a drastically reduced absolute poverty level, the COVID-19 pandemic, together with the Russian-Ukrainian war, dealt a historic blow to development, reversing decades of global development and poverty reduction. In particular, the World Bank estimates that the number of people living with less than \$1.90 per day in South Asia increased by 58 million after the pandemic, accounting for more than half of the global increase in poverty. The way things are unfolding in the major trading partners of South Asian nations (mainly with garments and IT services) and the retreat of migrant workers (from the Middle East and Malaysia) could turn into full-blown economic turmoil if the nations fail to prepare for the rough road ahead. It is clear by now that the region has gained economic growth in the latter part of the 20th century against all odds (e.g. corruption, administrative inefficiency, and overpopulation). However, serious adjustments to macroeconomic policies are needed to ensure macroeconomic and exchange rate stability and reduce inflation in the Asian region.

Thus, one must take a long and hard look at those countries that have managed to rebound their economies in the aftermath of various crises, such as the global financial crisis and pandemics. In this regard, the Southeast and East Asian financial crisis of 1997 immediately comes to mind. 'Bailout' is a popular term all over the globe nowadays, although it is not new. In this part of the world, bailing out nations from financial turmoil was witnessed first when the IMF and other friendly developed nations bailed Thailand, Korea, and Indonesia out from the crisis of 1997. Contrary to this, it was observed that Malaysia was also a crisis-hit nation that refused to be bailed out by the IMF in 1997.

The condition in 2008 and 2009 is somewhat different. This time the crisis began with the United States and other Organization for Economic Cooperation and Development (OECD) countries; thus, no IMF is available to bail them out. Plus, in the case of Southeast and East Asia, the amount of bailout money needed was in the billions, and now it is in trillions, at least in the cases of the United States and the EU. The bailout waves have hit South Asia as well. Some apex business bodies in the region are requesting the governments to bail them out from the present crisis with millions and billions of dollars. The IMF approved a bailout package for Sri Lanka in 2023, provided it managed to meet debt restructuring and revenue targets set under the programme when the country plunged into its worst economic crisis in 2022. As Sri Lanka appeared to have made substantial progress towards debt sustainability, raising domestic revenue, rebuilding foreign reserves, reducing inflation, and establishing external and internal stability, the second tranche of the \$2.9 billion bailout package was approved at the end of the year 2023. Relatedly, Pakistan also received a $6 billion bailout package from the IMF to support its BOP crisis in 2023.

It appears that the business of a bailout by the state is certainly not clear to the ordinary readers and students. In simple words, as they say, under the bailout plans, the incumbent government wants to support big businesses with the taxpayers' money or from borrowing it so that these businesses do not go broke and the workers can be kept on the payroll until a recovery is in sight. Nations such as the United States, Japan, and EU countries have bailed out private businesses in recent months. What awaits South Asia? This is certainly going to be the key question needing to be answered by the policies of respective governments in this respect in the near future.

Bailout or not, the present task is to keep the economy from bleeding from the Great Recession. For example, for a nation like Bangladesh, with the lowest credit rating and poor foreign reserves, the prospect of a bailout is very limited without indulging in printing money. It all depends on how hard the economy lands over the next two years and how the multilateral donors behave during the time of crisis for the nations such as Bangladesh. For the nations, rich or poor, at the end of the day, the major issue is recovering with minimum damage inflicted to the economy and recovering within the shortest possible time.

In this regard, the recovery in East Asia, particularly Korea, has been spectacular between 1997 and 1999, with bailout support by the IMF. In contrast, Malaysia's recovery in Southeast Asia from the Asian currency crisis, if not spectacular, was certainly remarkable without any support from the IMF or others. One should keep in mind here that the IMF support for Korea came in 1997 against some stringent conditions imposed by the IMF. The then government of Dr. Mahathir Mohammad, however, refused to accept such support for Malaysia. In the end, both Korea and Malaysia recovered, although Malaysia's recovery was slower by a few years. It is clear that by 2005, both Korea and Malaysia recovered. They have been growing again. Both the economies hit an almost 5 per cent growth level in 2003, and the inflation was brought down to below 3 per cent in 2005. During the crisis period (1997–1999), both countries were in deep recession. They, however, recovered from serious unemployment problems, which hit double digits during the crisis period in early 2000.

With the support of the IMF bailout package, the economic situation in Sri Lanka demonstrated a notable improvement towards the latter part of 2023, with 2023, the third quarter, reporting a 1.6 per cent year-on-year growth after six consecutive quarters of negative growth rate since 2022. Similarly, gross international reserves increased by $2.5 billion during 2023, and inflation remained contained. Pakistan has also demonstrated tentative signs of improving economic performance and easing external pressure.

It must be emphasized, once again, that for the recovery, the nations in question adopted contrasting policies. One can learn several lessons from both the experiences presented earlier. At this stage, the most important issue for South Asia is to ensure the current momentum continues and facilitate economic stability. A resilient recovery from pandemic- and war-related economic downturns and critical domestic economic mismanagement requires a wide range of policies, including carefully thought-through fiscal and monetary policy.

Reference

World Bank (2023) *World Development Indicators*, Washington, DC: The World Bank.

3

BENCHMARKING SOUTH ASIA'S HUMAN DEVELOPMENT IN THE ERA OF TURBULENCE

Moazzem Hossain

Introduction

Overall changes in selected social indicators

So far, the population statistics of the nations studied have indicated that remarkable improvements have occurred in demographic conditions over the last 30 years. In Table 3.1, a comparison has been made by country to show differences in various social indicators over the period between 2006 and 2021.

The longevity indicator in all eight nations shows an improving trend over this period. Bangladesh's average life expectancy over the last 15 years has increased by more than five years. Life expectancy in the rest of the South Asian nations, except Pakistan, increased by almost three years. Pakistan's life expectancy remains almost the same. The Philippines' life expectancy was

TABLE 3.1 Major social indicators, 2006 and 2021

Country	*Life expectancy at birth, total (years)*		*Infant mortality rate (per 1,000 live births)*		*Total fertility rate (birth per women)*		*Primary school completion rate (%)*		*Adult rate total (% of population ages 15+)*	
	2006	*2021*	*2006*	*2021*	*2006*	*2021*	*2005*	*2021*	*2006*	*2021*
Bangladesh	63.1	69	73	37	3.2	2.3	77	90.5	47.5	79.0
India	63.7	67	67	43	3.1	2.5	89	93.2	61	78.0
Pakistan	64.7	65	76	69	4	4.2	63	72.6	49.9	42.0
Sri Lanka	71.6	73	neg.	9	2	2.2	NA	98.9	90.7	98.9
Malaysia	74	75	12	7	2.7	NA	94	99.5	88	99.5
The Philippines	71	71	33	25	3.2	NA	97	98.7	93	90.7
Thailand	71	76	21	11	1.9	NA	82	89.6	53	90.9
Vietnam	71	74	19	18	1.8	NA	94	98.0	90	89.6

Sources: World Bank (2007), UNDP (2008, 2022)

DOI: 10.4324/9781032716244-4

not changed over the same period, and Malaysia's life expectancy increased by only one year. In Thailand, this increase has been by five years, while Vietnam shows an increase of three years. Infant mortality and fertility rates are in decline in all eight nations. However, in Bangladesh and India, the fertility rate continued declining. The rate of decline in Southeast Asia is not available but is certainly in decline. Primary school completion rates have been showing improvement in all the countries, and adult literacy ratios have been signalling improvement in all the nations except in Pakistan in South Asia between 2006 and 2021.

Development performance in health and education sector between 2006 and 2021

This section provides an overview of South and Southeast Asia's attempts to improve conditions in the areas of health and education over the last three decades. In other words, this makes intra-region and inter-region comparisons on social well-being.

Table 3.2 presents the basic health record in the eight countries under study. All the countries, as mentioned earlier, have increased their average life expectancy over the last 15 years, except the Philippines. All these countries recorded remarkable progress in life expectancy in recent years.

Access to overall health services has significantly improved in all countries. Access to improved water sources shows a moderate achievement by all these nations. Recently, Bangladesh provided improved water sources to 59 per cent of its population, Pakistan to 50 per cent, and Sri Lanka to 47 per cent. In Southeast Asia, Malaysia provides improved water sources to 94 per cent. The Philippines provide improved water sources to 48 per cent, and Thailand to 52 per cent. Malaysia's achievement in this sector remains at close to 100 per cent due to its strong per capita growth during the last three decades. Access to improved sanitation provided in 2021 by Bangladesh was 58 per cent, by India 75 per cent, by Pakistan 69 per cent, and by Sri Lanka 94 per cent. In Southeast Asia, improved sanitation provided in 2021 by Malaysia was 96 per cent, the Philippines 94 per cent, Thailand 99 per cent, and Vietnam 90 per cent.

Education

Government spending in education increased in India in 2021. Others in South Asia remained low for 2021. The use of the Internet increased in all these nations up to 2021. Malaysia was the highest user among the nations of these regions over this period.

Changes in poverty and income distribution

Poverty has many definitions; however, for the purpose of this section the following definition by Quibria is taken into consideration. Poverty can be defined as:

> the inability to achieve an acceptable living standard. Living standard may be thought of as real income, appropriately measured, after adjustments are made for goods and services produced and consumed at home, for income-in-kind, for cost-of-living differences and for household size and composition.
>
> *(1994: 188)*

TABLE 3.2 South and Southeast Asia's human development record, 2006 and 2021

Sector	*Bangladesh*		*India*		*Pakistan*		*Sri Lanka*		*Malaysia*		*The Philippines*		*Thailand*		*Vietnam*	
Human Development Index (HDI) (2021)	0.661		0.633		0.544		0.782		0.803		0.699		0.88		0.73	
Health																
Crude birth rate (per 1,000) (2006, 2021)	21	18	21	16	32	28	18	14	17	15	24	11	25	16	9	5
Crude death rate (per 1,000) (2006, 2021)	6	6	7	9	8	9	7	7	5	6	6	7	8	8	3	7
Contraceptive prevalence rate (% of women ages 15–49) (2006, 2021)	61	63	55	67	27	34	68	65	49	52	49	54	54	70	73	78
Access to improved water source (%) (2006, 2021)	55	59	NA	NA	39	50	46	47	93	94	45	48	52	52	NA	NA
Access to improved sanitation (%) (2006, 2021)	42	58	46	75	51	69	86	94	95	96	72	94	96	99	71	90
Physicians (per 1,000) (2006, 2021)	0.40	0.70	1.20	0.07	0.81	1.10		0.74	0.20	1.20	2.30	0.30	0.80	0.40	0.90	0.78
Health expenditure (% of GDP) (2006, 2021)	2.83	2.63	3.25	2.91	2.14	2.90	3.70	4.00	3.31	4.12	4.03	5.61	3.57	4.36	4.21	4.49
Education																
Primary enrolment ratio (2006, 2021)	90	50	90	93	71.5	72.6	99	96	99	97	99	96	91	89	99	98
Secondary enrolment ratio (2006, 2021)	53	70	65	78	30	42	95	99	98	99	97	99	96	95	91	89
Internet users (per 1,000) (2006, 2021)	5	39	10	46	NA	NA	NA	NA	61	97	29	53	24	85	35	74
Public expenditure on education (% of GDP) (2006, 2021)	2.1	1.8	3.8	4.6	2.2	1.7	1.7	1.5	5.8	4.3	2.5	3.9	4.8	3.0	3.8	3.0
Ratio of education and health expenditure and military expenditure (% of GDP) (2006, 2021)	1.2	1.2	2.7	2.5	3.3	3.0	2.2	1.9	1.6	1.0	1.2	1.4	1.5	1.3	2.0	2.3 (2018)

Sources: http://hdr.undp.org/reports/global/2004/pdf/hdr04.HDI.pdf,

http://devdata.worldbank.org/hnpstats/query/SMResult.asp.s

TABLE 3.3 Changing level of poverty

Country	*National measure: population below poverty line*						*International measure: $2/person/day*			
	Year	*%*	*Year*	*%*	*Year*	*%*	*Year*	*%*	*Year*	*%*
Bangladesh	2005	35.0*	2011	24.3	2022	18.7	2005	84.0	2022	18.7
India	2000	33.5*	2005	34.5*	2011	21.9	2005	80.	2022	21.9
Pakistan	2002	17.0*	2015	24.3	2018	21.9	2002	73.6	2018	4.9
Sri Lanka	2002	5.5*	2016	4.1	2019	14.3	2002	41.6	2019	1.0
Malaysia	1993	22.4	NA	NA	2021	6.2	1997	9.3	2018	0.0
The Philippines	1997	36.8	2011	25.2	2021	18.1	2003	30.6	2004	3.0
Thailand	1995	13.6	2010	13.2	2021	6.3	2002	25.2	2021	0.0
Vietnam	2002	28.9	2015	9.2	2020	4.8	1998	63.7	2020	0.7

Sources: World Bank (1990, 2004, 2007);

www.worldbank.org/data/wdi2004/pdfs/table2-5.pdf;
www.worldbank.org/wdr/2000/pdfs/engtable4.pdf;
www.worldbank.org/data/wdi2001/pdfs/tab2_6.pdf

Note:* Figures are $1/person/day.

TABLE 3.4 Eradication of extreme poverty

Country	*Year*	*Poverty (US$2 a day headcount ratio (%))*	*Share of consumption to poorest quintile (%), 2005*
Bangladesh	2022	9.6	9.0
India	2021	11.9	8.9
Pakistan	2018	4.9	9.3
Sri Lanka	2019	1.0	7.0
Malaysia	2018	0.0	4.4
The Philippines	2021	3.0	5.4
Thailand	2021	0.0	6.3
Vietnam	2020	0.0	9.0

Source: World Bank (2024)

Using US$1 per person per day as the poverty line, Table 3.3 shows that in 2005, Bangladesh had 35 per cent of its population living in poverty, India had 33.5 per cent, Pakistan had 17 per cent, and Sri Lanka had 5.5 per cent. However, in recent years, all these nations have experienced an increase in poverty due to an increase in the prices of food grains worldwide. In Southeast Asia, the international measure of poverty was considered at US$2 per person per day since in these countries the per capita income and cost of living are higher than in the South. The Philippines had 31 per cent of its population living in poverty in 2004, and Thailand had 25 per cent in 2002. The figures for Vietnam are unavailable for recent years. However, this nation's improvement in growth in recent years has contributed positively to the eradication of poverty (see Table 3.4).

Millennium development goals: a tale of two Asias

The MDGs were set by the international community led by the United Nations with a Millennium Declaration in 2000. In order to achieve the MDGs, the international community agreed that, for example, poverty will be halved by 2015 in developing nations, taking the 1990 level as a benchmark. On top of the goal of poverty reduction, there are seven more MDGs. Each of these goals, moreover, sets multiple targets to be achieved by 2015. Out of eight development goals, there are 18 targets to be met. The MDGs broadly include the areas covered under social and environmental goals with the partnership between developed and developing countries (World Bank 2006). In this section, an attempt is made to investigate the social goals and targets in some selected nations of Asia. The social goals cover five areas: eradicate extreme poverty, achieve universal primary education, promote gender equality, reduce child mortality, and improve maternal health.

The cut-off date for achieving the MDGs is 2015, yet many nations are finding major difficulties in living up to the commitments they made at the time of the declaration in 2000. There are many reasons for this; however, it appears that the Southeast Asian nations are ahead of their counterparts in South Asia. The results are presented in Tables 3.5 and 3.6.

Taking headcount ratio into consideration, it is expected that Bangladesh will bring down poverty by 20 per cent of its total population by 2015. For India it is 15 per cent, and for Pakistan this is about 8 per cent of the total population. In Southeast Asia, only the Philippines had more than 10 per cent of people suffering from poverty in headcount ratio terms in 2005. By 2015, this nation must bring down poverty to a level of 5 per cent. Other nations in this region have a negligible percentage of people suffering from poverty. Unfortunately, the information for Vietnam is not available currently.

Table 3.5 presents information on the status of these countries in terms of primary education completion rate and gender equality in education. Once again, the Southeast Asian nations have been ahead of the nations in South Asia. Primary education completion rates have been very high in all the nations in both regions except Bangladesh and Pakistan. However, Bangladesh and India have improved their completion rates significantly since 1991. In terms of gender ratio, all nations except Pakistan and India strongly recovered from education inequality between male and female students in 2005. Female enrolment is larger than male enrolment in all the nations except India and Pakistan. Thailand is marginally behind.

TABLE 3.5 Achieving universal primary education and promoting gender equality

Country	*Primary education completion (%)*		*Ratio of girls to boys in primary, secondary, and tertiary (%), 2021*		
	2010	*2020*	*Primary*	*Secondary*	*Tertiary*
Bangladesh	75.9	80.6	102	124	83
India	91.6	93.6	102	97	107
Pakistan	54.4	59.2	NA	NA	NA
Sri Lanka	NA	NA	NA	NA	NA
Malaysia	99.1	99.6	NA	106	NA
The Philippines	88.3	89.7	98	108	127
Thailand	98.4	99.4	99	103	127
Vietnam	96.7	97.8	102	NA	111

Sources: https//:www.globaleconomy.com/rankings/Female_to_male_primary_school_pupils/

https//www. Globaleconomy.com/rankings/Female-to_male_ratio_students_tertiary_level_educa/

TABLE 3.6 Reducing child mortality and improving maternal health

Nations due to a search for green fuel out of corn, soybean and sugarcane (ethanol)	*Nations due to a search for green fuel out of corn, soybean and sugarcane (ethanol)*			*Nations due to a search for green fuel out of corn, soybean and sugarcane (ethanol)*		
	2005	*2015*	*2021*	*2005*	*2015*	*2020*
Bangladesh	143	38	27.3	380	212	123
India	123	43.6	30.6	540	128	103
Pakistan	130	76.2	63.3	500	187	154
Sri Lanka	32	8.8	6.7	92	30	29
Malaysia	22	8.8	7.6	41	22	21
The Philippines	62	29.8	25.7	200	88	78
Thailand	37	10.8	8.3	44	30	29
Vietnam	53	21.9	20.6	130	109	124

Sources: World Bank (2024)

https://genderdata.worldbank.org/indicators/sh-dya-mort/?gender=total&year=2021
https://genderdata.worldbank.org/indicator/SH.STA.MMRI

In the case of child mortality and maternal mortality ratios, Table 3.6 presents figures for 2005. Once again, in terms of both the criteria, South Asia has been behind Southeast Asia. However, the South Asian nations have improved in both terms over 2005, 2021, and 2020. Maternal mortality rate is still very high in all the nations in South Asia except Sri Lanka. In Southeast Asia, this rate is relatively high in the Philippines.

Conclusion

Given the above information, it may be emphasized that in Southeast Asia the MDGs have been achieved by 2015. It is expected, however, that South Asia will cross the line in all the goals except poverty alleviation. In recent years, in relative terms, the poverty in headcount terms has increased in all the nations of South Asia for at least three reasons: increase in food prices, increase in fuel prices, and change in the food grain cultivation pattern in developed.

Bibliography

Quibria, M. G. (ed.) (1994) *Rural Poverty in Developing Asia*, Volume 1, Bangladesh, India, Sri Lanka and Manila: Asian Development Bank.
UNDP (2008) *Human Development Report 2007/2008*. http://undp.org
UNDP (2022) *Human Development Report 2020/2021*. http://undp.org
UNDP (2024) *Human Development Report 2023/2024*, Breaking the Gridlock: Reimagining Cooperation in a Polarized World, New York: The United Nations Development Programme.
World Bank (1990) *World Development Report 1990: Poverty*, Oxford: Oxford University Press.
World Bank (2004) *World Development Indicators 2004*, Oxford: Oxford University Press.
World Bank (2006) *Global Monitoring Report: Millennium Development Goals IBRD*, Washington, DC: The World Bank.
World Bank (2007) *The World Bank Development Report 2007: Development and the Next Generation*, Washington, DC: World Bank.
World Bank (2024) *World Development Report 2024: The Middle Income Trap*. https://worldbank.org

4

DEMOGRAPHIC DYNAMICS OF SOUTH ASIA

Maneka Jayasinghe, Saroja Selvanathan, and Eliyathamby A. Selvanathan

Introduction

It is well known that South Asia and Southeast Asia support more than one-fourth of the world's total population. The latest figures suggest that almost two billion people now populate the countries in these regions. More precisely, the figure was 2.7 billion in 2022 (see Table 4.1). Demographically, therefore, they are critical and alarming regions of the world. By world standards, South Asia is characterized by very high population growth, high density, and a high dependency rate. The reason for including this chapter in the present volume is to demonstrate the effect of the population problem in the course of the development of the countries studied. Also, it shows the severity of the population factor, which constrains economic development. An attempt is made, first, to outline the general demographic situation and then to analyse the effects of population growth on economic development.

The demographic conditions and trends

Table 4.1 shows that in 2022, the total population of all the countries studied is about one-third of the world's total. The average annual population growth rate for South Asia from 1995–2005 was 1.8 per cent per annum and has continued to decline to 1.3 per cent during 2005–2015 and 1.0 per cent per annum in 2015–2022. On the other hand, the average annual population growth rate for Southeast Asia during 1995–2005 was 1.7 per cent per annum and has continued to decline to 1.3 per cent during 2005–2015 and then to 0.9 per cent per annum during 2015–2022. Among the South Asian nations, Pakistan had the highest annual population growth rate between 1995 and 2022 (2.8 to 1.5 per cent), and Sri Lanka (0.9 to 0.5 per cent per annum) had the lowest population growth. Among the Southeast Asian countries, the Philippines had the highest annual rate of population growth (1.5 per cent), followed by Malaysia (1.1 per cent), while Thailand had the lowest of all countries (0.2 per cent) during the 2015–2022 period. In all countries under consideration in both regions, South Asia and Southeast Asia, the proportion of the population living in rural areas fell during 2005–2022.

DOI: 10.4324/9781032716244-5

TABLE 4.1 Demographic conditions in South Asia and Southeast Asia

Country	*Area (in '000 sq. km.)*	*Population (million)*				*Growth rate (%)*			*Rural/total population*		
		1995	*2005*	*2015*	*2022*	*1995–2005*	*2005–2015*	*2015–2022*	*2005*	*2015*	*2022*
South Asia											
Bangladesh	148	117.8	140.9	157.8	171.2	1.8	1.1	1.1	73.2	65.6	60.3
India	3,288	964.3	1154.6	1322.9	1417.2	1.8	1.3	0.9	70.8	67.2	64.1
Pakistan	882	133.1	174.4	211.0	235.8	2.8	1.9	1.5	66.0	64	62.3
Sri Lanka	66	18.0	19.7	21.3	22.2	0.9	0.7	0.5	81.7	81.7	81.0
Mean						1.8	1.3	1.0			
Southeast Asia											
Malaysia	331	20.1	25.9	31.1	33.9	2.6	1.8	1.1	33.4	25.8	21.8
The Philippines	342	69.3	86.3	103.0	115.6	2.2	1.8	1.5	54.3	53.7	52.0
Thailand	514	59.4	65.8	70.3	71.7	1.0	0.6	0.2	62.6	52.3	47.1
Vietnam	331	73.8	83.1	92.2	98.2	1.1	1.0	0.8	72.7	66.2	61.2
Mean						1.7	1.3	0.9			
Mean (overall)						1.8	1.3	1.0			

Sources: World Development Indicators; World Bank (2023)

TABLE 4.2 Population estimates and land use in South Asia and Southeast Asia

Country	*Total land in '000 sq. km*	*Population density (in per sq. km)*				*Land use (% of total)*			
	2022	*1995*	*2005*	*2015*	*2022*	*1995*	*2005*	*2015*	*2022*
South Asia									
Bangladesh	144	904	1082.5	1,212.5	1,301.0	64.6	61.1	59.4	62.3
India	3,288	324	388.4	444.9	473.4	54.5	53.6	52.6	51.9
Pakistan	796	172.7	226.2	273.7	300.2	39.5	27.6	39.4	39.6
Sri Lanka	66	289.9	313.7	344.7	358.2	14.1	14.2	21	22.1
Southeast Asia									
Malaysia	330	61.3	78.9	94.6	102.2	2.7	5.5	2.5	2.5
The Philippines	300	232.3	289.3	345.6	381.9	17.7	19.1	18.7	18.7
Thailand	510	116.3	128.8	137.6	140.1	33.4	27.7	33.1	33.6
Vietnam	330	226.6	265.8	294.2	311.0	16.6	21.3	22.3	21.7

Sources: World Development Indicators; World Bank (2023)

As can be seen in Table 4.2, population density has seen notable growth in all countries in both regions studied during 1995–2022. Population density in South Asian countries is generally higher than in Southeast Asian countries. In Bangladesh and India, over the last 30 years, the population density increased by more than 30 per cent, while in Pakistan, the density increased by 40 per cent. In Sri Lanka, the density increased by only 19 per cent. Among South Asian countries, in 2022, Bangladesh had the highest population density per square kilometre (1,301 persons per sq. km of land area), and Pakistan had the lowest (300 persons per sq. km of land area). Among the Southeast Asian countries, the Philippines had the highest population density per square kilometre (382 people per sq. km of land area), and Malaysia had the lowest (102 people per sq. km of land area) in 2022. Bangladesh has had the highest percentage of arable land (over 60 per cent of total land) during 1995–2022, followed by India (over 50 per cent of total land). In the Southeast Asian region, the land use in the arable category in 2005 was the highest in Thailand (27.7 per cent) and the lowest in Malaysia (5.5 per cent) out of the total surface land of these nations. By 2022, while the arable land in Thailand further increased to 33.6 per cent, Malaysia's declined to 2.5 per cent.

Population distribution

The distribution of population by age group and dependency ratio by country are presented in Table 4.3. As can be seen, children in the age group 0–14 years constitute the second largest proportion of the total population of each country. In 1996, this proportion was very high for all South and Southeast Asian countries. However, the proportion of children in the age group 0–14 years has seen a declining trend, with the most significant fall seen in Bangladesh, from 42 per cent in 1996 to 26 per cent in 2022. In South Asia, Sri Lanka has the lowest population proportion in the age group 0–14 years (23 per cent). In 2022, this was 37 per cent in Pakistan and 25 per cent in India. In 2022, these ranged from greater than 15 per cent in Thailand, greater than 20 per cent in Malaysia and Vietnam, and above 30 per cent in the Philippines. The overall figures suggest that the fertility rate in all these countries has declined over the last ten years. The issue of fertility rate is illustrated further in the last section of this chapter.

On the other hand, the proportion of the 65+ population has increased in all South and Southeast Asian countries, with Sri Lanka (12 per cent) having the highest and Pakistan having the

TABLE 4.3 Distribution of population by age and dependency ratio in South Asia and Southeast Asia, 1996, 2005, and 2022

Country	*Age group*									*Dependency ratio (% of working age population)*		
	0–14 years			*15–64 years*			*65+ years*					
	1996	*2005*	*2022*	*1996*	*2005*	*2022*	*1996*	*2005*	*2022*	*1995*	*2005*	
South Asia												
Bangladesh	42.3	35.5	26.0	56.8	60.9	68.0	0.9	3.6	6.0	76.1	64.2	47.1
India	35.8	32.1	25.3	60.2	62.7	67.8	4.0	5.3	6.9	66.1	59.6	47.5
Pakistan	45.5	38.3	36.6	51.1	57.9	59.1	3.4	3.8	4.3	95.7	72.7	69.2
Sri Lanka	31.7	24.1	22.8	64.2	68.6	65.6	4.1	7.3	11.5	55.8	45.8	52.3
Southeast Asia												
Malaysia	36.2	32.4	22.7	59.9	63.0	69.8	3.9	4.6	7.5	66.9	58.7	43.3
The Philippines	38.4	35.1	30.3	58.1	61.0	64.2	3.5	3.9	5.4	72.1	63.9	55.6
Thailand	26.2	23.8	15.5	68.2	69.1	69.3	5.6	7.1	15.2	46.6	44.7	44.3
Vietnam	36.0	29.5	22.4	58.5	65.0	68.5	5.5	5.4	9.1	70.9	53.7	46.0

Sources: World Development Indicators; World Bank (2023)

TABLE 4.4 Labour force participation rates in South Asia and Southeast Asia, by sector, 1980–2005

Country	*Agriculture*		*Industries*		*Services*	
	2010	*2022*	*2010*	*2022*	*2010*	*2022*
South Asia						
Bangladesh	47.3	37.1	17.6	21.7	35.1	41.2
India	51.5	44.0	21.8	25.3	26.7	30.7
Pakistan	43.4	37.5	24.8	25.2	35.2	37.3
Sri Lanka	30.9	25.7	21.4	27.9	44.2	46.4
Southeast Asia						
Malaysia	13.3	9.6	27.6	28.3	59.1	62.1
The Philippines	33.0	24.3	15.5	18.9	51.5	57.0
Thailand	38.2	31.6	20.6	22.5	41.1	45.9
Vietnam	48.7	29.0	21.7	33.1	29.6	37.8

Sources: World Development Indicators; World Bank (2023)

lowest (4.3 per cent) in South Asia and Thailand (15 per cent) having the highest and the Philippines having the lowest (5.4 per cent) in Southeast Asia.

The dependency ratio presented in Table 4.3 is calculated using the following formula:

$$\text{Dependency ratio} = \frac{\text{Persons } 0-14+65 \text{ and above}}{\text{Persons } 15-64} \times 1000$$

The dependency ratios presented in Table 4.3 show that children (aged 0–14 years) and older people (65 and above) constitute the dependency load for persons of the primary working ages (15–64 years). The figures reveal that generally, Pakistan had the highest dependency ratio (69 per cent in 2022), followed by Sri Lanka (52 per cent) in South Asia, and the Philippines has the highest (56 per cent), while Malaysia has the lowest (43 per cent) in Southeast Asia in 2022. However, the dependency ratio has declined for all the countries of these regions except in Sri Lanka and Thailand, potentially owing to a higher proportion of the aged population.

Table 4.4 presents the labour force participation rates for the eight countries in the two regions by sector for 2010–2022. The figures suggest that in 2010, the agricultural sector was the main source of labour force utilization for Bangladesh, India, and Pakistan in the South Asian region and Vietnam in the Southeast Asian region. During the same time, the services sector was the primary source of labour force utilization in Sri Lanka in South Asia and Malaysia, the Philippines, and Thailand in Southeast Asia. However, by 2022, labour force participation in the agriculture sector in all countries has dropped notably. On the other hand, during 2010–2022, the labour force participation in the industry and service sector increased in all countries under consideration.

Female labour force participation

In recent years, development literature has been inundated by studies on female participation in developed and developing countries (Agarwal 1989; Schultz 1990; Boserup and Harris 1990; Sen 1990; Bardhan 1993; Quibria 1993; UN Women 2018). During 2018–2023, the World Bank, UN agencies, and International Monetary Fund (IMF) undertook numerous studies on women and their role in the future development of developing countries. Table 4.5 presents some related information from selected Asian countries about the equality standard of women against that of men.

Women's participation in a country's labour force and women's health and literacy levels are some of the important indicators of the role of women in development. Table 4.5 depicts a notable increase in female life expectancy, particularly during 1990–2005 in all South and Southeast Asian countries under consideration. Similarly, female adult literacy rates have grown significantly over the last three decades.

Table 4.6 presents detailed comparative information on female labour force participation for the eight South and Southeast Asian countries between 1990 and 2022. In Bangladesh and Sri Lanka, over one-third of the labour force comprised of women in 2022. Almost half of the

TABLE 4.5 Women in development in South Asia and Southeast Asia, 1990, 2005, and 2022

Country	*Life expectancy of females as a % of males*			*Female adult literacy rate (% of people over 15)*		
	1990	*2005*	*2022*	*1990*	*2015*	*2022*
South Asia						
Bangladesh	96	104	105	26	44	72
India	103	104	105	34	51	69
Pakistan	104	105	108	21	35	47
Sri Lanka	114	113	109	84	89	92
Southeast Asia						
Malaysia	106	106	106	77	85	–
The Philippines	106	105	106	93	96	97
Thailand	111	111	111	90	92	93
Vietnam	114	114	113	83	91	95

Sources: Gender data portal; World Bank (2024)

TABLE 4.6 Female labour force in South Asia and Southeast Asia, 1990, 2005, and 2022

Country	*Total labour force (millions)*			*Female labour force (% of total labour force)*		
	1990	*2005*	*2022*	*1990*	*2005*	*2022*
South Asia						
Bangladesh	35.6	53.1	74.5	21.7	24.7	32.7
India	292.7	422	523.8	24.8	26.8	23.5
Pakistan	32	51.7	78.9	10.9	17.6	23.3
Sri Lanka	7.2	7.9	8.7	36.6	33.1	34.2
Southeast Asia						
Malaysia	6.9	10.8	17.3	35.1	35.2	39.2
The Philippines	22.5	33.7	47	38.7	38.3	39.1
Thailand	29	38.1	40.2	44.2	46.3	45.9
Vietnam	31.9	43.7	56	50.8	49	48.5

Sources: Gender data portal; World Bank (2024)

Vietnamese and Thai labour forces were made up of women in the same period. In the Philippines and Malaysia, women comprised almost 40 per cent of the labour force in 2022. In all the countries except India, Sri Lanka, and Vietnam, female participation has increased since 1990.

All values are expressed in relation to the male average, which is indexed to equal 100. The closer the value is to 100, the smaller the gap, and a value above 100 indicates that the female average is higher than that of the male.

Demographic challenges

Over the past 50 years, Asia has experienced rapid population growth. Today, its population stands at around 4.7 billion. The United Nations population projections suggest that Asia's population is expected to rise to 5.3 billion by 2050 (Ritchie 2019). It is a picture that is far less alarming than the other regions of Asia (the Far East), mainly when one looks at population densities (see Table 4.2).

On the one hand, during 1995–2005, population growth at an alarming rate was seen as the most significant obstacle in the South Asian region, particularly in India. On the other hand, policymakers began to consider the demographic dividend—the larger share of the working-age population than the non-working-age share of the population—as an engine for further economic development. However, during the last two decades, South and Southeast Asia have experienced a significant reduction in fertility rates. Most Southeast Asian countries have a fertility rate below the replacement level of 2.1 (Yeung 2022), while on average, South Asia's fertility rate stood at 2.56 during 2010–2015 (United Nations 2017). Rapid urbanization, increased female labour force participation, increased female median age at marriage, and higher cost of raising children have substantially contributed to the declining fertility rate. This situation can be further explained by the increasing or high contraceptive prevalence in the countries studied. As can be seen in Table 4.7, between 1995 and the latest year of data available, this has increased from 43 to 67 per cent of women aged between 15 and 49 in India, from 46 to 63 per cent in Bangladesh, and from 12 to 34 per cent in Pakistan. The contraceptive prevalence is lowest in Pakistan among the countries studied. Although the contraceptive prevalence has slightly

TABLE 4.7 Contraceptive use rates, 1995, 2005, and latest

Country	*Contraceptive prevalence (% of women aged 15–49)*		
	1995	*2005*	*Latest available*
South Asia			
Bangladesh	46	58	63 (2019)
India	43	47	67 (2021)
Pakistan	12	28	34 (2019)
Sri Lanka	62	70	65 (2016)
Southeast Asia			
Malaysia	56	49	52 (2014)
The Philippines	48	49	54 (2017)
Thailand	72	72	73 (2019)
Vietnam	75	77	73 (2021)

Source: World Bank (2023)

declined in Malaysia and Vietnam since 1995, that of Vietnam is still high, with almost 75 per cent of women aged between 15 and 49 using contraceptive methods.

It must be emphasized that in South Asia, particularly in Pakistan and Bangladesh, the population growth rate has been bouncing back in recent years after a significant slide in the final quarter of the 20th century. The increasing trend has been attributed to the lack of budget allocation and the decline in support by the international community for direct population control measures. A recent report by the population and family planning department of the government of Bangladesh identified several issues that are behind the collapse of the population programme implemented over the last two decades. These are a lack of sustained field-level workforce, corruption in the procurement of relevant effective population control devices, and declining morale of the existing workforce due to the lack of initiative by recent governments to keep the dedicated workforce in the departments. It has been reported that the success in the past had been brought by the field-level workers who visited the households in rural areas regularly. For example, out of the total rural households in Bangladesh, almost 43 per cent had been visited in 1993–1994. This dropped to 35 per cent in 1997–1998. In 1999–2000 this dropped even further to only 18 per cent. The major reason for such a drop in visits was the lack of condoms, pills, and other related population control devices. Moreover, out of more than 50,000 field workers, almost 7,500 positions are presently vacant (15 per cent of the total). This is no doubt contributing towards destroying the morale of the existing workers and results in the decline of service to rural areas, where demand for population control devices still exists.

In 2023, India surpassed China as the world's most populous country for the first time, with 1.4 billion people. India's population has grown by more than a billion since 1950. Although growth has slowed, owing to several national family planning programmes aimed at curbing its population growth since the 1950s, the number of people in the country is still expected to continue to rise for the next few decades, reaching its peak of 1.7 billion by 2064. Hansen (2002) suggests that in the last several decades, fertility control policies in India have failed to promote a sustainable solution to the problem of overpopulation. What factors have caused these efforts to disintegrate? The following have been suggested:

- It appears that the national sterilization scheme had not achieved a desirable outcome.
- Targeting female sterilization was a failure over the last few decades.

In addition, the major challenge for India is the family's strong preference for sons. This made the overall male-to-female ratio quite imbalanced in recent years (Begum and Singh 2007). The sex ratio in India during 2013–2015 was 900, suggesting that the number of females per 1,000 males was 900.

Pakistan is the world's fifth most populous country, and between 1951 and 2017, Pakistan's population grew over six-fold. As mentioned earlier, Pakistan has the highest population growth rate of 2.1 per cent during 2015–2022 among the South Asian countries. High birth rates, limited access to family planning services, cultural norms, and religious beliefs have been the main factors contributing to exponential population growth in Pakistan. In particular, the population control policy has been put on the back burner in Pakistan since the period after 11 September 2001. The United States Agency for International Development (USAID) was the major donor agency in Pakistan. It was the source of funds for the family planning department. There was a pause of USAID assistance in 2001–2003 since the agency closed its offices in Pakistan after 9/11. USAID was back again in 2008 and extended $60 million to Pakistan to address the population control issue. The country acknowledges the adverse effect of high population growth on the country's development and is committed to the FP2030 with the vision of empowering women and girls and all couples to enjoy the basic right to decide the number of their children freely and responsibly by maintaining a balance.

Sri Lanka was a high achiever in controlling population in the 1970s and 1980s. When the nation experienced civil war in the 1980s, it slipped from the demographic literature for this period. The population growth in Sri Lanka has been below 1 per cent since 2000. From 2019 to 2020, the population grew by only 0.42 per cent. The growing ageing population (the highest proportion in South Asia) and out-migration of the working-age population, especially due to the ongoing economic crisis, further shrinking the working-age population group, are the greater demographic challenges Sri Lanka is facing today (ILO 2023).

Bibliography

Agarwal, B. (1989) "Rural women, poverty and natural resources: Sustenance, sustainability and struggle for change", *Economic and Political Weekly*, WS46–WS65.

Bardhan, P. (1993) "Analytics of the institutions of informal cooperation in rural development", *World Development*, 21, 4: 633–639.

Begum, S. M. and Singh, C. (2007) "The economics behind son preference in South India", in A. Ahmed (ed.), *World Sustainable Development Outlook 2007* (pp. 391–400), London: University of Sussex.

Boserup, E. and Harris, D. (1990) "Population, the status of women and rural development", in G. McNicoll and M. Cain (eds.), *Rural Development and Population: Institutions and Policy* (pp. 45–60), New York: Oxford University Press.

Hannah Ritchie (2019) "More than 8 out of 10 people in the world will live in Asia or Africa by 2100," *Published Online at OurWorldInData.org*. https://ourworldindata.org/region-population-2100

Hansen, Z. (2002) Population Control in India, Colby College, USA.

ILO (2023) ILO Brief, Sri Lanka's Labour Market during the Economic Crisis of 2022–23, ILO.

Quibria, M. G. (ed.) (1993) *Critical Issues in Asian Development*, Hong Kong: Oxford University Press.

Schultz, T. P. (1990) "Women's changing participation in the labor force: A world perspective", *Economic Development and Cultural Change*, 38, 3: 457–488.

Sen, A. K. (1990) "How is India doing?", in *The Indian Economy and Its Performance since Independence*, Delhi: Oxford University Press.

UN Women (2018) *Turning Promises into Action: Gender Equality in the 2030 Agenda for Sustainable Development*, New York. www.unwomen.org/en/digital-library/publications/2018/2/gender-equality-in-the-2030-agenda-for-sustainable-development-2018

United Nations (2017) World Fertility Report 2015, Department of Economics and Social Affairs, United Nations.

World Bank (2023) *World Development Indicators*. Washington, DC: The World Bank.

The World Bank (2024) *Gender Data Portal*, https://genderdata.worldbank.org/en/home, accessed on 23 December 2023.

World Bank (2024) Gender Data Portal, Washington, DC.

Yeung, W. J. J. (2022) "Fertility", in *Demographic and Family Transition in Southeast Asia*, Cham: Springer. https://doi.org/10.1007/978-3-030-85679-3_4

PART II

South Asian economic development

5

LABOUR MARKET INSTITUTIONS AND ECONOMIC PERFORMANCE

Moazzem Hossain

Introduction

The labour market and economic development: two views

The notion that developing economies in general are characterized by labour market distortions is identified by Freeman (1993) as the 'distortionist view.' This, he claims, is typically associated with the work of the World Bank—although in more recent contributions the Bank offers a much more qualified view of its position (World Bank 1995a: Ch. 12). The alternative is the 'institutionalist' view associated with the work of the International Labour Organization (ILO). In the case of the former, such labour market interventions as minimum wage legislation, mandated contributions to social security, job security legislation, large-scale unionization, and collective bargaining impair the growth process through a variety of routes. These interventions, while 'intended to raise welfare and reduce exploitation . . . actually work to raise the cost of labour . . . and reduce labour demand . . . and labour incomes where most of the poor are found' (World Bank 1990: 63; ILO 1991: 5). On the other hand, there are claims that 'over the long run suppression of free industrial relations jeopardizes prospects for economic development' and that there is a 'need to re-regulate the labour market' (ILO 1991: 65).

Labour market institutions as impediments to growth: the 'distortionist' model

To appreciate the significance of this debate and its relevance to South Asia, it is necessary to offer a more detailed exposition of the alternative perspectives noted earlier. Consider the distortionist view, which interprets organized labour as the source of both market failure and government failure. Trade unions represent monopoly imperfections in labour markets. They also form part of protection-seeking distributional coalitions. Indeed, some models of trade union behaviour perceive them as 'insiders' primarily interested in seeking benefits for employed members and unconcerned about the interests of 'outsiders' (i.e. unemployed, new job-seekers) (Carruth and Disney 1987).

Apart from unions, minimum wage legislation and job security regulations may also cause unemployment by creating wage rigidities. In the context of developing economies, such

DOI: 10.4324/9781032716244-7

institutional variables are primarily responsible for the existence of a formal sector consisting of a white-collar labour market with fixed wages and an informal sector consisting of blue-collar, low-paid workers with flexible wages. In other words, sectoral wage differentials are higher in the presence, rather than the absence, of labour market institutions.

It is also alleged that organized labour leads to restrictive practices that impede job flexibility, constrain the capacity of management to cope with external shocks, and retard technological innovation. The net effect is to impede dynamic efficiency.

It also follows that labour market rigidities impair international competitiveness. By increasing labour costs above market-clearing levels and by retarding productivity, high union density, minimum wage legislation, and related regulations lead to adverse shifts in unit labour costs (i.e. nominal wages adjusted by productivity), a standard measure of trends in international competitiveness. More importantly, pro-labour legislation can offset the salutary effects on export competitiveness that can be generated by exchange rate policy. Thus, for example, devaluations typically enhance export competitiveness by engineering a fall in real wages. This presupposes the absence of real wage resistance by workers—an assumption that may not be valid in the presence of strong unions and wage indexation.

If the regulatory framework does not allow the unfettered operation of the labour market and leads to adverse consequences on competitiveness through multiple channels, does this mean that coercive labour legislation (e.g. a ban on unions, organized industrial action, elimination of minimum wage legislation and job security regulations) is the necessary price that industrializing economies must pay? One can detect an intriguing, but unintended, convergence of views on this issue between scholars who are advocates of the distortionist model and radical scholars who oppose coercive legislation—or 'labour subordination' as they prefer to call it—on ideological grounds but accept the economic logic behind it. Representative examples include Deyo et al. (1987) and although it must be noted that in a later contribution Deyo (1989) adopts a rather more circumspect view on the labour subordination hypothesis. Despite this caveat, the observation that 'foreign and local investors have an especially strong interest in low wages . . . in labour peace and a minimum of union interference in managerial autonomy' captures the spirit of the radical position, which maintains that state-imposed labour discipline is vital to the success of export-oriented industrialization.

Such an argument is largely inseparable from the position taken by Bhagwati (1986), an eminent economist steeped in the neoclassical tradition and presumably a natural ally of the distortionist model. Bhagwati (1986: 133–143, June), drawing on the experience of the East Asian NIEs, accepts the point that 'authoritarian methods to keep trade union wage demands under control' can pay substantial dividends in the form of low inflation and general macroeconomic stability.

Labour market institutions: the institutionalist perspective, political economy considerations, and a more eclectic paradigm

One problem with the distortionist model is that it represents selective use of economic theory and ignores, or abstracts from, the point that unemployment or an inefficiently low volume of employment (relative to the full employment norm) may emerge even in the absence of labour market distortions. Thus, it is well known that employers may pay workers efficiency wages (i.e. wages above the market-clearing norm) in order to reduce labour turnover and enhance labour productivity. It is also important to appreciate the links between product market imperfections and labour market regulations—a point that is analysed at some length in the next section.

It is worth remembering too that in developing economies with labour surplus conditions, interventionist labour market policies probably have limited impact. It is difficult to sustain the argument that non-union and union labour would be imperfect substitutes in the presence of an abundant supply of low-skilled workers. This would in turn act as a natural constraint on the market power of organized labour. Similar considerations allow one to understand why it is relatively easy to circumvent minimum wage and other employment regulations in labour-surplus economies.

The institutionalist view does not simply rely on a critique of the distortionist model. It tries to go beyond this position and develop an alternative framework for analysing the appropriate role of the labour market in economic development. The institutionalist view probably has not enjoyed much popularity among the community of economists and academic scholars. It deserves greater attention. Standing depicts this as a school of thought that interprets

> unions as a source of 'dynamic efficiency,' obliging enterprises to pay efficiency wages rather than 'market clearing' wages and inducing management to raise productivity by technological innovations and cost-saving practices rather than reliance on low-cost labour.
>
> *(1992: 327)*

Sengenberger (1991: 249) makes a very similar point when he argues that labour standards and other legally mandated benefits create pressures on employers to 'overcome the misguided preoccupation with cost-cutting . . . and (focus) attention to the strengthening of productive power (via training, technical innovation etc.).'

One could also invoke the notion of market failure in justifying labour market interventions. Such interventions—in the form of, say, mandated benefits or minimum standards for labour training—could be seen as producing positive externalities that cannot be internalized by firms. Hence, profit-maximizing employers do not provide such socially desirable benefits. Labour market interventions in such a situation could be regarded as one possible response to market failure rather than undesirable microeconomic distortions.

The argument that key labour market institutions, such as unions, can play a productive role in economic development is not merely confined to the work of the ILO. A variant of the institutionalist hypothesis is the voice/exit model of Freeman and Medoff (1984). Unions can provide a voice through which workers can air any grievances. The weakness or absence of unions may induce workers to take the exit option, leading to an increase in labour turnover. Higher labour turnover in turn impedes firm productivity.

Pencavel, in a careful review of the role of unions in economic development, reaches a conclusion that is similar in spirit to the institutionalist perspective:

> [U]nions have the potential to help raise productivity in the workplace by participating with management in search of better ways of organizing production. It is important for workers also not to feel alienated from the economic and social system and to believe they have a stake in it. Process matters: even if outcomes were identical, employees value the fact that they or their agents help to shape their working environment.
>
> *(1995: 23)*

Nelson (1991) emphasizes that if trade unions are structured as peak associations within a framework of democratic corporatism, then evidence from Europe shows that one can achieve the twin blessings of low inflation and low unemployment. A theoretical rationale can be provided in terms of game theory. A well-known result from such an analytical framework is that if bargaining partners (e.g. the government, peak employers, and workers associations) have long-term time horizons induced by repeated strategic interaction, they may arrive at co-operative solutions (e.g. collective wage restraint in the face of external shocks) that are able to take account of societal interest at the expense of sectional interests. Such a rationale resonates with Axelrod's (1984) theory of the evolution of co-operation in a context of repeated 'prisoner's dilemma' games.

One should, as Freeman (1993: 135–139) emphasizes, take account of a range of political economy considerations when interpreting the appropriate role of the labour market in economic development. The concept of corporatism noted earlier is part of this repertoire of political economy arguments. The point is that the exercise of inclusive politics, where organized labour is given access to the policymaking process as part of a tripartite dialogue between government, business, and labour may engender responsible unionism. Beyond this, there are other ways in which organized labour can play a productive role in the political management of economic policies.

It is now widely recognized that policymakers trying to implement a structural adjustment package (e.g. trade liberalization, macroeconomic stabilization) need political support to sustain this programme. One way of engendering such support is to provide compensatory labour market measures (e.g. severance pay, job re-training) in order to enhance the capacity of workers to cope in the post-reform phase. Other possibilities include ownership rights of workers through profit-sharing in public sector enterprises undergoing privatization as a means of reducing resistance to privatization. Finally, organized labour can contribute to the effective implementation of a structural adjustment package by offering feedback to the government on their social and income distribution effects—a point emphasized by Birdsall (1994: 442).

Labour market institutions and policies: the South Asian experience

The distortionist model appears to have been influential in the interpretation of the role of the labour market in economic development. This is typically done by comparing the labour market performance of East Asia with other developing economies. Thus, Adams and Davis, drawing on the work of Nugent (1991), Balassa (1988), uphold the conventional wisdom that:

> Asian labour markets are generally less regulated than in Latin America. While Latin American governments have often used wage regulations to promote different economic sectors, even when the result is wages above their market-clearing levels, East Asia has generally relied on market-determined wages and consequently kept costs down . . . and avoided the formation of entrenched labour groups.
>
> *(Adam and Davis 1994: 22)*

The message that follows from above is clear (Adam F. G and Davis, I, 1994). East Asia epitomizes the prescriptions of the distortionist model. The presence of a labour market relatively free of distortions constitutes one important reason why East Asia has consistently exhibited a superior performance compared to economies in other parts of the world.

The unflattering comparisons of labour market performance between East Asia and Latin America can easily be extended to South Asia. Consider, for example, the pioneering work of Agarwala (1983) on the degree of distortions in factor markets, foreign exchange markets, and product markets. Table 5.1 selectively reproduces the results compiled by Agarwal. On

TABLE 5.1 Distortion index for South Asia in factor markets in the 1970s

Country	*Distortion index: interest rate*	*Distortion index: wages*
Bangladesh	3	3
India	2	2
Pakistan	2	3
Sri Lanka	2	3
Korea	2	1
Malaysia	2	1
Thailand	1	1
Indonesia	2	1

Source: Selected extracts from Agarwala (1983)

Note: 1 = low; 2 = medium; 3 = high.

the basis of the distortion index as applied to factor markets (capital and labour markets), South Asia has 'high' to 'medium' distortion, while East Asia has 'low' to 'medium' distortion. Such a finding has inspired Lim (1994: 841) to suggest that 'factor pricing is more distorted in South Asian countries.'

A detailed analysis of labour market structures in specific South Asian countries provides interesting clues to the nature of labour market imperfections (World Bank 1995a). Thus, in the case of Sri Lanka, one can identify a regulated segment (approximately 25 per cent of the workforce) that includes government, public enterprises, and some medium and large enterprises. In this regulated segment, workers receive numerous wage and non-wage benefits, the latter primarily manifesting itself in the form of generous pension privileges. The primary labour legislation that governs job security is the Termination of Employment Workmen Act. It entails large severance payments and restrains firms from laying off workers without the prior written approval of the Commissioner of Labour.

Pencavel (1995: 2–3) extends this type of labour market regulation to include India and Bangladesh and characterizes them as 'patronage regimes.' In such regimes:

> [C]ollective bargaining is explicitly endorsed as a proper system for organizing labour markets and the state facilitates the unionization of new enterprises. . . . Firms are often required to pay substantial severance pay to workers laid off from their jobs, there are mandatory employer-financed fringe benefits, and firms may not close their plants without government permission.
>
> *(1995: 2–3)*

Pencavel's observations on India have been confirmed by other studies such as Lucas (1986), Fallon (1986), and Fallon and Lucas (1991). In the case of Bangladesh, the study by Mondol (1992) fits the Pencavel framework.

Another way in which one can uphold the view that labour markets in South Asia are more regulated than their East Asian counterparts is to offer a cross-country comparison of the ratifications of basic ILO conventions pertaining to forced labour, discrimination, child labour, and employment policy. The rationale is that countries that seek to uphold a broad range of

TABLE 5.2 Ratification of basic ILO conventions (as at 1994)

Country	*Total number of ratifications*
Bangladesh	31
India	36
Pakistan	31
Sri Lanka	33
Indonesia	10
Korea	4
Malaysia	11
Singapore	21
Thailand	11

Source: ILO (1995)

ILO-mandated conventions need to develop local regulations and mechanisms that enable governments to intervene in labour markets.

Table 5.2 suggests that (as recorded at 1994) the total number of ratifications in South Asia ranges from 31 (Bangladesh) to 36 (India). In selected East Asian economies, the corresponding numbers range from 4 (South Korea) to 21 (Singapore).

It seems, based at least on some indicators, that South Asian labour markets are more regulated than their East Asian counterparts. This in turn has been blamed as a key reason behind such problems as high unemployment (typically in the 10–13 per cent range in the case of Sri Lanka) in some countries of the region (World Bank 1995a). The temptation is to suggest that reform of labour market institutions to enhance their flexibility along East Asian lines is worth considering. Indeed, structural adjustment programs initiated by the World Bank and International Monetary Fund in South Asia have typically included labour market reform as part of the package.

There are, however, various reasons why such an inference should be treated with caution. First, a careful scrutiny of the institutional features of the labour market in East Asia and more recent developments in the region suggests that the contrast can be overdrawn. Second, one must distinguish between the facade of regulation and actual enforcement. The cross-country evidence shows that labour markets are highly flexible despite overtly interventionist labour legislation. Third, labour market imperfections need to be seen in the context of product market imperfections. Unionized firms in a context of protection from domestic and international competition (as in the case of import substituting industrialization) will behave rather differently compared with product markets exposed to both domestic and international competition. Finally, seeking to emulate East Asian-style labour markets, particularly as they prevailed during the take-off stage of industrialization in such policies as Taiwan and South Korea, entails an avoidable infringement of human rights. All these caveats deserve amplification.

Consider the recent labour market developments in Korea and Taiwan. Both countries have witnessed waves of industrial unrest (following the political liberalization of the late 1980s) that enabled them to break away from a historically entrenched tradition of strict controls on the labour movement. The role and power of unions in the two countries have now been substantially enhanced (Galenson 1992). A study of recent changes in labour legislation in Korea shows that in some respects it exceeds mandated ILO standards (Korea Focus 1995). Indeed, there is now a controversial move in Korea to deregulate the labour market and make it more flexible (*Korea Focus* 1997).

In Southeast Asia, Malaysia has been conspicuous for banning unions in the export-oriented, foreign direct investment-dependent electronics sector, but it agreed to allow unionization in 1988 (Standing 1992: 329). Minimum wage legislations exist in Thailand and Indonesia and have recently been increased (Islam and Chowdhury 1997).

Union densities are not necessarily lower in East Asia compared with South Asia. Frenkel (1993), for example, estimates union densities at 17 per cent in Singapore, 19 per cent in Hong Kong, 33 per cent in Taiwan, 24 per cent in South Korea, 14 per cent in Malaysia, and 6 per cent in Thailand. In Pakistan and India, union densities are below 10 per cent (World Bank 1995a: 82), although in the case of the latter, Joshi and Little (1994) suggest a higher value.

If one considers union wage differentials as an indicator of a regulated labour market, East Asia does not turn out to be an outlier. Thus, in Malaysia, the union wage premium is in the order of 15–20 per cent compared with 10 per cent in Mexico and 5–20 per cent in the developed economies of the United States, the United Kingdom, and Germany (World Bank 1995b: 81).

In the case of South Asia, found evidence in India of widening differentials of wages across firm size, but only a part of this differential can be explained by union influences. It has not been possible to identify comparable evidence for the rest of the region, although in the case of Sri Lanka, Fields (1986) makes the point that unions do not seem to be effective in the wage determination process. In sum, there is no clear evidence that South Asian labour markets generate union-influenced wage premiums that are above East Asian benchmarks.

Consider now the important distinction that one needs to make between the facade of regulation and its enforcement. As noted, in the presence of labour surplus conditions and the small size of the formal wage sector, vast segments of the labour market in developing economies remain unregulated, or at least enforcement of labour legislation becomes rather difficult. In South Asia, the size of the formal wage sector (as measured between 1986 and 1992) is quite small in Bangladesh (2 per cent) and India (3.7 per cent). It is moderate in Pakistan (13.8 per cent) and Sri Lanka (13.1 per cent) (ILO 1995). This means that well over 80 per cent of the workforce can be found in activities—in both rural and urban areas—that fall outside the pale of formal regulation.

Even in the formal wage sector, employers have found various ways in which they can circumvent stiff labour legislation. Edgren (1989) highlights the case of India, where such circumvention has occurred by, for example, paying workers to voluntarily quit and ensuring non-compliance with existing regulation without breaking the law!

It is this gap between appearance and reality that partly explains why cross-country evidence—assembled by Freeman (1993)—indicates a relatively high degree of real wage flexibility even in countries with apparently highly regulated labour markets. In fact, in many cases real wages actually fell and failed to keep up with the growth of per capita GDP.

Does South Asia follow this cross-country trend discovered by Freeman? Table 5.3 provides data on the behaviour of agricultural and manufacturing wages in South Asia for the 1960–1990

TABLE 5.3 Behaviour of real wages in South Asia (%)

Country	*Period*	*GDP per capita*	*Wages agriculture*	*Period*	*GDP per capita*	*Wages manufacture*
Bangladesh	1960–1991	0.81	−0.73	1976–1989	0.74	−1.05
India	1960–1990	1.93	1.82	1963–1990	1.94	1.74
Pakistan	1970–1992	2.32	2.94	1963–1988	3.00	4.89
Sri Lanka	1980–1990	2.96	−1.06	1966–1990	2.91	1.03

Source: World Bank (1995b)

period. Two features stand out. First, real wages seem to have fallen in Bangladesh and Sri Lanka (the latter in the agricultural sector), although in the case of India, Joshi and Little (1994: 29) highlight evidence of particular periods where real wages fell by as much as 12 per cent in the manufacturing sector and 17 per cent in the agricultural sector. Second, real wages have grown below the growth in per capita GDP, with the exception of Pakistan, where manufacturing wages have apparently grown above the rate of growth of GDP.

This admittedly crude and aggregate measure of real wage trends suggests that, despite both institutional and anecdotal evidence of a regulated labour market, the actual functioning of such a market does not show clear evidence of real wage inflexibility. Even in cases of sustained increases of real wages, there may well have been episodes of high variability of real wages (as in India).

The need to appreciate the link between labour market imperfections and product market imperfections is also crucial in understanding the South Asian experience. Product market imperfections arise primarily through state-sanctioned entry and exit barriers that afford a high degree of protection to firms in many industries. This has taken several forms: import protection through the route of import substituting industrialization, industrial licensing, and state-owned enterprises with monopoly or near-monopoly status. When product markets are imperfect, it creates an incentive structure in which both organized labour and employers engage in rent-sharing mechanisms either by dissipating excess profits or by extracting subsidies from the state. Such a line of analysis suggests that the inefficiencies that one ascribes to labour market regulations are a reflection of deep-rooted protection of domestic industries. Such an approach also suggests an obvious solution to labour market rigidities: creating a greater degree of competition in product markets through a combination of trade liberalization, domestic deregulation, and privatization.

Suggestive evidence that this policy approach works can be found in South Asia. In the case of Sri Lanka, Rodrigo (1983) draws attention to the fact that the industrial and political power of the trade unions declined substantially after 1977, reflecting the impact of the economic liberalization efforts at the time. It is important to emphasize that, while organized labour apparently seems to lose out in such a strategy, the beneficiary is the average worker. On the basis of a sample size of 37 countries and observations spread over 1970–1990, one can find a correlation between real wage growth (approximately 3 per cent a year) and greater exposure of the domestic economy to international competition (as measured by export-GNP ratios). In other words, the greater the degree of export orientation (which is an aggregate proxy for product market competition), the greater the degree of real wage growth (World Bank 1995b: 5).

Even if one accepts the fact that South Asian labour markets work by default (because of a lack of enforceability of labour standards) and even if one acknowledges that creating a competitive product market represents one solution to labour market rigidities, can one still mount a case for East Asian-style suppression of unions or at least a system in which the state co-opts the labour movement?

The weight of theory and evidence now suggests that this approach represents a misreading of the East Asian experience and represents an avoidable infringement of human rights. One often overlooks the fact that the attempt to control the labour movement in East Asia had political motives—a point highlighted by Deyo (1989). Certainly, in the East Asian NIEs, the initial phase of coercive legislation had political origins because of the perceived association of organized labour with communist dissidents. Furthermore, several commentators (e.g. Lee 1984; Manning and Fong 1990; Addison and Demery 1987) note that there is no evidence that the East Asian economies have deliberately tried to suppress wages in the export-oriented sectors in order to maintain and prolong their competitive advantage in labour-intensive manufacturing. In other words, suppression or control of the union movement did not entail attempts to regulate the wage determination process.

A more positive reason why attempts to control the labour movement are misguided stems from studies that actually demonstrate the productive role that unions can play. Thus, Freeman (1993: 134) highlights the fact that 'extant studies reject the claim that unions are a general impediment to macro adjustments or to enterprise performance in developing countries, although they may be so in particular cases.'

Standing (1992) represents one of the very few studies that try to test the role of unions in affecting enterprise performance using firm-level data generated from a large-scale 1988 survey of Malaysian establishments. He arrives at the following conclusions on the relationship between unionization and labour market outcomes:

- Unionized firms were more likely to engage in training and thus improve worker productivity.
- Product innovations and work re-organization were much more prevalent in unionized firms.
- There appears to be a positive correlation between the unionization and labour productivity.
- There is no clear-cut evidence that unions represent a source of employment rigidity.

In sum, there is a case for rejecting the view that coercive labour legislation to remove or alleviate distortions in the labour market is the necessary price to pay for rapid industrialization. Such legislation probably represents an avoidable infringement of human rights. These ideas are now ratified by the World Bank, which is often perceived to be an advocate of the distortionist view. Thus the Bank observes (1995b: 86): 'Denial of workers' rights is not necessary to achieve growth of incomes. It is possible to identify the conditions and policies under which free trade unions can advance rather than impede development.' What are these 'conditions?' One of them has already been identified. If product markets are competitive, organized labour loses its capacity to impose deleterious effects on the economy, but the average worker gains.

Another point to note is that unions work best when they face incentives to focus on the workplace. An unfortunate feature of labour regimes in South Asia—particularly in Bangladesh and India—is that unions become highly politicized. They are more concerned with cultivating their political affiliations than dealing with enterprise-level issues (Pencavel 1995; Bardhan 1993). The results are invariably deleterious, as a study on Bangladesh by Mondol (1992) demonstrates. The regime of Hussain Muhammad Ershad in Bangladesh in the 1980s, in seeking the political support of the union movement, ended up granting unsustainable public sector wage increases, severance pay, and non-wage benefits. A viable and desirable alternative to breaking this unfortunate link between unions and politics is to develop a regulatory framework that encourages decentralized bargaining between independent, politically non-affiliated unions (based on voluntary membership) and firms.

The discussion so far has focused on policies pertaining to the collective bargaining process that primarily affect wages and working conditions in the formal wage sector. What about the large majority of workers in rural and informal areas who often work under hazardous and insecure conditions? What about such issues as health and safety standards, gender discrimination, and child labour?

To begin with, one has to accept the harsh fact that South Asian economies, in common with other developing economies, lack enforcement capacities and have scarce administrative capabilities that undermine the effectiveness of well-intended protective labour legislation. Furthermore, workers themselves are not aware of existing labour standards. In Bangladesh, for example, a survey of female workers in the garment industry revealed that most were not aware that they were entitled to maternity leave (Chowdhury and Mazumdar 1991; Rahman 1995). Even if workers are aware of employers' neglect of government-legislated standards, they are prepared to accept such neglect as the price to pay for a remunerative formal sector job. Any policy initiative to improve wages and working conditions in the informal sector must therefore start with the acceptance of the constraints noted earlier. Fortunately, economic logic and evidence suggest that general-purpose policies have favourable side effects on labour standards. Thus, public actions that aim to enhance the provision of safe drinking water, improve sanitary conditions, or eradicate infectious diseases feed into an improved working environment for the rural and informal sector workers. In the case of child labour, measures that improve access to education (e.g. construction of schools closer to children's homes) and reduce the cost of schooling can go some way towards alleviating the worst forms of child labour—as the experience of the Indian state of Kerala has shown (Boyden and Myers 1994). In the case of gender discrimination, efforts to improve female education and enhance access to productive employment opportunities can have a bigger impact on the living standards of women than elaborate, but inadequately enforced, equal pay legislation. A good example is the case of the export-driven garment industry in Bangladesh—a notable success story. Ninety per cent of the workers are female. Evidence also reveals that women in this industry are better educated and receive on-the-job training (Khan 1993; UNDP 1994).

Within the framework of general-purpose policies, there is still a role for government-legislated labour standards and the ratification of ILO conventions. At the very least, they have symbolic value. However, governments in South Asia, mindful of their limited enforcement capacities, should work imaginatively to improve the effectiveness of labour standards. One mechanism is to engage in widespread dissemination of information on minimum labour standards, particularly pertaining to health and safety, child labour, and gender discrimination, as a means of creating community awareness of these issues. In the area of monitoring and compliance, public officials can work closely with labour unions and other civic organizations whose activities can supplement the watchdog functions of the government.

Concluding comments

The notion that labour market inflexibilities are a characteristic feature of South Asian economies is well-entrenched among many practitioners. Whether this has led to real wage inflexibility cannot be demonstrated, at least at the aggregate level. This can be regarded as an outcome by default simply because there is a conspicuous gap between regulation and reality. Most of the workforce in South Asian economies is engaged in activities outside the pale of regulation. Admittedly, one can describe labour institutions as 'patronage regimes' in South Asia, and legitimate concerns have been raised about the political affiliations of trade unions. The solution is not to engage in East Asian-style coercive legislation but to refocus the attention of unions to the workplace. Both theory and evidence suggest that unions can be a productive force when they face the appropriate incentives. More generally, South Asian governments should refrain from adopting an overly legislative approach towards labour market issues. A lot can be achieved through fostering greater competition in the product market through general-purpose policies that impinge on human development and by working closely with unions and civic organizations in raising community awareness on appropriate labour standards. This message is quite distinct and richer than the distortionist model that entails an uncritical embrace of a fully deregulated labour market as the panacea for enhancing the welfare of workers in South Asia.

Bibliography

Adams, F. G. and Davis, I. (1994) "The role of policy in economic development: East Asia and Latin America", *Asian Pacific Economic Literature*, 8, 1: 8–24.
Addison, T. and Demery, L. (eds.) (1987) *Wages and Labour Conditions in the Newly Industrialising Countries of Asia*, London: Overseas Development Institute.
Agarwala, R. (1983) "Price distortion and growth in developing countries", World Bank Staff Working Paper No. 575, Washington, DC: World Bank.
Axelrod, R. (1984) *The Evaluation of Cooperation*, New York: Oxford University Press.
Balassa, B. (1988) "The lessons of East Asian development: An overview", *Economic Development and Cultural Change*, 36.
Bardhan, P. (1993) "Analytics of institutions of informal cooperation in rural development", *World Development*, 21, 4: 633–639.
Bhagwati, J. N. (1986) "Splintering and disembodiment of services in developing Nations", *The World Economy*, 7, 2: 133–144.
Birdsall, N. (1994) "Roundtable discussion on employment and development: Growth inequality and the labour market", Proceedings of the World Bank Annual Conference on Development Economics, World Bank, Washington, DC.
Boserup, E. and Harris, D. (1990) "Population, the status of women and rural development", in G. McNicoll and M. Cain (eds.), *Rural Development and Population: Institutions and Policy* (pp. 45–60), New York: Oxford University Press.
Boyden, J. and Myers, W. (1994) *Exploring Alternative Approaches to Combating Child Labour*, Stockholm: UNICEF.
Carruth, A. and Disney, R. (1987) "Where have two million trade union members gone?" *Economica*, 55, 217: 1–17.
Chowdhry, A. and Mazumdar, P. P. (1991) *The Condition of Garment Workers in Bangladesh – An Appraisal*, Dhaka: Bangladesh Institute of Development Studies.
Deyo, F. (1989) *Beneath the Economic Miracle: Labour Subordination in the New Asian Industrialism*, Berkeley: University of California Press.
Deyo, F. (ed.). (1987) "State and labour modes of political exclusion in East Asian Development", in F. Deyo (ed.), *The Political Economy of the New Asian Industrialism*, Ithaca and London: Cornell University Press.
Edgren, G. (ed.) (1989) *Restructuring, Employment and Industrial Relations: Adjustment Issues in Asian Industries*, Geneva: ILO.
Fallon, P. R. (1986) "The effects of labour regulation upon industrial employment and output in India", Development Research Department Discussion Paper 296, Washington, DC: World Bank.
Fallon, P. R. and Lucas R. E. B. (1991) "The impact of changes in job security in India and Zimbabwe", *The World Bank Economic Review*, 5, 3: 395–413.
Freeman, R. B. (1993) "Labour market institutions and policies: Help or hindrance to economic development?" Proceedings of the World Bank Annual Conference on Development Economics, 1992, Washinton, DC: World Bank.
Freeman, R. B. and Madoff, R. J. (1984) *What Do Unions Do?* New York: Basic Books.
Frenkel, J. (1993) "Is Japan creating a yen bloc in East Asia and the Pacific?" in J. Frankel and M. Kahler (eds.), *Regionalism and Rivalry: Japan and the US in Pacific Asia*, Chicago: University of Chicago Press.
Galenson, W. (1992) *Labour and Economic Growth in Five Asian Countries*, South Korea, Taiwan, Malaysia, Thailand, and the Philippines, New York: Praeger.
ILO (1991) *World Labour Report 1991*, Geneva: International Labour Organisation.
ILO (1995) *World Labour Report 1995*, Geneva: International Labour Organisation.
IMF (2004) *World Employment Report 2004–2005, Employment, Productivity and Poverty Reduction*, Oxford: Oxford University Press.
Islam, I. and Chowdhury, A. (1997) *The Newly Industrialising Economies of East Asia*, London and New York: Routledge.
Joshi, V. and Little, I. M. D. (1994) *India: Macroeconomic and Political Economy, 1964–1991*, Washington, DC and New Delhi: World Bank and Oxford University Press.
Khan, A. A. (1993) *Bangladesh Labour and Industrial Law*, Dhaka: Pragati Prakashani.
Korea Focus (1995) A Journal that focuses on Korea, *Scholarly articles of Korea Focus Journal*. See Korea Focus Journal (1995).
Lee, E. (1984) "Introduction", in E. Lee (ed.), *Export Processing Zones and Industrial Employment in Asia*, Bangkok and Geneva: ILO-ARTEP.

Lim, D. (1994) "Explaining the growth performance of Asian developing economies", *Economic Development and Cultural Change*, 42, 4: 829–844.
Lucas, R. E., Jr. (1986) "On the mechanics of economic development", *Journal of Monetary Economics*, 10, 1.
Manning, C. and Fong, P. E. (1990) "Labour market structure in ASEAN and the East Asian NIEs", *Asian-Pacific Economic Literature*, 4, 2: 59–89.
Mondol, M. A. S. (1992) "Impact of new technology in production variability in Bangladesh Agriculture", *Bangladesh Journal of Agricultural Economics*, 18, 2: 1–13.
Nelson, J. (1991) "Organised labour, politics, and labour market flexibility in developing countries", *The World Bank Research Observer*, 6, 1: 37–56.
Nugent, J. B. (1991) "The demise of economic development in Latin America and its implications for other developing countries", *Journal of Economic Development*, 16, June: 7–35.
Pencavel, J. (1995) "The role of labour unions of fostering economic development", Policy Research Working Paper Series 1469, Washington, DC: The World Bank.
Prothom, A. (2009) "Growth of population by Shir Kumar", *Bangla Daily*, Dhaka.
Quibria, M. G. (1993) "The gender and poverty nexus: Issues and policies", Economics Staff Paper No. 51, Manila: Asian Development Bank.
Rahman, M. (1995) *Structural Adjustment and Employment of Workers: Public Policy Issues and Choices for Bangladesh*, Dhaka: University Press Limited.
Schultz, C. (1989) "The impossibility of 'involuntary unemployment' in an overlapping generation model with rational expectations", Discussion Paper 5–89–18, University of Copenhagen, Department of Economics.
Sen, A. K. (1990) "How is India doing?", in *The Indian Economy and Its Performance since Independence*, Delhi: Oxford University Press.
Sengenberger, W. (1991) "The role of labour market regulation in industrial restructuring", in G. Standing and V. Tokman (eds.), *Towards a Social Adjustment: Labour Market Issues in Structural Adjustment,* Geneva: ILO.
Standing, G. (1992) "Do unions impede or accelerate structural adjustment? Industrial vs company unions in industrialising labour market", *Cambridge Journal of Economics*, 16, September: 327–354.
UNDP (1994) *Human Development Report 1994*, New York: Oxford University Press.
UNDP (2008) *Human Development Report 2007/2008*. http://hdr.undp.org.
UNDP (2022) *Human Development Report 2022*. http://hdr.undp.org.
Uppal, J. S. (1977) *Economic Development in South Asia*, New Delhi: Tata McGraw-Hill Publishing Company.
World Bank (1990) *World Development Report 1990: Poverty*, Oxford: Oxford University Press.
World Bank (1995a) Sri Lanka: Recent Economic Development and Prospects, Washington, DC: World Bank, April.
World Bank (1995b) *Economic Development in India: Achievements and Challenges*, A World Bank Country Study, Washington, DC: World Bank.

6

THE MILLENNIUM DEVELOPMENT GOALS (MDGS) PERFORMANCE AND THE WAY FORWARD

Saroja Selvanathan, Maneka Jayasinghe, and Eliyathamby A. Selvanathan

Introduction

It is well known that Southeast, East, and South Asia carry more than half of the total population of the world. The latest developments suggest that all the countries studied in this chapter (China, Indonesia, Malaysia, the Philippines, Thailand, Vietnam, India, Pakistan, Bangladesh, Nepal, and Sri Lanka) are now populated by more than three and a half billion people. More precisely, the population was 3.6 billion in 2022 (see Table 6.1). Demographically, therefore, Southeast, East and South Asia are critical and alarming regions of the world. By world standard, except China (due to single child policy), the region is characterized by very high rates of population growth, high density, and high dependency. The main objective of this chapter is to investigate the achievements and the non-achievements in meeting important targets of the Millennium Development Goals (MDGs) in Asia during the period 2000 to 2015, the terminal year for achieving the MDGs. To investigate such an issue, it is important first to clearly understand the population and demographic issues of the countries under study. The reasons for analysing the demographic dynamics (see Chapter 4) are to demonstrate the effect of the population problem while achieving MDGs. Also, it shows how serious the population factor is as a constraint to achieving MDGs. The attempt is made, first, to outline the general demographic situation in Asia. Next, an analysis on achieving MDGs is attempted against the backdrop of the population dynamics of the regions. In 2015, Sustainable Development Goals (SDGs) replaced MDGs, and SDGs are a global agenda with 17 goals to be achieved by 2030. The SDGs seek to end poverty and hunger, realize the human rights of all, achieve gender equality and the empowerment of all women and girls, and ensure the lasting protection of the planet and its natural resources. In the final section of this chapter, the trajectory of these countries towards achieving the United Nations SDGs is briefly discussed.

The demographic conditions and trends

Table 6.1 shows population growth data in Southeast, East, and South Asian nations under study. The populations of all Southeast and South Asian countries in Table 6.1 have increased

DOI: 10.4324/9781032716244-8

TABLE 6.1 Demographic conditions, Asia

Country	*Area (in '000 sq. km.)*	*Population (million)*				*Annual growth rate (%)*			*Rural/total population*			
		1995	*2005*	*2015*	*2022*	*1995–2005*	*2005–2015*	*2015–2022*	*1990*	*2005*	*2015*	*2022*
South Asia												
Bangladesh	148	117.8	140.9	157.8	171.2	1.8	1.1	1.1	80.2	73.2	65.6	60.3
India	3,288	964.3	1,154.6	1,322.9	1,417.2	1.8	1.3	0.9	74.5	70.8	67.2	64.1
Nepal	147	19.6	26.3	27.6	30.6	3.1	0.4	1.4	91.1	84.9	81.4	78.6
Pakistan	882	133.1	174.4	211.0	235.8	2.8	1.9	1.5	69.4	66.0	64.0	62.3
Sri Lanka	66	18.0	19.7	21.3	22.2	0.9	0.7	0.5	81.5	81.7	81.7	81.0
East and Southeast Asia												
China	9,597	1,135.0	1,304.0	1,380.0	1,412.0	1.4	0.5	0.3	73.6	57.5	44.5	36.4
Indonesia	1,919	182.2	228.8	259.1	275.5	2.3	1.2	0.8	69.4	54.1	46.7	42.1
Malaysia	331	20.1	25.9	31.1	33.9	2.6	1.8	1.1	50.2	33.4	25.8	21.8
The Philippines	342	69.3	86.3	103.0	115.6	2.2	1.8	1.5	53.0	54.3	53.7	52.0
Thailand	514	59.4	65.8	70.3	71.7	1.0	0.6	0.2	70.6	62.6	52.3	47.1
Vietnam	331	73.8	83.1	92.2	98.2	1.1	1.0	0.8	79.7	72.7	66.2	61.2

Sources: Human Development Indicators (2004); FAOSTAT: World Bank (2024);
www.infoplease.com/ipa/A0004379.html

TABLE 6.2 Population estimates and land use 1995–2022

Country	*Population density (in per sq. km)*				*Arable land (% of total)*				*Arable land per person (hectares/100 people)*			
	1995	*2005*	*2015*	*2021*	*1995*	*2005*	*2015*	*2022*	*1995*	*2005*	*2015*	*2022*
South Asia												
Bangladesh	904.0	1082.5	1,212.5	1,301.0	64.6	61.1	59.4	62.3	6.1	5.7	4.9	4.8
India	324.0	388.4	444.9	473.4	54.5	9.8	52.6	51.9	15.5	14.8	11.8	11.0
Nepal	156.0	183.0	193.0	210.0	16.3	15.9	14.7	14.7	10.5	8.7	7.7	7.0
Pakistan	172.7	226.2	273.7	300.2	39.5	27.6	39.4	39.6	15.2	14.1	14.4	13.2
Sri Lanka	289.9	313.7	344.7	358.2	14.1	14.2	21.0	22.1	4.7	4.8	6.1	6.2
East and Southeast Asia												
China	126.0	140.0	147.0	150.4	11.1	11.1	12.2	12.0	8.1	8.0	8.3	7.7
Indonesia	101.0	122.0	138.0	144.6	11.2	12.7	12.7	13.9	10.3	10.6	9.2	9.6
Malaysia	61.3	78.9	94.6	102.2	2.7	5.5	2.5	2.5	5.3	3.7	2.7	2.5
The Philippines	232.3	289.3	345.6	381.9	17.7	19.1	18.7	18.7	7.4	7.1	5.4	4.9
Thailand	116.3	128.8	137.6	140.1	33.4	27.7	33.1	33.6	25.6	22.4	24.1	24.0
Vietnam	226.6	265.8	294.2	311.0	16.6	21.3	22.3	21.7	8.2	8.0	7.6	7.0

Source: UNDP (2024); World Bank (2024)

over the period 1990–2022 by more than one and a half times (World Bank 2024). The average population growth rate for Southeast and East Asia over 1990–2005 was 1.9 per cent and during 2005–2015, it was reduced to 1.2 per cent and then was further reduced to 1 per cent during 2015–2022. The population growth rate for China alone was 1.4 per cent in 1995–2005, and then it reduced to 0.5 per cent and 0.3 per cent during 2005–2015 and 2015–2022, respectively. Among the Southeast and East Asian nations, the Philippines had the highest rate of growth (1.5 per cent during 2015–2022), and in South Asia, the highest rate of growth has been witnessed in Pakistan (also 1.5 per cent).

Table 6.2 provides further disaggregated estimates on population and land use in the countries under study. In 2021, the population density per square kilometre was very high in Bangladesh (1,301), followed by India (473), and moderately high in the Philippines (382), Vietnam (311), and Pakistan (300). In Southeast Asia, the land use in the arable category in 2022 was highest in Thailand (33.6 per cent) and lowest in China (12 per cent) out of the total surface land of these nations. Arable land use in 2022 was highest in Bangladesh (62.3 per cent) and lowest in Nepal (14.7 per cent).

Population distribution

The distribution of population by age group and dependency ratio by country are presented in Table 6.3. In Southeast and East Asia, children in the age group 0–14 years constituted the second largest proportion of the total population of each country. In 1996, this proportion was very high for all the countries. In 2022, this ranged from less than 20 per cent in China and Thailand to above 25 per cent in Indonesia and the Philippines. In South Asia, the number of children below 14 years in 2022 is highest in Pakistan (36.6 per cent) and lowest in Sri Lanka (22.8 per cent). A reduced fertility rate also helped reduce the population in South Asia. The overall

TABLE 6.3 Distribution of population by age and dependence ratio, 1996, 2005, and 2022

Country	*Age group*									*Age dependency ratio (% of working age population)*		
	0–14 years			*15–64 years*			*65+ years*					
	1996	*2005*	*2022*	*1996*	*2005*	*2022*	*1996*	*2005*	*2022*	*1996*	*2005*	*2022*
South Asia												
Bangladesh	42.3	35.5	26.0	56.8	60.9	68.0	0.9	3.6	6.0	761	642	471
India	35.8	32.1	25.3	60.2	62.7	67.8	4.0	5.3	6.9	661	596	475
Nepal	–	39.0	28.9	-	57.3	65.0	-	3.7	6.1	-	745	538
Pakistan	45.5	38.3	36.6	51.1	57.9	59.1	3.4	3.8	4.3	957	727	692
Sri Lanka	31.7	24.1	22.8	64.2	68.6	65.6	4.1	7.3	11.5	558	458	523
East and Southeast Asia												
China	27.2	21.4	17.2	66.5	71.0	69.0	6.3	7.6	13.7	504	408	448
Indonesia	32.2	28.3	25.2	64.0	66.2	67.9	3.8	5.5	6.9	563	511	473
Malaysia	36.2	32.4	22.7	59.9	63.0	69.8	3.9	4.6	7.5	669	587	433
The Philippines	38.4	35.1	30.3	58.1	61.0	64.2	3.5	3.9	5.4	721	639	556
Thailand	26.2	23.8	15.5	68.2	69.1	69.3	5.6	7.1	15.2	466	447	443
Vietnam	36.0	29.5	22.4	58.5	65.0	68.5	5.5	5.4	9.1	709	537	460

Sources: US Bureau of the Census, International Data Base, www.census.gov/cgi-bin/ipc/idbagg; Hossain et al. (1999), World Bank (2024)

values, however, suggest that the fertility rate in all these countries has declined over the last ten years. The issue of fertility rate is illustrated further in a subsequent section. The dependency ratio is defined as

$$\text{Dependency ratio} = \frac{\text{Persons } 0-14+65 \text{ and above}}{\text{Persons } 15-64} \times 1000 \tag{6.1}$$

In Table 6.3, the dependency ratio shows that children (aged 0–14 years) and older people (65 and above) constitute the dependency load for persons in the primary working ages (15–64 years). The dependency ratios provided in Table 6.3 reveal that the dependency has declined for all the countries over the period of 1996–2022. Among the countries studied in Southeast and East Asia, the Philippines have the highest ratio of dependency of 721, 639, and 556 (per 1,000), respectively, in 1996, 2005, and in 2022. The highest dependency ratio in South Asia was in Pakistan (692), followed by Nepal (538) in 2022. Sri Lanka also demonstrated a higher dependency ratio than India and Bangladesh, but this was mainly driven by the higher proportion of the population aged 65 and above. Population ageing (65+) appears to be a major concern in China and Thailand in the East and Southeast Asian region and in Sri Lanka in South Asia, with a double-digit portion of the population aged 65 and above in 2022.

Table 6.4 presents the labour force participation rates for the Asian countries studied by sectors between 2010 and 2022. The values for most countries in 2010 suggest that the agricultural sector was the major source of labour force utilization. This picture radically changed for every country in 2022 with increased labour force participation in the services sector; however, the changes were prominent for Bangladesh, China, Indonesia, and Vietnam.

Female labour force participation

In recent years, development literature has been flooded with studies on female participation in development in developing countries. From the 1990s, UN agencies undertook numerous studies on women and their role in the future development of developing countries.

Women's participation in a country's labour force is one of the important indicators that measure the role of women in development. Table 6.5 presents detailed comparative information on female labour force participation for a sample of 11 countries of Southeast, East, and South Asia over 1990 and 2022.

In Southeast and East Asia, almost half of the Vietnamese, Chinese, and Thai labour force was made up of women. In Indonesia, Malaysia, and the Philippines, women constitute about 40 per cent of the labour force. In all the countries in East Asia, female participation has been stable since 1990. In South Asia, the female labour force participation is highest in Nepal (38.1 per cent in 2022) and lowest in Pakistan and India (about 23 per cent in 2022). India's female labour force participation rates experienced a slight drop between 2005 and 2022.

Asia's demographic challenges

By 2022, Southeast and East Asia's population reached more than 3.9 billion as compared to 2.8 billion in 1995. World Bank (2024) projections suggest that by 2030, the total population of the region will reach well over 4.5 billion. It is a somewhat less alarming picture than in the other regions of Asia, as far as the population densities are concerned. As can be seen in Table 7.2,

TABLE 6.4 Labour force participation rates, by sector 2010–2022

Country	*Agriculture*		*Industries*		*Services*	
	2010	*2022*	*2010*	*2022*	*2010*	*2022*
South Asia						
Bangladesh	47	37	18	22	35	41
India	52	44	22	25	27	31
Nepal	68	62	14	16	18	22
Pakistan	43	38	25	25	35	37
Sri Lanka	31	26	21	28	44	46
East and Southeast Asia						
China	37	24	29	28	35	47
Indonesia	39	29	19	22	42	49
Malaysia	13	10	28	28	59	62
The Philippines	33	24	16	19	52	57
Thailand	38	32	21	23	41	46
Vietnam	49	29	22	33	30	38

Sources: World Bank (2024)

TABLE 6.5 Female labour force 1990–2022

Country	*Total labour force (millions)*			*Female labour force (% of total labour force)*		
	1990	*2005*	*2022*	*1990*	*2005*	*2022*
Southeast Asia						
Bangladesh	35.6	53.1	74.5	21.7	24.7	32.7
India	292.7	422	523.8	24.8	26.8	23.5
Nepal	4.7	6.5	8.7	25	27.7	38.1
Pakistan	32	51.7	78.9	10.9	17.6	23.3
Sri Lanka	7.2	7.9	8.7	36.6	33.1	34.2
East and Southeast Asia						
China	639	769	782	45.6	44.9	45.2
Indonesia	78	105	137	38.3	35.8	39.5
Malaysia	6.9	10.8	17.3	35.1	35.2	39.2
The Philippines	22.5	33.7	47	38.7	38.3	39.1
Thailand	29	38.1	40.2	44.2	46.3	45.9
Vietnam	31.9	43.7	56	50.8	49	48.5

Sources: http://genderstats.worldbank.org; World Bank (2024)

by 2021, Vietnam's population density per square kilometre reached almost 311 persons, while China had 150, Indonesia had 145, the Philippines had 382, and Thailand had 140. By 2021, South Asia's population reached 3.7 billion. In terms of density of population in 2021, while Nepal (210 per sq. km), Pakistan (300), Sri Lanka (358), and India (473) have tolerable density, Bangladesh is certainly in a challenging position (1301 per sq. km).

The contraceptive prevalence has been increasing substantially in the populous nations of the regions. For example, between 1995 and recent years, this in fact increased from 46 to 63 per cent in Bangladesh. However, it is very much stagnated in Thailand (72–73 per cent) during the

TABLE 6.6 Fertility and contraceptive use rates 1990–2021

Country	*Contraceptive prevalence (% of women aged 15–49)*			*Total fertility rate (birth per woman)*		
	1995	*2005*	*Latest available*	*1990*	*2005*	*2021*
South Asia						
Bangladesh	46	58	63 (2019)	4.3	3	2
India	43	47	67 (2021)	3.8	2.8	2
Pakistan	12	28	34 (2019)	5.8	4.1	3.5
Sri Lanka	62	70	65 (2016)	2.5	1.9	2
Nepal	29	38	47 (2019)	5.1	3.5	2
East and Southeast Asia						
China	*90*	*87*	*85 (2017)*	2.1	1.8	1.2
Indonesia	*55*	*57*	*59 (2015)*	3.1	2.3	2.2
Malaysia	56	49	52 (2014)	3.4	2.3	1.8
The Philippines	48	49	54 (2017)	4.3	3.2	2.7
Thailand	72	72	73 (2019)	2.2	1.9	1.3
Vietnam	75	77	73 (2021)	3.6	1.8	1.9

Sources: World Bank (2024)

last 25 years (see Table 6.6). Since the contraceptive prevalence has been increasing substantially in most countries in this region, such development certainly would have helped in reducing the growth rate of the population in the region as predicted by the World Bank. In terms of reduction in fertility rate, the Asian region is doing extremely well, better than expected.

Achievements in MDGs in 2000–2005

In this section, an attempt is made, given the conditions in population growth in Southeast, East, and South Asia, to investigate how the countries studied cope with their commitments in achieving MDGs by 2015. The investigation is carried out by analysing the achievements between 1990 and 2022 (based on the availability of data), comparing the period before and after the implementation of the MDGs strategy by 2015.

In terms of eradicating extreme poverty, all countries have managed to drastically reduce the proportion of the population below $1 a day during 1990–2022. Certainly, Southeast and East Asian nations are ahead of South Asia (see Table 6.7). Since 1990, the international poverty line has risen from $1 a day to $1.25 a day, and in 2015 to US$1.90 a day. On the basis of the latest $1.90-a-day poverty line, about 15 per cent of the population in Nepal was living with under US$1.25. About 10 to 12 per cent of the population in Bangladesh (2022) and India (2021) was living below US$1.90 a day. The performance in Sri Lanka is outstanding in this regard, where only 0.6 per cent of the population was living below US$1.90 a day in 2019. However, many economists have predicted that several million people would have slipped into poverty due to the economic crisis in Sri Lanka in 2022. When considering the US$3.20 cut-off—the lower-middle income cut-off—the figures suggest that a considerable proportion of the population in South Asia is below the lower-middle income cut-off.

As can be seen in Table 6.7, all East and Southeast Asian nations have achieved remarkable outcomes in reducing poverty levels. While Malaysia has 6.3 per cent of its population living on less than US$1.90 a day, in all other countries under consideration, only 1 per cent or below 1

TABLE 6.7 Eradication of extreme poverty

Country	*Share of population below $1 a day (2011 prices)*			*Share of population below $1.90 a day (2011 prices)*			*Share of population below $3.20 a day (2011 prices)*		
	1990	*2005*	*Latest*	*1990*	*2005*	*Latest*	*1990*	*2005*	*Latest*
South Asia									
Bangladesh	3.0	0.8	0.4 (2022)	35.0	25.1	10.1 (2022)	74.8	65.8	43.0 (2022)
India	6.0	3.6	0.4 (2021)	47.6	39.9	11.9 (2021)	82.0	76.3	45.9 (2021)
Nepal	19.8	12.1	1.1 (2010)	66.0	49.9	14.9 (2010)	88.7	77.9	50.8 (2010)
Pakistan	17.4	0.3	0.005 (2018)	60.6	16.6	3.6 (2018)	87.9	60.7	34.4 (2018)
Sri Lanka	0.3	0.1	0.003 (2019)	9.3	4.4	0.6 (2019)	44.5	25.7	9.1 (2019)
East and Southeast Asia									
China	21.0	2.2	0.02 (2020)	66.3	18.5	0.08 (2020)	90.0	43.2	1.00 (2020)
Indonesia	10.0	1.0	0.004 (2022)	54.9	18.0	1.5 (2022)	85.4	57.3	15.8 (2022)
Malaysia	0.0	0.1	0 (2018)	1.3	0.6	0.01 (2018)	11.8	3.8	0.1 (2018)
The Philippines	2.9	0.9	0.34 (2021)	26.3	14.4	6.3 (2021)	53.4	41.3	28.3 (2021)
Thailand	0.6	0.0	0.005 (2021)	9.2	0.7	0.01 (2021)	35.9	6.1	0.3 (2021)
Vietnam	10.6	2.4	0.08 (2020)	52.3	18.8	1.0 (2020)	79.7	50.6	5.00 (2020)

Source: World Bank (2024)

per cent of the population is under the US$1.90-a-day poverty line by 2022. When considering the population below the middle-income cut-off (US$3.20 a day), about one-third of the population in the Philippines and one-sixth of the population in Malaysia are below this cut-off. In all other Southeast and East Asian countries, only a small proportion (0.1–5 per cent) of households are currently sitting below US$3.20 a day. Overall, it is disturbing to see that the populous nations in South Asia (Bangladesh and India), in population density terms, have been making slow progress in eradicating absolute poverty. The lasting effects of the COVID-19 pandemic and global geopolitical instability may have further impeded the progress of these countries to eradicate extreme poverty.

The achievements in universal primary education and the promotion of gender equality as targets of the MDGs are presented in Table 6.8. By 2022, the Southeast and East Asian nations were ahead and have made strong progress since 1991. The overall figures suggest that the Philippines need further investment in the primary education sector in order to catch up with the rest of the nations.

Table 6.9 presents the child mortality rate and the maternal mortality ratio of the two regions. As far as child mortality is concerned, there was strong achievement made in all the nations. Bangladesh, Nepal, India, China, and Thailand recorded a greater than 75 per cent reduction in child mortality during 1990–2022. All the other nations have seen greater than 50 per cent reduction during the same period. The same trend can be observed with respect to maternal mortality. Outstanding performance on reducing maternal mortality rates could be observed in India and Nepal (with greater than 75 per cent) and Bangladesh and Sri Lanka (greater than 67 per cent). In absolute terms, however, Sri Lanka has the lowest maternal mortality rate compared to its South Asian neighbours, whose maternal mortality ratio is still greater than 100. All Southeast and East Asian nations have seen a greater than 50 per cent reduction in maternal mortality ratio during 2000–2020. However, in absolute values, the maternal mortality ratio in Indonesia and Vietnam is still greater than 100.

TABLE 6.8 Achieving universal primary education and promoting gender equality

Country	*Primary education completion (%)*			*Ratio of girls to boys in primary and secondary school (%)*	
	1991	*2005*	*2022*	*2005*	*2022*
South Asia					
Bangladesh	49	77	108	106	114
India	68	89	–	88	99
Nepal	51	76	101	90	95
Sri Lanka	94	97	99	102	102
East and Southeast Asia					
China	106	92	–	99	101
Indonesia	91	99	103	98	99
The Philippines	89	93	88	102	103
Thailand	88	82	97	98	103
Vietnam	90	100	116	103	–

Source: World Bank (2024)

TABLE 6.9 Reducing child mortality and improving maternal health

Country	*Child morality (<5 morality rate per 1,000)*			*Maternal morality ratio (per 100,000 live birth)*	
	1990	*2005*	*2020*	*2000*	*2020*
South Asia					
Bangladesh	146	65	29	380	123
India	127	74	32	540	103
Nepal	139	59	28	740	174
Pakistan	140	97	66	160	154
Sri Lanka	23	14	7	92	29
East and Southeast Asia					
China	54	24	7	31	23
Indonesia	84	42	23	230	173
Malaysia	17	8	8	–	21
The Philippines	57	34	27	200	78
Thailand	37	17	9	44	29
Vietnam	52	25	21	130	124

Source: World Bank (2024)

Concluding comments

The comprehensive analysis in this chapter reveals that South Asia, East Asia, and Southeast Asia have made considerable progress towards achieving MDGs since 1990. Consequently, by the end of the MDG campaign (2015), they had caught up with more affluent regions on many critical social indicators. For example, the Asia and Pacific region reduced extreme poverty by half even before the 2015 deadline. In particular, the proportion of people living below \$1.25 a day in the Asia Pacific region drastically reduced from 55 per cent in 1990 to 24 per cent in 2008. This was mainly driven by the reduction in extreme poverty rates in China (with annual reductions of 28.3 million during 1990–2008) and India (with annual decreases of 4.2 million in 1994–2010). The region also demonstrated remarkable achievement in reducing the proportion of people without access to safe drinking water by half, reversing the prevalence of HIV/AIDS, and slowing the spread of tuberculosis in some countries. Gender parity has been achieved in primary and secondary education in most of the countries in the region.

Nevertheless, the Asia-Pacific region, the world's most populous region, still faces many challenges concerning economic development and human well-being. For example, the region accounts for almost two-thirds of the world's poorest people, most of whom live in the South Asia region. Inequality is rising within sub-regions and countries in the region. The progress towards health targets, such as child and maternal mortality, is slow in all sub-regions, in particular in South Asia. Though the region is performing comparably better in education than health, the progress towards primary school completion in South Asia has been slow. In the post-pandemic era, the Asia and Pacific region will continue to face substantial development challenges, such as eradicating extreme poverty, addressing rising inequality, enhancing sustainable economic development, ensuring external and internal economic stability amid global uncertainties, balancing economic and environmental interests, and mitigating the impact of climate change and thereby ensuring human development and well-being. The SDGs, the UN's 2030 agenda, focus on addressing these challenges.

Bibliography

Hossain, M., Islam, I. and Kibria, R. (1999) *South Asian Economic Development: Challenges, Opportunities, and Transformation*, 1st Edition, London and New York: Routledge.

Hossain, M., Kathuria, R. and Islam, I. (2010) *South Asian Economic Development*, 2nd Edition, London and New York: Routledge.

UNDP (2024) Human Development Indicators, New York.

World Bank (2024) World Development Indicators, Washington, DC.

7

MACROECONOMIC MANAGEMENT IN THE ERA OF THE INFORMATION REVOLUTION

Maneka Jayasinghe, Saroja Selvanathan, and Eliyathamby A. Selvanathan

Introduction

This chapter deals with the macroeconomic management of the four South Asian economies studied. The objective is to see how these economies are doing on the macroeconomic front under the present era of the information revolution. Macroeconomic treatment of the selected countries with specific major macro indicators over time will provide an understanding about the overall economic performance of the countries and will also focus on their achievements and non-achievements in economic development during 1990–2022. The analysis is conducted with an open economy trade-dependent framework. All four economies fall within the categories of trade-dependent and open economy structures. The analysis of the macroeconomy of the four countries helps to identify the right macroeconomic balance and policies.

Money supply, inflation, and growth of output

A major issue addressed here is the relationship between inflation and monetary expansion over time. The issue of monetary expansion and inflation for an economy is important for various reasons. The most important among them is aggregate domestic savings affected by the rapid expansion of money for deficit financing. It is well established in the literature that a growing public sector or fiscal deficit has repercussions on private savings and investment, as well as on the current account balance. The extent of the public sector deficit managed through monetary expansion in turn affects the adjustments on the above three macro variables. It is, therefore, money supply that plays a major role in determining these variables for an economy. It is in the deficit-financing environment that monetary policy assumes a greater role in the macroeconomic management of South Asian nations (Raghavan 1990; Frain 2004).

The major objective of the monetary policy is to ensure a supply of liquidity in the economy to satisfy the demand for money arising mainly from the transactions demand of both producers and consumers. An economy, however, suffers from inflationary pressure at a point where the money supply significantly exceeds the growth in real output. The undesirable inflation pressures take their toll in various ways, particularly making the economy suffer from a regime of low investment and high consumption, thereby reducing the level of domestic savings. Inflation

DOI: 10.4324/9781032716244-9

also adversely affects the purchasing power of the low-income group of a nation. The South Asian nations are not exceptions to the above consequences of monetary policy.

Table 7.1 summarizes the trends in inflation rate, output growth, and monetary expansion in four countries. Table 7.1 and Figure 7.1 establish that there is a close relationship between

TABLE 7.1 Trends in inflation rates, GDP growth, and monetary expansion in selected countries 1990–2022

Country	*Inflation (annual % change)*				*Average rate of growth (GDP in %)*					*Money supply (annual % growth)*			
	1990	*2005*	*2019*	*2022*	*1990*	*2000*	*2010*	*2019*	*2022*	*1990*	*2000*	*2010*	*2022*
Bangladesh	6.1	7	5.6	7.7	5.6	5.3	5.6	7.9	7.1	10.4	18.6	22.4	9.5
India	9.2	4.3	3.7	6.7	5.5	3.8	8.5	3.9	7.2	15.1	16.8	16.1	9
Pakistan	9.1	9.1	10.6	19.9	4.5	4.3	1.5	2.5	4.7	11.6	9.4	13	13.1
Sri Lanka	21.5	11.6	3.5	49.7	6.4	6.0	8.0	−0.2	−7.8	19.9	13	18	8.9

Source: World Bank (2023)

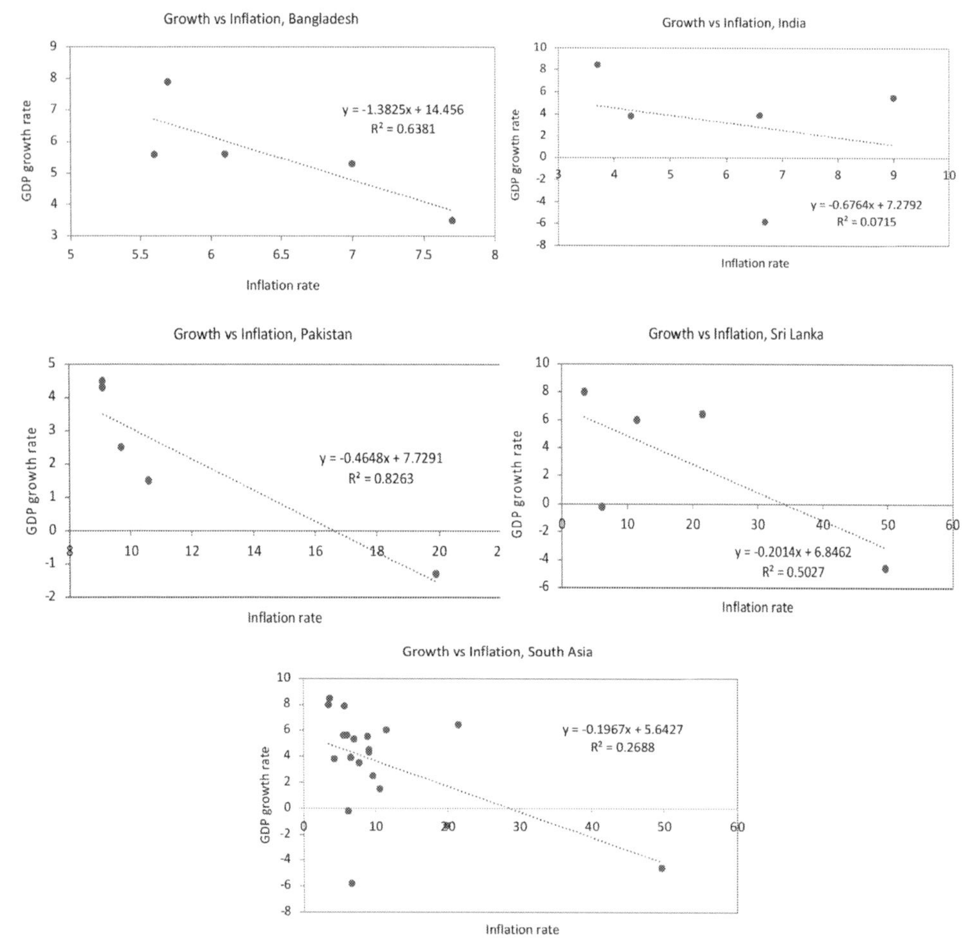

FIGURE 7.1 Relationship between inflation rate and GDP growth rate

inflation and monetary expansion, on the one hand, Table 7.1 shows that during the last three decades, Bangladesh has been experiencing a moderate level of inflation together with a fairly high level of money supply and moderate GDP growth. However, in 2022, immediately after the pandemic, Bangladesh experienced a slightly higher than usual inflation rate and substantially lower than usual money supply growth rate. In the case of India, the results were the same except that the inflation rate in India has been substantially lower than that of Bangladesh (and other South Asian countries), and the rate of growth (GDP) was very high (8.5 per cent) in 2010. This was mainly due to this nation's economic reform measures and the fact that information economy reforms commenced in the 1990s and 2000s. For Pakistan, it is evident that the economy has been suffering from high inflation, low growth, and a high money supply. Since 9/11 and the subsequent wars in Afghanistan and Iraq until now, the Pakistan economy has had major adverse effects. The political uncertainty with hand, and inflation and the growth in output, on the other hand. Figure 7.1 suggests that there is a negative relationship between inflation and GDP growth rate.

Pakistan's neighbours in the western front have not been subsiding in recent years. The political crisis and civil war that ravaged Sri Lanka over the last three decades brought the nation to its knees, and, as a result, inflation remained high in the 1990s and early 2000s, with a relatively moderate rate of growth (before the pandemic period and during recent political unrest) with a high money supply. Nevertheless, the economic crisis in 2022, the worst in its history, resulted in an unprecedented hike in inflation to 50 per cent and a negative growth rate of 7.8 per cent. The above analysis makes one point clear: it appears that there is feedback between money supply and prices as well as money supply and output growth in these countries.

Exchange rate policy

The exchange rate regime and the related issues are important yardsticks of measuring macroeconomic management in order to strive for economic development. The exchange rate policies can exert a powerful role in managing the balance of payments instrument of an economy. In South Asia, historically, at least two exchange rate regimes existed between the nations. All the nations have been governed by pegged (fixed) rates in the past. Since the mid-1990s, all the nations have gradually embraced a flexible rate regime. However, under the flexible regime, all the nations have closely followed the directions and conditions imposed by the International Monetary Fund for borrowing from the Fund in recent years.

Table 7.2 presents a detailed picture of the currency fluctuations of various currencies of the South Asian nations. The evidence is presented in nominal terms, capturing the movements in relation to the US dollar, although it is recognized that such information may not adequately capture movements in real exchange rate terms. Table 7.2 captures the movement in nominal exchange rates since 1990. The trends in depreciation in nominal exchange rates are estimated for the period between 2004 and 2022 in Table 7.3.

The nominal exchange rate in relation to the US dollar has depreciated by about 43 per cent in Bangladesh in the period between 2004 and 2022. During the same period, India experienced a 73 per cent depreciation. The currencies of Pakistan and Sri Lanka experienced a depreciation of 252 and 262 per cent, respectively, during this period.

External sector

The current account as a macroeconomic indicator mainly provides a picture of an economy's performance in the external sector. The trade balance (i.e. exports and imports difference at a

TABLE 7.2 Exchange rates 1990–2022 (in national currencies per US$)

Currency	*1990*	*2005*	*2019*	*2020*	*2022*
Bangladesh	34.6	64.3	84.5	84.5	91.7
India	17.5	44.1	70.4	74.1	78.6
Pakistan	21.7	59.5	150	161.8	204.9
Sri Lanka	40.1	100.5	178.7	185.6	367

Source: World Bank (2023)

TABLE 7.3 Trends in depreciation in nominal exchange rates in relation to US$ in South Asia

Country	*Period*	*Annual rate of depreciation/ appreciation (%)*
Bangladesh	2004–2005	7.2
	2009–2010	0.9
	2014–2015	0.4
	2021–2022	7.8
India	2004–2005	−2.7
	2009–2010	−5.5
	2014–2015	5.1
	2021–2022	6.3
Pakistan	2004–2005	2.1
	2009–2010	4.1
	2014–2015	1.6
	2021–2022	20.5
Sri Lanka	2004–2005	−1.1
	2009–2010	−1.6
	2014–2015	4.1
	2021–2022	84.6

Source: World Bank (2023)

Note: Positive sign reflects domestic currency depreciation.

particular point of time) shows the economy's direction and effects of its macro management to achieve the desired goals. The yardsticks of measuring the trade balance and performance of an economy in the external sector are of two types: current account deficit as a percentage of GDP and the trade deficit as a percentage of GDP. This text relates to deficit instead of surplus ratios because the South Asian nations expected to carry deficits. Here, it is the magnitude of the deficit historically that matters more than analysing the ways of abolishing the deficits.

Table 7.4 provides a clear picture of the trade deficit/surplus in four countries over time. The trade deficit/surplus of all countries studied has been fluctuating wildly over time. Bangladesh recorded a lower trade deficit during 1995 and 2005. However, the trade deficit marginally increased in 2015 to 7.5 per cent and increased further to 8 per cent immediately after the pandemic. Among the four South Asian countries studied, India has the lowest trade deficit, ranging from 1.2 to 2.8 per cent during 1990 and 2015. After the pandemic, India's trade deficit marginally increased to 3.6 per cent. Pakistan's trade deficit has seen substantial fluctuations between 2.7 and 6.7 during

TABLE 7.4 Trends in external trade and trade balance (annual change, % of GDP), selected years, 1990–2022

Country	*Exports*	*Imports*	*Trade balance deficit*	*Current account deficit*
Bangladesh				
1990	5.9	13.1	7.2	1.3
1995	10.9	17.3	6.4	2.2
2005	14.4	20.0	5.6	0.3
2015	17.3	24.8	7.5	−1.3
2022	12.9	20.9	8.0	3.1
India				
1990	7.1	8.5	1.4	2.2
1995	10.8	12.0	1.2	1.5
2005	19.6	22.4	2.8	1.3
2015	19.8	22.1	2.3	1.1
2022	22.8	26.4	3.6	2.3
Pakistan				
1990	14.8	20.3	5.5	4.2
1995	16.7	19.4	2.7	5.5
2005	12.3	17.6	5.3	2.5
2015	10.0	16.7	6.7	0.9
2022	10.5	22.5	12.0	3.2
Sri Lanka				
1990	30.2	38.1	7.9	3.7
1995	35.6	46.0	10.4	5.9
2005	32.3	41.3	9.0	2.7
2015	19.9	27.0	7.1	2.2
2022	21.5	25.0	3.5	2.0

Source: World Bank (2023)

TABLE 7.5 Ratios of export to imports (%)

Country	*1990*	*1995*	*2005*	*2015*	*2022*
Bangladesh	45.0	63.0	72.0	69.8	61.7
India	83.5	90.0	87.5	89.6	86.4
Pakistan	72.9	86.1	69.9	59.9	46.7
Sri Lanka	79.3	77.4	78.2	73.7	86.0

Source: World Bank (2023)

1990–2015. However, during the post-pandemic period, Pakistan reported the highest trade deficit of 12 per cent. Sri Lanka has had a relatively higher trade deficit during the 1990–2015 period. However, in 2022, Sri Lanka reported the lowest trade deficit (after India), mainly owing to the import ban of a wide variety of goods to address the foreign reserves crisis in the country. The ratio of exports to imports in Table 7.5 implies that Bangladesh and Pakistan fell behind in exports relative to imports in the recent years. Despite some fluctuations, India and Sri Lanka had a relatively stable export-to-import ratio during 1990–2022.

The changes in current account ratios over time provide a picture of a country's external debt situation in that period. The final issue under analysis in this chapter is each country's external debt position between 1990 and 2022. The ratio of external debt to GDP is often used as an indicator to assess a country's capacity to generate income in order to meet outstanding debt-servicing capacity. Table 7.6 shows a clear picture of debt by all the countries in US$ billions. Out of all the nations studied, India has the highest level of debt in terms of dollars, followed by Pakistan. However, during the period 2015 and 2022, Bangladesh's debts have increased by 147 per cent and Pakistan's debts have increased by 90 per cent. India and Sri Lanka recorded only 18 and 36 per cent growth rates in debts, respectively, during the same period. It must, however, be mentioned that these figures do not provide a meaningful measure for external indebtedness or the consequences of a large amount of debt in macroeconomic management. These are just indications of the situation of the debt level of each country, and they provide information about the level of debt changes over time to show the need for external resources in servicing the current account deficit.

However, to evaluate the economic implications of such a large dependence on external resources, it is necessary to investigate various other macroeconomic indicators of each nation, such as debt-service ratio and the proportion of aid to the total external resources made available to individual countries. The creditworthiness of various countries is evaluated by the debt-service ratio. In other words, this shows the capacity of a country to service the interest and amortization of loans through earnings from exports of goods and services of the country. The aid share of the total external resources of a country is required to be known by the donors, whether the aid money is used for servicing the outstanding debt and current account deficit or to meet the basic needs of the poor people.

Table 7.7 presents the trends in debt-service ratios over the last three decades. This ratio has been within a comfortable reach for Bangladesh and India in 2022, while that has increased out of proportion for Pakistan and Sri Lanka in 2022.

TABLE 7.6 External debt stocks, long-term 1990–2022 (US$ billion)

Country	*1990*	*2005*	*2015*	*2022*
Bangladesh	11.5	17.4	30.5	75.5
India	72.2	111.4	391.8	465.7
Pakistan	16.6	31.6	55.9	106.7
Sri Lanka	5.1	10	35.1	47.8

Source: World Bank (2023)

TABLE 7.7 Trends in the debt-service ratio 1990–2022 (% of exports)

Country	*1990*	*2005*	*2015*	*2022*
Bangladesh	33.7	7.3	3.8	5.9
India	27.2	9.7	3.1	2.4
Pakistan	22.7	10.2	12.3	29.5
Sri Lanka	14.8	4.6	17.4	49.7

Source: World Bank (2023)

TABLE 7.8 Official Development Assistance (ODA*) received (net disbursement)

Country	*Total (US$ million)*		*Net ODA received per capita (US$)*		*Net ODA received (% of GNI)*	
	2015	*2021*	*2015*	*2021*	*2015*	*2021*
Bangladesh	2,593	5,041	16.4	29.8	1.25	1.15
India	3,174	3,119	2.4	2.2	0.15	0.1
Pakistan	3,764	2,698	17.8	11.7	1.27	0.78
Sri Lanka	445	153	20.9	7.0	0.54	0.18

Sources: UNDP (2024); World Bank (2023)

Note: * ODA is defined as those concessional flows of resources that contain a grant element of at least 25 per cent of flows under this category.

More specifically, Sri Lanka is carrying a huge burden in debt-service terms. Among the nations studied, Sri Lanka has been utilizing almost 50 per cent of its export earnings for servicing debt. Bangladesh and India have been utilizing only 6 and 2.4 per cent, respectively, of their export earnings for this purpose. It is, of course, very hard to estimate the optimum level of a particular country's borrowing, but an ever-increasing debt-service ratio signals that a country's drop in either export earnings or the rate of growth in borrowing has outpaced the rate of growth in export earnings. In both these terms, the country in question could prematurely step into major macroeconomic imbalance, a crisis that has been witnessed in Sri Lanka in recent years.

Table 7.8 illustrates the Official Development Assistance (ODA) in the countries studied between 2015 and 2021. In per capita terms, the ODA has been stable in India and marginally increased in Bangladesh. In Pakistan, the ODA decreased by about 35 per cent, and Sri Lanka experienced a fall in ODA of about 67 per cent from 2015 to 2021. However, the absolute value of the ODA was substantial for nations such as Bangladesh, India, and Pakistan. All these nations attracted more than US$10 billion in total as ODA in 2022. Table 7.8 further suggests that the ODA declined in all countries under consideration as a percentage of Gross National Income (GNI).

Managing the macroeconomy in the context of trade dependence and external indebtedness

Finally, Table 7.9 summarizes the performance of the major fiscal indicators of four countries studied. The period considered is 1990–2021. In other words, this shows the fiscal performance of all the nations. The values show that Bangladesh experienced a decline in its current account deficit as a percentage of GDP before increasing again in 2021, after the pandemic. Similarly, Bangladesh's fiscal deficit also reduced to −3.2 per cent of the GDP in 2015. In the case of India, the values suggest that the nation's current account deficit and budget deficit declined between 1990 and 2015. In Pakistan, both the current account and budget deficits declined over this period. While Sri Lanka's current account deficit declined over the period under investigation, the budget deficit increased from −7.6 in 2015 to −10.2 in 2021.

TABLE 7.9 Fiscal indicators 1990–2021 (% of GDP)

Country	*Indicators*	*1990*	*2005*	*2015*	*2021*
Bangladesh	Current account balance	−1.3	−0.3	1.3	−3.8
	Government exp./GDP	17.1	8.1	9	8.3
	Total revenue/GDP	9.3	7.1	8.5	7.6
	Budget balance/GDP	−7.7	0.7	−3.2	–
India	Current account/GDP	−2.2	−1.3	−1.1	−2.3
	Government exp./GDP	15.5	15.2	15.1	15.7
	Total revenue/GDP	10	10.1	10.6	12
	Budget balance/GDP	−8.5	−3.6	−3.5	–
Pakistan	Current account/GDP	−4.2	−2.5	−0.9	−3.2
	Government exp./GDP	25.9	14.5	–	–
	Total revenue/GDP	13.7	12.9	–	–
	Budget balance/GDP	−6.5	−3.2	−4.6	−7.9
Sri Lanka	Current account/GDP	−3.7	−2.7	−2.2	−2
	Government exp./GDP	24.6	20.2	17.1	17.5
	Total revenue/GDP	19	13.7	11.7	7.4
	Budget balance/GDP	−10.0	−7.3	−7.6	−10.2

Sources: ADB (2024); World Bank (2023)

Concluding comments

In view of the above, while the macroeconomic analysis earlier in this chapter shows an impressive recovery in almost all indicators in a macro sense, it unfortunately failed to impact the bottom section of the income ladder. After almost two decades of reasonable growth, the lowest 20 per cent of the population in the region has not benefitted as per the top deciles of the income group. Any progress towards this has been substantially reversed due to the adverse economic implications of the COVID-19 pandemic, global demand, and supply shocks linked to the Russian-Ukrainian war. Thus, it is premature to begin celebrating the recent macroeconomic successes of the region. Half of the population has yet to fully benefit from the growth, which began almost two decades ago.

Bibliography

ADB (Asian Development Bank) (2024) Asian Development Outlook 2024, Metro Manila.

Frain, J. C. (2004) "Inflation and money growth: Evidence from multi-country data set", *The Economic and Social Review, Economic and Social Studies*, 53, 3: 251–266.

Raghavan, S. N. (1990) *Macroeconomic Performance and Policy Framework in the SAARC Countries: A Review*, New Delhi: Interest Publications.

UNDP (United Nations Development Programme) (2024) Human Development Report 2023–24: Breaking the Gridlock: Reimagining Cooperation in a Polarized World, New York.

World Bank (2023) *World Development Indicators*, Washington, DC: The World Bank.

8

ECONOMIC REFORMS AND FOURTH INDUSTRIAL REVOLUTION IN SOUTH ASIA

Post-pandemic SDG 2030 agenda

Moazzem Hossain

Introduction

With all these in mind, now nations are already serious about the Fourth Industrial Revolution, particularly South Asia. For example, taking India into consideration, it faced hardships, but this nation showed the pathway to prosperity. India's economic journey began, in fact, with the vision of one Prasanta Chandra Mahalanobis, an Indian applied statistician during the Third Industrial Revolution. He founded the Indian Statistical Institute (ISI) in Kolkata and contributed to the design of large-scale sample surveys. In later life, Mahalanobis was a member of the Indian planning commission and contributed prominently to newly independent India's five-year plans starting from the early 1950s.

In the second five-year plan of India, he emphasized industrialization by proposing a two-sector model, which worked towards the rapid industrialization of India. In the 1950s, Mahalanobis played a critical role in the campaign to bring India its first digital computers too. It is also known that, with the creation of ISI in Kolkata, he approached the then prime minister of India, Pandit Jawaharlal Nehru, and said that if India were to become industrialized, it needed to produce hundreds and thousands, if not millions, of technical and skilled workers. The Nehru government in 1952 accepted this proposal and established the Indian Institute of Technology (IIT) in almost all forward-looking state capital cities. At present, the IITs of India are known worldwide and are the engines of India's progress over the last 70 years; they were graduates and PhDs from IITs (Hossain and Chatterjee 1996).

Currently, cities like Bengaluru, Hyderabad, Delhi, Chennai, Kolkata, and Mumbai are the genuine IT hubs of the world. The products of IIT migrated to the United States to work and lead the start-ups at Silicon Valley. It was Mahalanobis' vision 70 years back that well and truly began India's industrialization during the Third Industrial Revolution.

Fourth Industrial Revolution and role of private sector

This is a huge topic in terms of policy contrast since now and post-WW II, post-oil crisis of the early 1970s, the global financial crisis (GFC), and now the COVID-19 pandemic. More

DOI: 10.4324/9781032716244-10

importantly, it deals with the UN Agenda 2030 and the role of the private sector, keeping in mind the Fourth Industrial Revolution. Thus, it includes the following issues:

- What role does the private sector play under the Sustainable Development Goal (SDG) framework?
- What motivates private sector actors to engage with the UN 2030 agenda?
- Learn how sustainability can influence the future of the private sector.
- Learn about what the UN can do to engage the private sector under the 2030 agenda.
- Income Inequality: what is it and why does it matter under the 2030 agenda?

2015 was the end of the Millennium Development Goals (MDGs) launched by the United Nations under the Millennium Declaration 2000. There were eight goals of the MDGs, and the aim was to reduce each, for example, by half by 2015 from the 1990 level.

It is now established that in the era of the Third Industrial Revolution, Bangladesh, among the seven member nations of South Asian Regional Cooperation, has its share of achievements in meeting all the MDGs by 2015. This makes Bangladesh a role model for the medium developing world in two Millennium Development Goal (MDG) fronts: improved sanitation access and poverty reduction (Hossain and Howard 2014).

In this chapter, the author makes an attempt to investigate industrialization under the framework of the UN 2030 agenda, or SDGs, with 17 goals. In particular, the Goal 17: Partnership. More clearly, what role do private sector actors play as partners under the SDG framework? It is important to remember there is a huge difference in entrepreneurial activities between the SDG approach and the Conglomerate approach of the miracle nations of East and Southeast Asia (NICs).

What role does the private sector play under the SDGs framework?

The 2030 Agenda for Sustainable Development is a useful framework for defining a business' place in society, and the SDGs allow companies to identify areas to focus on from 'do not harm' to 'do good' (e.g., GFC and Asian Conglomerate or Winner takes it all attitude). Conglomerate is a large business organization consisting of several different types of firms, such as Samsung and Keema of Korea, which promotes a shared value approach. Makes goal setting easier and allows companies to align their efforts with clearly articulated goals and report results and has allowed companies to articulate and quantify their efforts on sustainable development. This highlights that sustainable development is a common responsibility shared by ALL. It refers to indicators helpful for entrepreneurs in measuring impact (see Impact Hub's 2018 Impact Report).

Bangladesh: a test case?

In view of the above, this author was looking closely at the PM's Vision 2041 agenda. In one sentence, as gathered, Bangladesh in 2041 would enter a Golden Age. Indeed, the momentum the nation gathered over the last 15 years in both social and economic terms, the opportunities certainly have opened up towards 2041. This is also recognized by the multilateral development agencies and the bilateral development partners. For example, among other recognitions, the PM was invited by a G7 nation to attend the Outreach of 2018 summit in Canada on 12 June. However, the time has come to see the other side of the coin closely, the challenges, from the viewpoint of the election of the 12th parliament, which was held on 7 January 2024. In the present time, politics matter most for obvious reasons. This will be addressed in short at the end of this chapter.

Having said all this, in the non-political arena, a new volume just released has a comprehensive analysis of Bangladesh's socio-economic issues and the achievements over the last few decades authored by an eminent economist of the nation, Dr. Qazi Kholiquzzaman Ahmad, Chairman of Dhaka School of Economics. The volume is titled *Socioeconomics of Bangladesh Through the Decades*, published by Pathak Shamabesh, Dhaka, 2018. It is indeed an excellent overview of the author's contribution in the field of development, spreading from 1979 to 2017. The book has 26 selected articles published over 37 years at home and abroad. Here, no space is available to provide an extensive review of the volume; however, I will try to illustrate the main challenges of the nation Dr. Ahmad articulated for the next 20 years. This volume certainly unpacked the power of the private sector for the next wave of growth in Bangladesh.

In the concluding chapter of the above volume (Chapter 26), the author presented what needs to be done for marching ahead from here. Since the agriculture sector is the backbone of the Bangladesh nation, the agricultural wage growth is important too. It says, 'The daily wage rate in rural areas is now, on an average, the equivalent of 10/11 kgs of rice. It may be recalled that, in the 1980s it was only 3.5 kgs' (page 560). The power sector, which makes the industrial growth sustainable, has been showing major strides. For example, electricity generation has enjoyed a phenomenal increase from only 3,300 MW in 2000–2001 to 9,036 MW in 2015–2016. This contributed to the industrial sector flourishing, which accounts for more than 32.50 per cent of GDP at this stage. Social indicators such as 'education, health services, poverty reduction, maternal mortality etc., enviable improvement have been achieved' (page 261).

Given all those indicators, the volume claims the nation is no doubt marching forward. This indeed is a people-driven growth, particularly initiated by the post-liberation generation together with the private sector. Credit also goes to the incumbent for creating people-friendly investment in infrastructure and employment opportunities created at home and abroad. Now, what are the challenges for 2041? The volume makes some observations for both social and economic sectors for the future. Observations on the major economic challenges are highlighted as follows:

- Needs to develop skilled persons for all the sectors. The National Skills Development Policy 2011 provides a basic framework. However, a study by the Bangladesh Institute of Development Studies (BIDS) suggests that 90 per cent of workers in ten major industries have no skill and clearly have little facility available to enrich skill. Due to a lack of skills, production and productivity have been falling behind what was expected. Ten industries were surveyed in 2013, and the results were published recently. These are agri-processing, construction, health, tourism, information technology, leather, light engineering, ready-made garments, textiles, and shipbuilding. Among these, the study refers to leather having the most unskilled workers. All these sectors are private sector driven.
- Climate change induced by global warming is regarded as one of the major hurdles of the future, where the nation contributing little to CO_2 emissions is the main cause of global warming. Due to this global phenomenon, Bangladesh becomes one of the most vulnerable countries on the planet. The achievements so far are in great danger due to climate change, particularly agriculture and related industries to 2041.

- Finally, the volume identified a major issue, which is the responsibility of the public sector but has major implications for the private sector going forward. It has been found that only 27 per cent of the total development budget has been utilized in the first six months of 2017–2018. In other words, there was a cause of concern among the economists that implementation and monitoring of national budget spending is very ineffective and wastage-ridden.

Finally, Dr. Ahmad made some observations in the non-economic areas, most importantly on the politics that exists at present, which has a major bearing on the stride of long-term economic growth. He mentions that political destabilization is a cause of major concerns for the private sector in terms of harassment, violence, destruction of infrastructure, and so on. This affects the growth and spirit of the private sector, which is recognized as the major driver of the future wave of growth. In conclusion, any nation needs to overcome the challenges professionally to attain prosperity under democratic governance.

The Conference of Parties 26 (COP26) was held in Glasgow in November 2021. The last UN General Assembly in September 2021 covered extensively the agenda for Net Zero Emissions by 2050. The heads of the UN member states discussed this agenda with great optimism. It appears, however, that the COP26 was not a success as far as the use of non-renewable global energy, coal, and gas are concerned. Given this outcome, uncertainty remains in achieving the global goal of Net Zero Emissions by 2050.

In the COVID-19 front, the world is going to open up with full force as soon as the nations reach 80–90 per cent of their citizens having double doses of vaccines by the end of 2021. It was expected that, once world economies were in business again in the beginning of 2022, industry and agricultural development would get top priority in the developing world, preparing them for the next stage of growth and wealth creation. Bangladesh is no exception too.

Bangladesh has been enjoying more than 8 per cent growth in the pre-pandemic period. However, COVID-19 brought down the growth rate to half, to 4 per cent or even less, as 2021 data show. It remains to be seen in a few years' time how the nation performs on an economic front: soft or hard landing. As one knows well, economies certainly run with cycles in macroeconomic terms: expansionary, peak, and contractionary. The truth is policymakers and governments of developing nations want to keep expanding as long as possible without pause or interruption.

Economists are of the view that, historically, the present Organization for Economic Cooperation and Development (OECD) nations took almost 200 years to reach the peak, but China and Korea took only 40–50 years and have been continuing to grow with 6 to 7 per cent per year until COVID-19 struck in 2020. Historically, the nations that had experienced industrial revolutions, for example, the second and third, witnessed two world wars in the 20th century, including the Great Depression of the 1930s and the GFC of 2007–2008. Providing with huge economic stimulus packages, the world had ultimately recovered out of these crises within a relatively short period of time. Contrary to that, the pandemic of early 2020 is having catastrophic impacts on global economic prosperity and stability over the last two years, and now it is uncertain again how long the pandemic will last; in turn, the economic recovery of nations becomes uncertain.

Historically, on the one hand, post-Second World War Japan and Germany, two defeated forces, took the lead in pathways to industrialization with the support of the Allied forces, particularly the United States. On the other hand, the colonies of Asia, Africa, and Latin America at last got freedom from the clutches of centuries-old colonial rules in the post-Second World War period. Moreover, the newly industrialized countries (NICs) of East and Southeast Asia went for growth with a big bang in the 1970s, 1980s, and 1990s with the support of foreign direct investment from Japan, Germany, and the United States. Within two decades, the NICs hit double-digit growth by the end of the 20th century. This is indeed called prosperity in the modern world with the Third Industrial Revolution (3rd IR).

The Conference of Parties 26 (COP26) was held in Glasgow in November 2021. The last UN General Assembly in September 2021 covered extensively the agenda for Net Zero Emissions by 2050. The heads of the UN member states discussed this agenda with great optimism. It appears, however, that the COP26 was not a success as far as the use of non-renewable global energy, coal, and gas is concerned. Given this outcome, uncertainty remains in achieving the global goal of Net Zero Emissions by 2050.

In the COVID-19 front, the world was going to open up with full force as soon as the nations reached 80–90 per cent of their citizens having double doses of vaccines by the end of 2021. Once world economies were in business again in the beginning of 2022, industry and agricultural development would get top priority in the developing world, preparing them for the next stage of growth and wealth creation. The four South Asian nations are no exception too.

Moreover, internationally recognized scholars, scientists, writers, and speakers, who have been contributing many reports published by the Intergovernmental Panel on Climate Change (IPCC), and as a result, the IPCC had been awarded the Nobel Peace Prize as an institution recognizing the UN serving the world community. One of the important areas the IPCC has been working with is climate change and publishing assessment review reports on climate change issues of the world at regular intervals. The AR6 was published before COP26. AR6 was mainly engaged with climate adaptation issues. In the meantime, W. Clark, one of the IPCC experts on climate adaptation we were working with, said, 'The Green Industrial Revolution (GIR) is a major paradigm changer in that it examines globally what is already one of the most transformative changes in world history.' Clark said. "The GIR argues that countries around the world have already moved dramatically from their dependency over the last century, on carbon-based energy generation to one powered by renewable energy in order to provide the means that are both economical and mitigate against climate change."

According to Clark, "While others have written about climate change and renewable energy, his studies integrate the individual industrial sectors together within the context of major public policy, economic, environmental, and social change, to grow a "green" economy in all areas of industrial development from automobiles and construction to electronics and systems which all depend on energy" (Clark 2014).

Concluding comments

While to some it is a tall talk, the PM is right to claim this given the backdrop to make Vision 2021 a reality. This agenda surpassed all the records of the major socio-economic criteria articulated in Vision 2021, ahead of time. Given such a record under the belt, the PM is convinced and highly positive about the outcome in the year 2041. In the development literature, however, there are always some reservations about the success of a long-term vision as opposed to achieving short- and medium-term goals (see more on this topic contributed by this writer having the Sheikh Mujibur Rahman (SMR) Professorial Fellowship at the University of Hull, UK, in 2001 called Bangladesh's Development Agenda and Vision 2020, UPL, 2003, page 10). In the literature of development, it has also been shown that the long-term planning and development approach certainly has some merit covering the challenges and identifying the opportunities of a nation for the future. For example, Malaysia 2020, World Bank's China 2020, OECD's The World in 2020—Towards a New Global Age, and so on.

Bibliography

ADB (Asian Development Bank) (1996) *Asian Development Outlook 1995–96*, Oxford: Oxford University Press.

Ahmad, Q. K. (2018) *Socio Economics of Bangladesh through the Decades*, Dhaka, Bangladesh: Pathak Shamabesh (Readers Guild).

Balassa, B. (1977) *Policy Reform in Developing Countries*, Oxford and New York: Pergamon Press.

Behrman, J. R. (1990) *Human Resource Led Development? Review of Issues and Evidence*, New Delhi and Geneva: ILO-ARTEP.

Bhagwati, J. N. (1993) *India in Transition: Freeing the Economy*, Oxford: Clarendon.

Clark, G. (2014) *The Industrial Revolution decisively changed economywide productivity growth*, 2: 217–262, Elsevier.

Enos, J. (1989) "Transfer of technology in the Asia Pacific Region", *Asia Pacific Economic Literature*, 11, 1: 56–66.

Hossain, M. M. and Chatterjee, S. (1996) "India's liberalisation in Communications: Some preliminary observations", Conference proceedings of the Asian Studies Association of Australia Inc.

Hossain M. and Howard P. (2014), The sanitation access to developing Asia: India's performance over 2001 and 2011. *World Journal of Science, Technology and Sustainable Development*, 11(2), pp. 93–101.

Impact Hub's (2018) Impact Report, London.

James, W. E., Naya, S. and Meier, G. M. (1989) *Asian Development: Economic Success and Policy Lessons*, Madison: University of Wisconsin Press.

Kawan, Y. (1996) "Korean economic development and prospects", *Asian Pacific Economic Literature*, 11: 15–39.

Lim, D. (1983) *Explaining Economic Growth*, London: Edward Elgar Publishing.

Rodrik, D. (1993) "The positive economics of policy reform", *The American Economic Review, Papers and Proceedings*, 83, 2: 357–361.

UNDP (1995) *Human Development Report 1995*, Oxford: Oxford University Press.

Woodrow, C. and Grant, C. (2015) *The Green Industrial Revolution: Energy, Engineering and Economics*, Elsevier Press.

9

TRADE AND ECONOMIC INTEGRATION

Saroja Selvanathan, Maneka Jayasinghe, and Eliyathamby A. Selvanathan

Introduction

Industrialization and trade prospects in South Asian nations will be influenced not only by their attempts at stabilization and the SAP policies but also by the changes in the external environment they face and their policy adjustments to those changes. The principal external environments that need to be watched closely are economic growth, inflation and interest rates of industrial countries, world commodity prices, international capital flows, and world trade.

Issues in international trade and economic integration are investigated in this chapter. The objective of this investigation is to show what prospects the South Asian nations have for expanding their current trade and to integrate the region with the world economy and within the region in the first quarter of the 21st century.

World merchandise trade (exports and imports) has increased phenomenally during the last several decades. In the late 1990s, merchandise trade grew between 8 and 9 per cent on average compared to about a 4 per cent increase during the early 1990s because most of the industrial nations were in recession in this period (World Bank 1995). The factors that drove the merchandise trade growth in the late 1990s include

- economic recovery witnessed in industrial countries over 1995–1996;
- appreciation of Yen and further opening up of Japanese market;
- higher world prices for primary products (which contribute to the increased purchasing power of primary exporters);
- a faster growth witnessed in developing countries in the long run;
- world capital market integration;
- further acceleration in trade liberalization in both developed and developing countries.

However, the global financial crisis (2008–2009) time witnessed the most notable drop in merchandise trade. The collapse in global demand brought about by the biggest economic downturn in decades resulted in about a 12.2 per cent decline in trade volume in 2009 and a 2.3 per cent fall in the GDP, reflecting the biggest economic contraction since the Second World War (WTO 2010).

DOI: 10.4324/9781032716244-11

Global trade flows rebounded strongly in 2010 following the 2009 collapse. The volume of trade rose by 14.5 per cent—the largest on record—driving world trade to return to its pre-crisis level. The world GDP recorded a 3.5 per cent growth in 2010. Economic conditions continued to improve in both developed and developing economies, but the recovery of both trade and output proceeded more slowly in developed countries. The trade growth in Asia, driven by the fastest-growing economies in the region, such as China and India, contributed substantially to the world trade growth during the post-financial crisis period. During 2015–2019, the merchandise trade grew at about 2.4 per cent on average.

Nevertheless, the volume of world merchandise trade declined by 5.3 per cent in 2020 as the COVID-19 pandemic severely jolted the global economy. This was accompanied by a 3.6 per cent contraction in world real GDP at market exchange rates. The trade decline was therefore 1.5 times larger than the decline in output. This is, however, smaller than in 2009 following the global financial crisis, when trade volumes fell about six times more than the slump in GDP.

Merchandise trade made a strong recovery in 2021, as demand for imported goods continued to rebound from the pandemic-induced slump of 2020. The volume of world merchandise trade grew 9.7 per cent in 2021. Trade growth in 2021 was well above the 2.7 per cent average rate for 2010–2019, the period between the global financial crisis and the onset of the pandemic. Growth in merchandise trade was accompanied by a 5.8 per cent increase in world GDP at market exchange rates, well above the 3.0 per cent average rate for 2010–2019. Overall, Asia reflected the strongest recovery in trade and the weakest recovery in regions that rely on exports of natural resources (WTO 2023).

Trade and output growth slowed again in 2022 and remained weak in 2023 owing to the Russian-Ukrainian war, high inflation, and monetary policy tightening in major economies. Merchandise trade volume growth fell to 2.7 per cent in 2022 while GDP growth at market exchange rates dropped to 3.0 per cent. The World Trade Organization (WTO) forecasts a merchandise trade volume growth of 1.7 per cent in 2023 and 3.2 in 2024, accompanied by real GDP growth of 2.4 per cent in 2023 and 2.6 per cent at market exchange rates. The global geopolitical tensions, food insecurity, potential financial instability stemming from monetary policy tightening, and increasing levels of debt are the main factors linked with slower growth forecasts in 2023 and 2024.

The trade in services continues to be a critical force in global trade. After the notable drop in services trade (by 12 per cent) during the global financial crisis, it rebounded strongly thereafter before declining sharply (by 20 per cent). The large decline in services trade is mainly attributed to travel restrictions and lockdowns.

South Asia's integration with the world economy in terms of trade can be measured as the ratio of trade to GDP, and the speed of integration can be measured from the growth rate of trade and the growth rate of output. Table 9.1 shows the figures for the speed of integration by four South and East Asian nations. Most countries in the region have demonstrated a slower integration with the world economy. In particular, the speed of integration has substantially slowed down in the South Asian region during the pandemic, with the slowest integration seen in Bangladesh and Sri Lanka, compared to Southeast Asian countries under consideration.

Doha round and trade issues

The General Agreement on Tariffs and Trade (GATT) was created as one of the UN institutions after the Second World War. The GATT was replaced by the WTO after the Uruguay Round

TABLE 9.1 Trends in South and East Asia's trade integration (%)

Country	*Output (GDP) growth*				*Trade growth**				*Speed of integration***			
	1990	*2000*	*2010*	*2020*	*1990*	*2000*	*2010*	*2020*	*1990*	*2000*	*2010*	*2020*
South Asia												
Bangladesh	5.6	5.3	5.6	3.5	3.5	3.3	−5.7	−16.8	−2.1	−2.0	−11.3	−20.3
India	5.5	3.8	8.5	−5.8	2.2	8.4	6.4	−5.3	−3.3	4.6	−2.1	0.5
Pakistan	4.5	4.3	1.5	−1.3	1.8	−33.6	−4.0	−7.6	−2.7	−37.9	−5.5	−6.3
Sri Lanka	6.4	6.0	8.0	−4.6	6.6	12.6	–	−25.1	0.2	6.6	–	−20.5
Southeast Asia												
Malaysia	9.0	8.9	7.4	−5.5	7.5	1.3	−2.8	−5.1	−1.5	−7.6	−10.2	0.4
The Philippines	3.1	4.4	7.3	−9.5	4.0	10.4	8.6	−15.5	0.9	6.0	1.3	−6.0
Thailand	11.2	4.5	7.5	−6.1	4.7	20.4	6.7	−10.8	−6.5	15.9	−0.8	−4.7
Vietnam	5.1	6.8	6.4	2.9	40.4	8.4	−15.4	−0.9	35.3	1.6	−21.8	−3.8

Sources: Tables 2.1 and 2.4

Note: * Growth rate of sum of merchandise exports and imports volume;
** Growth rate of trade minus growth rate of output.

concluded in 1993 after almost eight years of negotiations. The WTO, like GATT, is primarily responsible for the following roles and activities for the member nations:

- WTO polices the world trading system.
- WTO makes sure member states adhere to the rules laid down in trade treaties signed by the members at the WTO.
- Presently, 161 member nations collectively account for almost 99 per cent of the world trade.
- While the WTO has been working on lowering the barrier on trade and the liberalization of trade among member nations, some critics are of the view that this organization is also promoting conflicts in certain circumstances and areas (www.wto.org).

WTO: Doha Round

The WTO Doha Round, known as the 'Doha Development Round,' commenced in 2001 in Doha, the capital of Qatar, located in the Arab Peninsula. This round is still current. The major objective of the Doha Round is to introduce discipline into world agricultural trade since the Uruguay Round was unsuccessful in finalizing the agricultural issues in 1993 before its conclusion. In Doha, negotiations in agricultural trade liberalization and the direct inclusion of the developing nations in the negotiations have been major breakthroughs. This round is also regarded as the Doha Development Round due to the leading role played by the developing nations in the negotiations. There are five major actors in the negotiations: the United States, the EU, Japan, the Cairns Group of nations led by Australia, and the G20. The G20 nations have been led by four large developing nations: Brazil, India, South Africa, and China.

At Doha, all members of the WTO agreed upon a far-reaching mandate for agricultural trade reform in addition to other mandates. Trade ministers committed to negotiations aimed at 'substantial improvements in market access; reductions of, with a view to phasing out, all forms of export subsidies, and substantial reductions in trade distorting domestic support' (www.wto.org; WTO Agriculture Negotiations).

In the Doha mandate, it is clear that the member nations have committed themselves to comprehensive negotiations aimed at achieving a meaningful trade reform in agriculture, covering market access, domestic support, and export subsidies. These are also known as the three pillars of negotiations.

Market access

At present, agricultural products are only protected by tariffs in WTO member nations (except for Chinese Taipei, the Republic of Korea, and the Philippines for rice). There are also some non-tariff barriers in the form of sanitary and phytosanitary measures, technical barriers, BOP payment conditions, and general safeguards. In addition to the above, it is also mandated that all other non-tariff barriers have to be eliminated or converted into tariffs as a result of the Uruguay Round's 'tariffication' measure (Hossain and Maswood 2005).

In the Doha Round, the negotiations on existing tariff reduction mainly involve general tariffs, tariff quotas, and tariff quota administration in two phases. In the first phase, discussion on tariffs covered both tariffs on quantities within quotas and those outside. In the second phase of discussions, two proposals emerged for tariff reduction in general. One, mainly, copied the Uruguay Round reduction method, and the other, known as a 'cocktail' approach, endorsed a flat-rate percentage reduction for all products (see www.wto.org).

The other, so-called Swiss formula suggests that there should be steeper cuts on higher tariffs. It was supported by the countries previously advocating the cocktail approach. One must note that the Swiss formula was first proposed by Switzerland in the Tokyo Round negotiations in the 1970s for industrial tariff reduction. Switzerland does not support this approach in the agriculture negotiations.

Domestic support

This is regarded as the second pillar of the agriculture negotiations, and many WTO members provide support in the form of subsidies to the producers. In WTO terminology, subsidies in general are identified by 'boxes,' representing the colours of traffic signals. These are:

- Green: subsidies are permitted to those products designated under the green box.
- Amber: the present subsidies need to be reduced on the products designated under the amber box.
- Red: subsidies are totally forbidden under the red box. However, in agriculture, there is no product under red box.
- Blue: subsidies are allowed on the products under the blue box, but there exists a limit on the production of such products.

Export subsidies and competition

Under the export subsidy pillar, discussions have taken place in five separate headings: export subsidies; export credit, guarantees, and insurance; food aid; exporting state trading enterprises and export restrictions; and taxes.

Table 9.2 presents agricultural producer support in some selected developed nations. From South Asian member nations, India has been playing a major part in the negotiations together

TABLE 9.2 Agricultural producer support (in US$ millions), selected OECD nations

Country	*1990*	*2000*	*2010*	*2022*
Australia	1,640	916	2,300	3,971
New Zealand	169	101	413	447
Canada	8,184	5,159	8,745	7,251
The US	45,134	71,675	79,404	134,142
EU	125,704	91,166	117,097	101,196
Japan	47,470	63,947	58,529	31,582
Korea	9,920	20,192	21,854	25,345
Norway	3,843	2,459	3,950	3,164

Source: OECD (2023)

with Brazil and South Africa in the Doha Round. The negotiations are almost dead at the present moment due to the uncompromising stand taken by the developed nations on the demand for access to the developing nations' industrial goods market in return for offering some access to agriculture in developed nations.

Composition and magnitude of South Asian trade

The composition of South Asian trade can be presented in two forms: commodity trade and trade with services.

Commodity trade

The composition of South Asian trade has changed substantially over the last three decades. All the countries studied have undergone changes in their commodity exports and imports. A country-specific illustration on commodity trade is provided later.

Bangladesh's imports in recent years comprise more manufactured goods and food items. In the recent years, there has been a growth in fuel imports in Bangladesh. More recently, however, the food grain imports have been taking a major share of the total imports of goods and services—durum wheat comprises 10 per cent of total imports (value) in 2015. Bangladesh is also at present less dependent on traditional exports such as jute, leather, and tea. The non-traditional garment industry overtook jute as a major export earner.

A major feature of India's trade in recent years has been the radical change in its composition. Jute and tea were the major export items in the 1960s, but at present, major export items include petroleum oil preparation, medicaments, jewellery made of precious metal, and milled rice. On the import side, the process of import substitution of food grains and finished manufactured goods has led to a sharp fall in the proportion of imports of consumer goods with a rise in the share of raw materials and intermediate goods led by petroleum and uncut diamonds. The demand for imported monolithic integrated circuits and gold has risen in recent years.

Pakistan's trade with the outside world has diversified in recent years. Pakistan's major export items consist of men's or boys' ensembles, milled rice, and various types of linen. Pakistan's largest imports are petroleum and petroleum products, natural gas, palm oil, and vaccines for human medicine in 2021.

In Sri Lanka, agricultural exports have remained at about one-fourth of total exports in recent years. Two major traditional exports dominate the sector. These are tea and rubber products. But in the last two decades, garments have also become a leading export item. Petroleum, semi-finished products of iron, transmission apparatus, and fabric were the main import goods in Sri Lanka in 2021.

Trade with services

It can be seen from the previous section that not only are the market and volume of trade widening, but more and more products are becoming internationally tradable. In South Asia, a significant shift has been noticed in the services sector, where both trade and foreign direct investment (FDI) have been growing very rapidly. The reasons for such growth are:

- Many services were considered non-tradable only a few years ago, but they are now being actively traded. Rapid expansion of telecommunications and information technology are central forces underlying these changes.
- By competing with more and more products and contesting in the industrial countries on these products, new opportunities for long-distance service exports have been created.
- These opportunities have contributed to the efficiency and competitiveness in trade with services in the region.
- This trend will grow further with the region's recent adoption of a liberal trade and investment regime.

Services comprise a wide range of economic activities, and the services products can be divided into two distinct parts: knowledge-based services (e.g. professional and technical services, banking and insurance, modern health care and education, financial products, and chemical processes) and information technology-based services (e.g. computing facilities and software services). In recent years, India captured the leading role in the South Asian region for exporting these services to the outside world. Within the region, the demand for service products has been growing strongly. For example, computer reservation systems for airlines have contributed to a great increase in air travel in the region. India provides a large number of health and education services to neighbouring countries.

Since South Asia is a labour-abundant region, its growth in the services trade has been centred on remittances from skilled and unskilled labourers temporarily working in foreign countries. All four countries studied have substantial workforces temporarily working in the Middle East and Southeast Asian countries. Table 9.3 shows the growth in remittances for the four countries in the region over the last 22 years.

Regional trade in South Asia

Growth in trade

Trade growth, particularly export growth, is a necessary condition for a country to achieve a high rate of economic growth. This has been demonstrated by the high-growth countries of East Asia over the last quarter of a century. From Table 9.4, it can be seen that in Southeast Asia, Malaysia, Thailand, and Vietnam experienced double-digit export growth in 1990, while

TABLE 9.3 Personal remittances received (as a % of GDP) 2000–2022

Country Name	*2000*	*2010*	*2020*	*2022*
South Asia				
Bangladesh	3.69	9.41	5.82	4.67
India	2.75	3.19	3.11	3.26
Sri Lanka	7.07	7.03	8.46	5.13
Pakistan	1.08	4.93	8.68	7.97
Southeast Asia				
Malaysia	0.37	0.43	0.42	0.40
The Philippines	8.28	10.35	9.64	2.24
Thailand	1.34	1.30	1.65	1.80
Vietnam	4.30	5.14	3.04	3.22

Source: World Bank (2023)

TABLE 9.4 Growth rates of merchandise trade of South and East Asian economies, 1990–2022 (% per annum)

Country	*1990*		*2005*		*2019*		*2020*		*2022*	
	Exports	*Imports*	*Exports*	*Imports*	*Exports*	*Imports*	*Exports*	*Imports*	*Exports*	*Imports*
South Asia										
Bangladesh	17.8	9.3	43	38.1	11.5	0.5	−17.5	−11.4	29.4	31.2
India	11.1	3.4	26.1	32.3	−3.4	−0.8	−9.1	−13.7	13.6	17.1
Pakistan	1.1	−3.5	17.6	35.1	13.2	7.6	1.5	−5.1	5.9	11
Sri Lanka	6.7	7.9	6.7	2.7	1.7	−3.5	−29.6	−20.1	10.2	−19.9
Southeast Asia										
Malaysia	17.8	26.3	8.3	8.9	−1.0	−2.4	−8.6	−7.9	14.5	15.9
The Philippines	2.3	9.9	12.5	3.7	2.6	2.3	−16.1	−21.6	10.9	13.9
Thailand	13.4	23.7	7.8	16.2	−3	−5.2	−19.7	−13.9	6.8	4.1
Vietnam	12.9	−4.5	17.8	14.2	6.2	4.9	4.1	3.3	5.7	3.7

Source: Table 2.5

in South Asia, only Bangladesh and India showed double-digit export growth. While Pakistan and the Philippines showed slower export growth in 1990, Sri Lanka showed moderate growth. However, by 2005, exports in South Asia experienced a notable growth compared to Southeast Asia, with Bangladesh showing a 43 per cent year-on-year growth in 2005, followed by 26 per cent growth in India and 17.6 per cent growth in Pakistan. Nevertheless, export growth declined in 2019 and 2020 in all countries, with some countries even recording a negative growth. In the post-pandemic period, exports have seen growth in all countries under consideration. Apart from the pandemic-related downturn, overall, South Asian countries have surpassed the Southeast Asian countries under consideration in exports.

The export growth in South Asia was accompanied by a notable growth in imports in 2005. However, 2019 and 2020 import growth also demonstrated a negative growth rate owing to the pandemic-related global economic slowdown. Similar to exports, imports also mostly restored in all countries in South and Southeast Asia, except in Sri Lanka. The negative import growth rate in 2022 in Sri Lanka is due to severe import restrictions imposed by the government to address the economic crisis in the country.

Table 9.4 further shows that between 1990 and 2022, India showed a continuous growth in exports as a percentage of GDP from 7 per cent in 1990 to 22.8 per cent in 2022. However, exports as a percentage of GDP fluctuated substantially in all other South Asian countries. In 2022, exports as a percentage of GDP were higher than 20 per cent in India and Sri Lanka and higher than 10 per cent in Bangladesh and Pakistan. Exports as a percentage of GDP have been much higher in all Southeast Asian countries, particularly in Malaysia and Vietnam.

Trade within South Asia

South Asia's regional trade performance is presented in Table 9.5. The region's trade has been dominated by India as expected. The value of trade has continuously grown over time. However, this growth was more dramatic between Bangladesh and India than in any other pair of nations. The second highest growth was between India and Sri Lanka. This pattern has not changed in recent years, although some disruptions could be observed during the pandemic year.

The trade balance figures reported in Table 9.6 suggest that India is in the most advantageous position in the region. It had trade surpluses with all three nations. The highest trade surplus was seen between India and Bangladesh, followed by between India and Sri Lanka. Bangladesh had a trade deficit with all countries, with the largest deficit seen with India, followed by Pakistan. Pakistan experienced a trade surplus with Bangladesh and Sri Lanka and a large deficit with India. Sri Lanka recorded a moderate trade surplus with Bangladesh, a moderate deficit with Pakistan, and a large deficit with India during 2014–2022.

TABLE 9.5 Regional trade in South Asia (US$ million), 2014–2022

	Bangladesh			*India*			*Pakistan*			*Sri Lanka*		
	2014	*2018*	*2020*	*2014*	*2018*	*2020*	*2014*	*2018*	*2020*	*2014*	*2018*	*2020*
Exports to South Asian counterpart countries (US$ million)												
Bangladesh				432	877	879	48	71	60.6	22	24	37
India	6,580	8,827	7,851				2,182	2,362	283	6,433	4,662	3,225
Pakistan	688	746	586	392	377	0.17				266	367	255
Sri Lanka	90	135	153	625	768	605	74	76	75			
Imports from South Asian counterpart countries (US$ million)												
Bangladesh				6,174	8,642	6,290	484	575	505	68	52	105
India	557	899	1,029				529	543	3	592	1,319	689
Pakistan	61	72	62	2,105	1,992	243				63	103	71
Sri Lanka	26	35	48	3,977	4,168	3,008	280	432	325			
Trade balance with South Asian counterpart countries (US$ million)												
Bangladesh				−5,742	−7,764	−5,410	−435	−504	−444	−46	−28	−69
India	6,023	7,927	6,822				1,653	1,820	280	5,841	3,344	2,536
Pakistan	627	675	523	−1,713	−1,615	−243				203	264	183
Sri Lanka	64	101	106	−3,352	−3,400	−2,404	−205	−356	−250			

TABLE 9.6 South Asia's trade balance (exports minus imports) with other regions, 2010 and 2015 (US$ million)

Region	*Bangladesh*		*India*		*Pakistan*		*Sri Lanka*	
	2010	*2015*	*2010*	*2015*	*2010*	*2015*	*2010*	*2015*
South Asia	−3.7	−6.2	9.05	25.69	1.06	0.81	−2.26	−3.89
East Asia and Pacific	−15.32	−23.24	−48.63	−122.1	−9.71	−28.7	−4.48	−8.33
Europe and Central Asia	7.39	13.62	−25.59	−15.88	0.9	2.55	1.78	2.39
North America	4.27	5.48	3.68	30.97	1.81	2.09	1.44	2.95
Middle East and North Africa	−2.1	−2.87	−51.97	−79.84	−10.36	−16.03	−0.52	−1.21
Sub-Saharan Africa	−0.15	–	−12.01	−7.28	0.32	−2.15	–	−0.06

Source: IMF (2023) (https://data.imf.org)

Trade between regions

Trade investigation between regions contributes to the knowledge of the big picture of trade in terms of direction and share. Table 9.6 presents the trade balance of the four South Asian countries with other regions: South Asia, North America, East Asia and the Pacific, Europe and Central Asia, North America, the Middle East and North Africa, and Sub-Saharan Africa. While India and Pakistan recorded a trade surplus with the rest of South Asia, Bangladesh and Sri Lanka reported a trade deficit with the rest of South Asian countries. All four countries demonstrated a trade deficit with East Asia and Pacific countries, while the deficit of India was substantially higher (US$ −122 million) than that of other countries. India also showed a trade deficit with Europe and Central Asia, while all other countries experienced a trade surplus. All countries reported a trade surplus with North America and a trade deficit with the Middle East and North African and Sub-Saharan African regions.

The relative share of South Asian trade (exports and imports) with major trading partner countries is presented in Figure 9.1. The composition of South Asia's major export partners has not seen a notable change during the last decade. The United States is South Asia's largest trading partner country, followed by the UAE, China, Hong Kong, and the United Kingdom. However, the composition of South Asia's major import partner countries has seen some changes during 2010–2021. For example, in 2010, imports from China constituted only 12 per cent of total imports into South Asia. By 2021, the value of imports to South Asia from China has seen more than two-fold growth (26 per cent). Furthermore, by 2021, South Asia's share of imports from the top five importing countries—China, the UAE, Saudi Arabia, Switzerland, and the United States—has increased from 36 to 62 per cent, suggesting a substantial concentration of imports to these five countries.

Figure 9.2 depicts the trade (exports plus imports) share of four South Asian countries with other regions, including South Asia. The inter-regional trade analysis reveals that regional trade within South Asia is substantially low in India and Pakistan. Over the 2010–2015 period, India's trade share within South Asia has remained at 3–4 per cent. The trade share of Pakistan with South Asia is particularly concerning, since this has seen a substantial drop from 8 per cent in 2010 to 3 per cent in 2015. Bangladesh has managed to maintain a 10 per cent share of its trade with South Asia, while Sri Lanka is the only South Asian country that has a 20 per cent trade share with the South Asian region in 2015. The East Asia and Pacific region is the

FIGURE 9.1 South Asia trade with major trading partners (US$ million)

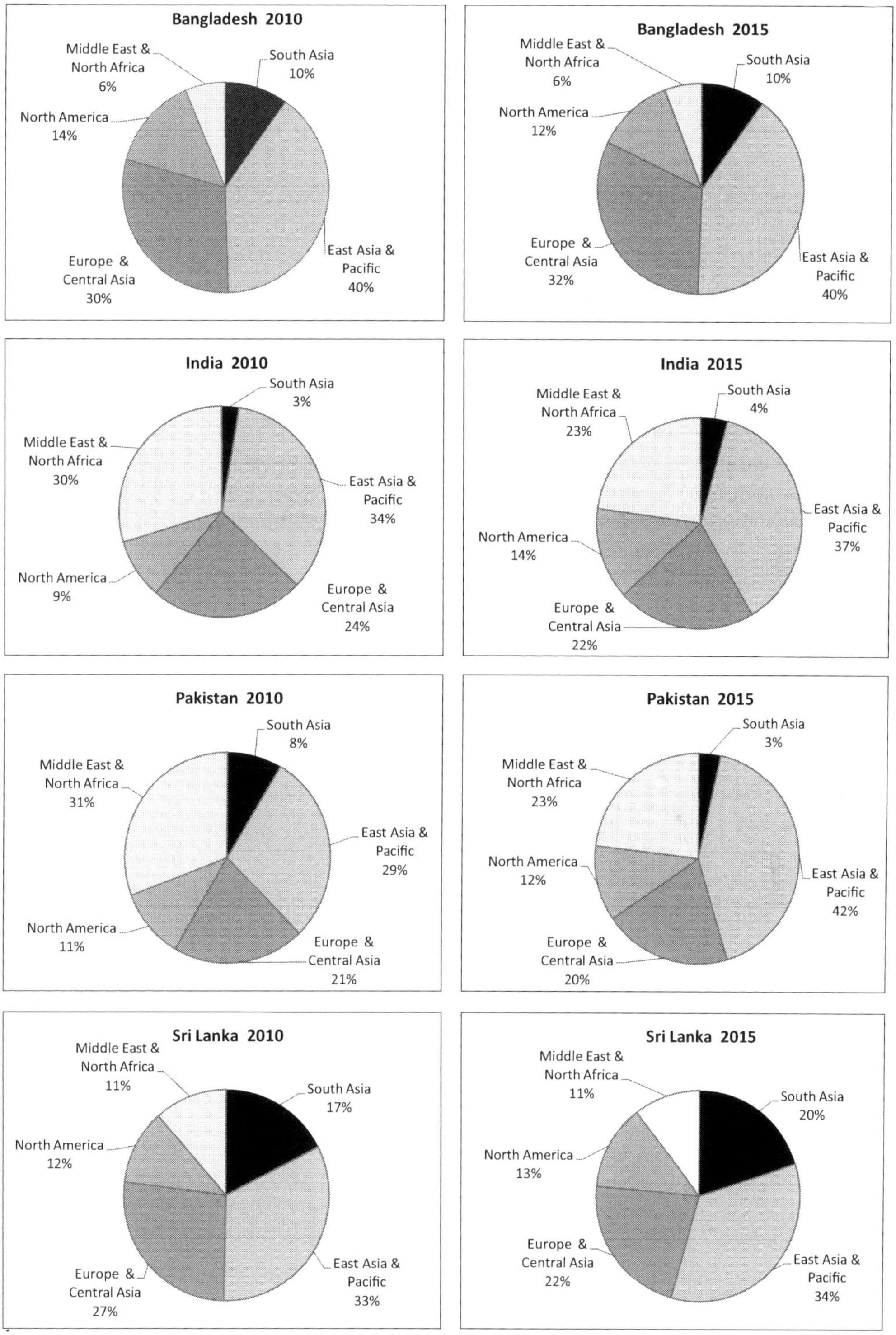

FIGURE 9.2 Global trade and South Asia (imports plus exports, US$ million)

largest trading partner region with all South Asian countries. In addition, Europe and Central Asia is the second largest trading region for Bangladesh in 2015. For India and Pakistan, Europe and Central Asia and the Middle East and North Africa regions are the second largest trading partners, while Europe and Central Asia and South Asia are the next largest trading partners of Sri Lanka.

Trade opportunity analysis by country

Opportunities for more trade in the region can be analysed by considering three major measures of trade: country-wise balance of trade, country-wise exports, and commodity-wise exports.

Bangladesh

Bangladesh's trade figures presented in Table 9.7 show that Bangladesh's exports share to the United Kingdom and Germany has increased while that to the United States, France, and the Netherlands has decreased. Bangladesh's export share to the rest of the world has increased slightly from 40.4 to 43.6 per cent during the 2010–2015 period. When considering imports, Bangladesh's imports from China, India, Singapore, and Hong Kong further increased during 2010–2015 while Indonesia replaced Thailand within Bangladesh's top five import partners in 2015. The major concern with Bangladesh's trade area is the continuous growth in deficit with East Asian countries and with India. Almost half of the country's trade deficit in recent years was with China and India.

The destination of Bangladesh's exports over 2010–2015 has not changed dramatically; however, the trade figures suggest it exported more than half of its exports to G7 nations during 2010–2015. If Bangladesh carefully nurtures these markets in the future, there will be some scope to make additional exports to these countries. The country should also take steps to explore export markets in East Asia's fastest-growing nations.

Figure 9.3 presents the export and import share of Bangladesh's major commodities in 2015. As can be seen, ready-made garments and related textile exports are the top export items in Bangladesh. Petroleum oils dominate the imports of Bangladesh.

Table 9.8 presents Bangladesh's structure of merchandise and services trade in recent years. Manufactured goods and food are the major items that are traded under the merchandise goods category. The services trade, particularly transport and ICT goods, also gained prominence in recent years.

TABLE 9.7 Bangladesh's trade with major destinations (% of total), 2010 and 2015

Country	*Exports (2010)*	*Country*	*Exports (2015)*	*Country*	*Imports (2010)*	*Country*	*Imports (2015)*
The USA	24.2	The USA	19.4	China	17.5	China	21.5
Germany	13.8	Germany	14.7	India	11.5	India	12.2
The UK	8.9	The UK	11	Singapore	5.4	Singapore	9.2
France	6.4	France	5.5	Thailand	5.7	Hong Kong	5.5
The Netherlands	6.3	Spain	5.8	Hong Kong	5.1	Indonesia	4.6
Other	40.4	Other	43.6	Other	54.8	Other	47

Source: World Integrated Trade Solution Data (2023)

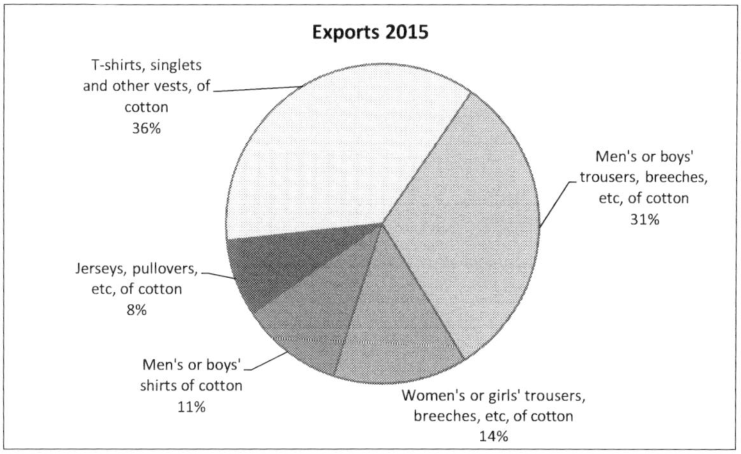

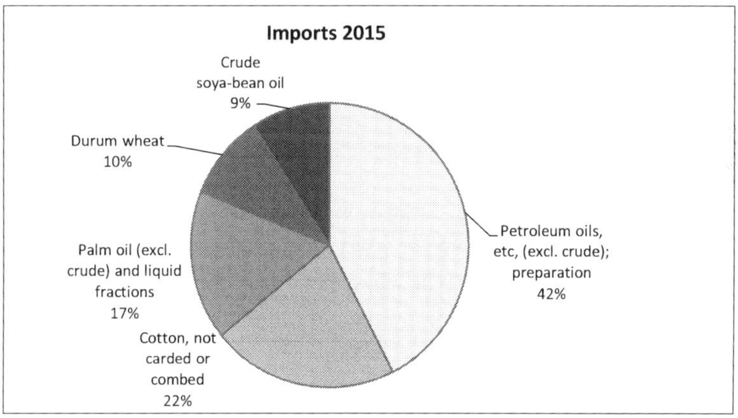

FIGURE 9.3 Bangladesh's major export and import products (US$ thousand)

TABLE 9.8 Structure of merchandise and services trade, Bangladesh, 2010 and 2015 (% of total*)

Merchandise goods and services	*Exports*		*Imports*	
	2010	*2015*	*2010*	*2015*
Agricultural raw materials	1.95	0.75	8.11	6.41
Food	4.03	2.71	17.42	16.56
Fuel	1.87	0.56	8.36	10.92
Manufactures	91.69	95.81	64.07	63.16
Ores and metals	0.46	0.17	2	2.68
Services goods**				
Transport	14.22	23.94	83.50	78.11
Travel	6.57	8.92	6.32	5.78
Insurance and finance	3.86	4.24	1.74	6.67
Information and communications	75.36	62.90	8.44	9.43

Source: World Integrated Trade Solution Data (2023)

*Note:** The share of total merchandise trade (export or import) accounted for by the product in a given year.

** Percentage of commercial services only

India

India's trade figures are shown in Table 9.9. As can be seen, India's exports to the United States have increased by about 8 per cent during 2010–2021, while exports to the UAE, China, and Hong Kong have decreased. Bangladesh has become one of the top five exporting countries of Bangladesh in 2021, replacing Singapore. While India has maintained a trade surplus with South Asia and North America, notably in 2015, its trade deficit with East Asia and the Pacific and the Middle East and North Africa has increased notably during 2010–2015. However, the trade deficit with Europe and Central Asia and Sub-Saharan Africa have decreased slightly during the same period. The major concern about India's balance of trade is with East Asia and Pacific countries, where the trade deficit has seen more than a two-fold increase during 2010–2015. This is due to its huge import of raw materials and intermediate goods. China is India's largest import partner country, accounting for about 15 per cent of India's imports. Such concentration of imports in a single country is somewhat concerning for India, as any disruptive event may adversely affect India's supply chain, compromising its economic and strategic interests. Therefore, exploring further export opportunities with the fastest-growing East Asian nations and considering import market diversification in the future seem critical for India.

Figure 9.4 presents the export and import share of India's major commodities in 2011. More than one-fifth of India's export earnings have been generated by the gems and jewellery sector, and almost 50 per cent of exports consist of petroleum oils. Gems and jewellery sector and petroleum oils are also the major import items in India in 2021.

Table 9.10 presents a breakdown of India's merchandise and services trade in recent years. Manufactured goods, fuels, and food are the major items that were traded under the merchandise goods category in recent years (2010–2021). The services trade, particularly transport and ICT goods, has also gained prominence in recent years.

Pakistan

Table 9.11 shows Pakistan's import and export figures with its major trading partners. The major destinations of Pakistan's exports have seen some changes during the period 2010–2021. In 2010, the major export partners were the United States and the UAE, which constituted about one-fourth of export value, while in 2021, the United States remained as the largest export partner, covering one-fifth of export values, and China became the second largest export partner, with Pakistan accounting for about 11 per cent of total export value.

TABLE 9.9 India's trade with major destinations (US$ million), 2020 and 2021

Country	*Exports (2010)*	*Country*	*Exports (2021)*	*Country*	*Imports (2010)*	*Country*	*Imports (2021)*
The UAE	12.4	The USA	18.1	China	11.8	China	15.4
The USA	10.7	The UAE	6.5	The UAE	8.8	The UAE	7.6
China	7.9	China	5.8	Saudi Arabia	5.8	The USA	7.3
Hong Kong	4.3	Bangladesh	3.6	The USA	5.5	Switzerland	5.2
Singapore	2.7	Hong Kong	2.9	Switzerland	6.3	Saudi Arabia	4.9
Other	62.0	Other	63.1	Other	61.8	Other	59.6

Source: World Integrated Trade Solution Data (2023)

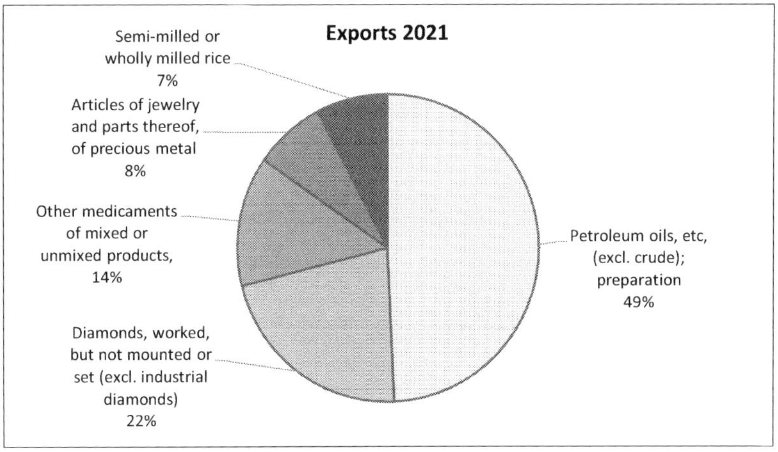

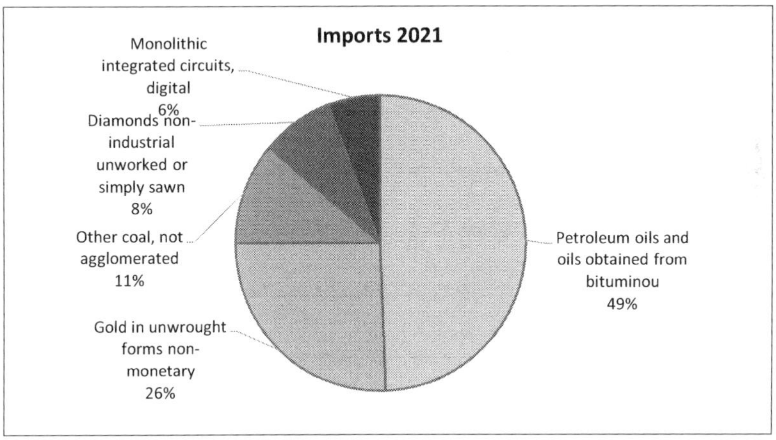

FIGURE 9.4 India's major export and import products (US$ thousand)

TABLE 9.10 Structure of merchandise and services trade, India 1990–2005 (% of total*)

Merchandise goods and services	*Exports*			*Imports*		
	2010	*2015*	*2021*	*2010*	*2015*	*2021*
Agricultural Raw Materials	1.98	1.49	1.36	1.58	1.84	1.47
Food	8.25	11.32	11.31	3.52	5.24	5.05
Fuel	17.24	11.88	14.29	31.71	26.84	29.92
Manufactures	62.85	68.99	68.16	44.93	47.86	48.08
Ores and Metals	7.59	3.38	4.8	4.79	6.47	5.45
Services goods**						
Transport	11.39	9.20	12.23	18.27	18.87	22.23
Travel	12.43	13.49	3.61	13.41	18.15	10.42
Insurance and finance	6.53	4.71	3.41	10.50	5.21	5.64
Information and communications	69.65	72.60	80.75	57.82	57.78	61.70

Source: World Integrated Trade Solution Data (2023)

Note: * The share of total merchandise trade (export or import) accounted for by the product in a given year.

** Percentage of commercial services only.

TABLE 9.11 Pakistan's exports to major destinations (US$ million)

Country	*Exports (2010)*	*Country*	*Exports (2021)*	*Country*	*Imports (2010)*	*Country*	*Imports (2021)*
The USA	17.2	The USA	21.1	China	13.98	China	28.32
The UAE	8.6	China	10.5	The UAE	13.98	The UAE	10.09
China	6.7	The UK	7.3	Saudi Arabia	10.22	Saudi Arabia	5.75
The UK	5.2	Germany	5.4	Kuwait	6.95	Kuwait	5.25
Afghanistan	7.9	The Netherlands	4.9	Malaysia	5.47	Malaysia	5.17
Other	54.4	Other	50.8	Other	49.4	Other	45.42

Source: World Integrated Trade Solution Data (2023)

It has further potential to improve its export share with the United States and with the EU nations.

On the import front, China has been Pakistan's main import partner for decades, and the share of imports from China has seen more than two-fold growth during 2010–2021. The share of imports from all other major partners, the UAE, Saudi Arabia, Kuwait, and Malaysia, and the rest of the world has marginally declined during the same period. The considerable reliance of Pakistan on Chinese imports is also reflected in the increasing trade deficit (see Table 9.7) with the East Asia and Pacific region during the 2010–2015 period. The trade deficit with the Middle East and North African region has also marginally increased during 2010–2015.

The country's major achievement on the trade balance front has been with North America and Europe and Central Asian regions. In 2010, Pakistan had a trade surplus of almost $1.81 million with the North American region, and in 2015, the surplus further increased to almost $2.09 million. Similarly, the trade surplus with Europe and the Central Asian region increased from $0.9 million to $2.55 million during the same period.

Figure 9.5 shows that the country's major export products are concentrated within the cotton and textile industries. On the other hand, the major import products consist of petroleum, natural gas, palm oil, and vaccines in 2021.

Table 9.12 presents Pakistan's structure of merchandise and services trade during the last decade. Manufactured goods and food are the major items that were traded under the merchandise goods category. The services trade, particularly transport and information and communications technology goods, has also gained prominence in recent years. Although travel services gained momentum during the 2010–2015 period, they experienced a drastic drop in 2021, particularly due to the aftermath of the pandemic.

Sri Lanka

Sri Lanka's trade with major destinations is given in Table 9.13. As can be seen, the composition of Sri Lanka's export destinations has remained mostly unchanged during the period 2010–2021, with the United States, the United Kingdom, India, Italy, and Germany being the major export partners. Nevertheless, import partners have notably changed during the same period. In 2010, India was the largest import partner, covering about 21 per cent of import share, and

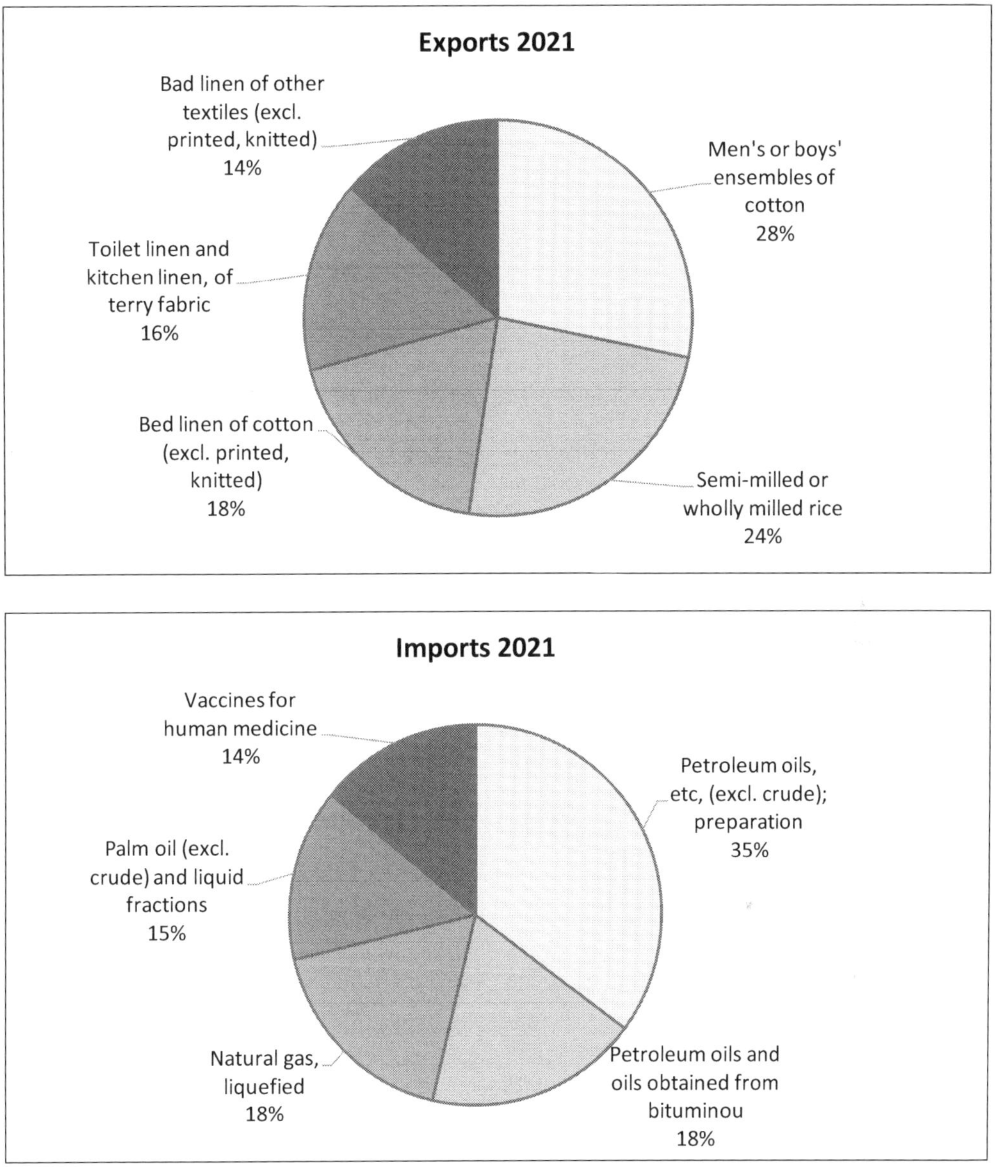

FIGURE 9.5 Pakistan's major export products (US$ thousand)

China was the third largest import partner accounting for 10 per cent of import share. By 2021, China has become Sri Lanka's largest import destination, accounting for almost one-fourth of import share, surpassing India. The share of imports from Singapore has declined notably during the same period. Overall, the imports of Sri Lanka are mainly concentrated in China and India, accounting for almost 50 per cent of imports. Figure 9.6 shows that slightly less than 50% of the country's export products consist of tea. On the other hand, petroleum is the major import product.

TABLE 9.12 Structure of merchandise and services trade, Pakistan 1990–2005 (% of total*)

Merchandise goods and services	*Exports*			*Imports*		
	2010	*2015*	*2021*	*2010*	*2015*	*2021*
Agricultural Raw Materials	1.77	1.18	1.69	4.9	4.26	5
Food	16.48	19.74	17.16	13.03	12.05	12.85
Fuel	5.6	1.2	0.7	30.47	22.9	26.55
Manufactures	74.56	76.26	75.87	48.3	56.75	51.17
Ores and Metals	1.55	1.55	4.55	2.94	3.87	4.32
Services goods*						
Transport	48.58	33.94	11.08	57.17	45.17	52.89
Travel	10.41	9.16	10.14	14.12	20.18	9.61
Insurance and finance	3.21	4.68	3.61	3.74	5.79	6.99
Information and communications	37.80	52.21	75.17	31.48	33.63	33.58

Source: World Integrated Trade Solution Data (2023)

Note:* The share of total merchandise trade (export or import) accounted for by the product in a given year.
** Percentage of commercial services only.

TABLE 9.13 Sri Lanka's trade with major destinations (US$ million)

Country	*Exports (2010)*	*Country*	*Exports (2021)*	*Country*	*Imports (2010)*	*Country*	*Imports (2021)*
The USA	21.3	The USA	24.8	India	20.6	China	23.7
The UK	12.3	The UK	7.5	Singapore	13.1	India	22.1
India	5.6	India	6.7	China	10.1	The UAE	6.6
Italy	5.6	Germany	6.1	Iran	5.3	Malaysia	3.9
Germany	4.8	Italy	4.7	Japan	4.7	Singapore	3.6
Other	50.4	Other	50.2	Other	46.2	Other	40.1

Source: World Integrated Trade Solution Data (2023)

This is also reflected in the increasing trade deficit with South Asia (particularly with India) and East Asia and the Pacific (particularly with China). Sri Lanka records a moderate increase in trade surplus with North America and the Middle East and North Africa regions during 2010–2015.

Prospects of regional integration

The term 'regional integration' encompasses the broad areas of socio-political, economic, and cultural links among the nations joining together in a forum and generally belonging to one or several regions. The ASEAN is one example of such an integration. The purpose in this part of the book is to make an assessment on the prospects of a workable economic integration among the countries of the South Asian region. Economic integration as a separate area of study under international economics has been thriving in recent years (Salvator 1995; Carbough 2009). Two major conferences have been held on this topic: one by the former GATT (Anderson and Blackhurst 1992) and the other by the World Bank (de Melo and Panagariya 1993). The term 'economic integration' has been defined by various experts

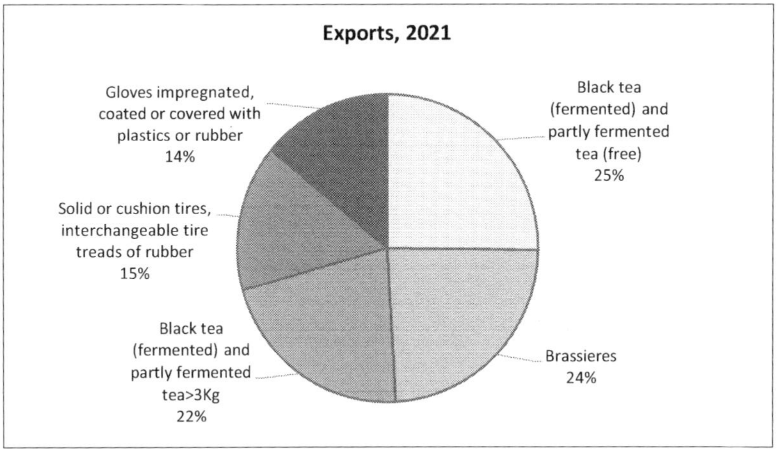

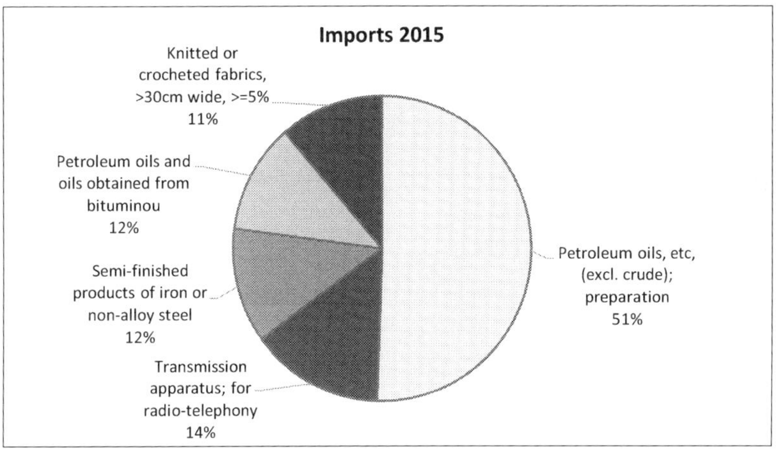

FIGURE 9.6 Sri Lanka's major export and import products (US$ thousand)

TABLE 9.14 Structure of merchandise and services trade, Sri Lanka, 2010–2021 (% of total*)

Merchandise goods and services	*Exports*			*Imports*		
	2010	*2015*	*2021*	*2010*	*2015*	*2021*
Agricultural Raw Materials	3.95	2.46	3.01	1.44	2.18	1.37
Food	26.89	25.12	25.38	15.25	13.12	13.37
Fuel	0.16	1.77	1.91	16.75	14.04	15.85
Manufactures	66.53	70.1	69	64.06	69.06	67.61
Ores and Metals	0.88	0.54	0.67	1.79	1.35	1.79
Services goods*						
Transport	47.34	33.06	39.1	65.94	39.54	49.37
Travel	23.47	46.52	22.68	14.72	35.56	20.91
Insurance and finance	3.28	5.86	4.49	5.99	11.81	14.08
Information and communications	25.91	14.26	33.82	13.34	13.10	15.64

Source: World Integrated Trade Solution Data (2023)

Note:* The share of total merchandise trade (export or import) accounted for by the product in a given year.
** Percentage of commercial services only.

and authors. Balassa (1962), however, provided a comprehensive definition for the term. Balassa defines it as:

> economic integration as a process and as a state of affairs. As a process, it encompasses measures designed to abolish discrimination between economic units belonging to different national states; as a state of affairs, it can be represented by the various forms of discrimination between national economies.
>
> *(Balassa 1962: 1)*

The degree of economic integration ranges from preferential trade arrangement (PTA) to free trade area (FTA), customs union (CU), common market (CM), and economic union (EU).

The four South Asian countries studied are loosely connected with a PTA under the present framework of a South Asian regional organization called the South Asian Association for Regional Cooperation (SAARC). The PTA arrangement within SAARC is discussed later. As mentioned earlier (see Chapter 1), the four countries studied are the four influential members of the eight SAARC nations. Nepal, Bhutan, and the Maldives are also included in the SAARC (see Madan 1996 for further details on SAARC). In 2007, Afghanistan was invited to be one of the full members. It became the eighth member of SAARC.

Integration of South Asian nations

Since the formation of SAARC in 1985, almost four decades ago, the pace of integration among the South Asian nations has not been satisfactory. Political and religious tensions still run high in the region, particularly between India and Pakistan. However, on other fronts, India-Bangladesh and India-Nepal relations have improved substantially since 1996–1997 (see below). The major objectives of regional integration are to achieve, within a certain period of time, a freer movement of goods, services, people, and capital in the region. In South Asia, despite the SAARC arrangement and subsequently with the present PTA and other developments, South Asia is one of the least integrated regions in the world.

So far, research initiatives on South Asian regional integration have been very few. However, the World Bank's South Asian Region Unit initiated a study on the subject in the early 1990s (World Bank 1993). This study identified four preconditions that bring significant success in integrating a region, particularly to becoming an FTA among a group of nations:

> First, the pre-FTA tariffs should be high. Second, the members of the FTA should be important trading partners before entering into an arrangement. Third, there should be complementarity in demand. For South Asian countries this by and large means entering an arrangement with countries that have different economic structures. Fourth, the differences in economic structure should be based on the 'true' competitiveness of the countries involved. This means that arrangements with countries that have substantially different factor endowments are superior to those with similar endowments.
>
> *(cited by Srinivasan and Canonero 1995: 29 from World Bank 1993: 16)*

As to the possibility of forming a possible South Asian FTA, South Asia hardly satisfies any of the above conditions except the first. As shown in the previous sections of this chapter, South Asian countries trade little with each other. They mainly trade with G7 nations, particularly with North America and Europe. The composition of each country's exports to these regions is similar, with an overwhelming share accounted for by RMG. The trade between South Asian countries is largely competitive, not complementary. Under these circumstances, it is unlikely to maximize gain from a South Asian FTA. However, a comprehensive study by Srinivasan and Canonero concluded that:

> The most preferred option for South Asia is to liberalize their external trade in a coordinated manner and extending the liberalized market access to the rest of the trading world on a Most Favoured Nation (MFN) basis. . . . The suggested coordinated liberalization should be viewed as an integral part of extending and deepening the ongoing economic reform process in South Asia.
>
> *(Srinivasan and Canonero 1995: 36)*

This proposal can also be interpreted on the principle of open regionalism.

This prescription is more likely to be obtained through a bilateral agreement of any two nations than through multilateral means. In this connection, Bhagwati and Srinivasan (1993) make the following recommendations specifically on India's trade reform:

> Finally, if we are to move to an outward-oriented strategy, seeking to exploit trade and investment opportunities provided by the world economy, then we must take appropriate action to ensure that these opportunities are available to us maximally. Otherwise, we would be operating with one blade of the scissors and ignoring the other . . . more important, we recommend that India now actively start exploring the options of joining in the free-trade blocs that are in place (EC and NAFTA) and which might emerge (in Asia). Else, it stands in danger of losing out to other countries, members of such blocs, in trade access and in attracting investment.
>
> *(cited by Srinivasan and Canonero 1995: 33, from Bhagwati and Srinivasan 1993: vi)*

The major reason behind these recommendations was India's—and other regional nations'—trade relations with NAFTA and the EC. India's trade (imports plus exports) with NAFTA and the EC comprised more than 42 per cent of the total in 1994, and recently this has increased to half of the total trade. In contrast, India's trade with the countries of the South Asian region is no more than 10 per cent of the total. Therefore, Srinivasan and Canonero (1995) conclude that the most preferred option for South Asia is to liberalize their external trade in a co-ordinated manner and extend the liberalized market access to the rest of the trading world on an MFN basis. Co-ordination of liberalization policies of each country in the region is needed, mainly to achieve the objectives of expansion of the currently low level of trade within the region and to avoid political opposition to liberalization by a country if its imports from neighbours rise faster than its exports to them.

South Asian Preferential Trade Agreements (SAPTA)

The regional trade analysis within the four countries studied has shown that South Asian trade makes up no more than 10 per cent of the total trade of any pair of nations. There are many reasons for such a low outcome; however, the major reason is the closed-door trade policies adopted by these countries since gaining independence in the late 1940s. Almost 50 years of restrictive trade policies, particularly among themselves, was mainly due to the apprehension that India, a large nation in the region, could swamp the markets of other smaller nations under a liberalized regime. However, under the SAARC arrangements, the countries of South Asia began working together, particularly co-operating in the areas of cultural and technical affairs after 1985. A limited economic co-operation began in the region in 1993, when the South Asian Preferential Trade Agreement (SAPTA) came into place and were signed by all members of SAARC nations.

Under SAPTA, Bangladesh, India, Pakistan, and Sri Lanka committed to establishing PTAs among their countries. Almost 300 commodities were identified for which restrictions have been reduced. In the past, India has offered tariff concessions to 106 items, Bangladesh to 120 items, Pakistan to 53 items, and Sri Lanka to 31 items (Madan 1996). It was also proposed in 1995 at the eighth SAARC summit in New Delhi that measures should be taken at the appropriate level to bring the region under a free trade regime called the South Asian Free Trade Area (SAFTA).

This proposition cannot be regarded as new in the region. In the pre-partition period of the Indian sub-continent (pre 1947), India, Bangladesh, and Pakistan were part of the same country and were operating like a CM with a single currency. This experience in the region could be useful to forming a possible SAFTA. To explore this matter further, one must look at it from a historical perspective and explore the arrangements the colonial government put in place with respect to trade and governance of the sub-continent. The southeastern region was divided into three presidencies: Bengal, Madras, and Bombay (see Map 9.1). These were the coastal regions of British India with four major seaports: Chittagong, Calcutta (Kolkata), Madras (Chennai), and Bombay (Mumbai). These coastal cities were full of life, servicing the intra- and inter-regional trade of British India (see more in Bhagwati and Desai 1970). However, it would be a monumental task at the present time to bring the whole region under FTA, mainly due to the political tensions between major countries of the region (e.g. India and Pakistan). Forming a full-scale FTA in the region seems very remote. Alternatively, it is better to create a manageable and workable sub-regional group within and beyond the South Asian region. Such a move has already been taken recently by five nations: Bangladesh, India, Myanmar (Burma), Sri Lanka, and Thailand. This is a move in the right direction. It has been argued that this forum will ultimately work as a bridge between the fastest-growing nations of East Asia and emerging nations of South Asia. A similar attempt could be made in the west, involving India, Pakistan, and Tajikistan, to connect South Asia with the newly independent transitional nations of Central Asia.

SAPTA and SAFTA results to date have fallen short of meeting expectations due to complex safeguard measures and NTBs among the SAARC member countries. Various SAARC meetings and summits have raised the issues of acceleration of economic integration in goods and services in the region, such as improving trade facilitation and reduction in sensitive lists. More specifically, the Eighteenth SAARC Summit held in Kathmandu, Nepal, in 2014 stressed the need for 'the elimination of all non-tariff and para-tariff barriers and smooth and efficient transit of transport to accelerate the process for South Asian Economic Union (SAEU) in a phased and planned manner.' Nevertheless, global, regional, and domestic political and economic turbulences have hampered the progress in liberalizing trade, investment, and other dimensions of regional economic co-operation within SAARC to date.

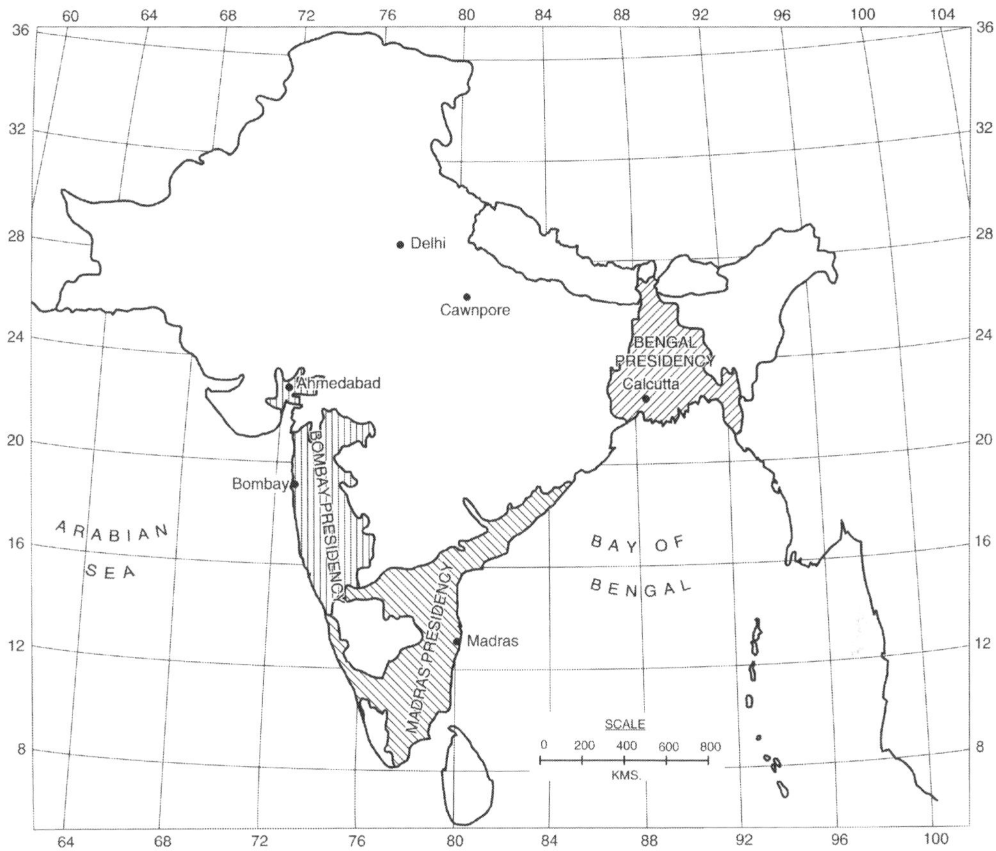

MAP 9.1 The three presidencies of British India: Bombay, Bengal, and Madras

SAARC Agreement on Trade in Services (SATIS)

The lack of progress in regional trade in South Asia through various regional initiatives such as SAPTA and SAFTA discussed earlier led the governments in the member countries to initiate another SAARC regional agreement, South Asian Trade in Services (SATIS), at the 16th SAARC summit held in Thimphu in 2010. The agreement entered into force on 29 November 2012. The objectives of this agreement are to

> promote and enhance trade in services among the SAARC countries in a mutually beneficial and equitable manner by establishing a framework for liberalising and promoting trade in services within the region in accordance with Article V of General Agreement on Trade in Service.

SATIS is following the GATS-plus 'positive list' approach for trade in services liberalization. This was particularly driven by the evidence of more complementarities in services than in goods in South Asia and the trade imbalance with India of other South Asian countries to be much lower than in goods (ADB 2004).

Concluding comments

The major aims of India, Bangladesh, and Sri Lanka in joining Thailand and Myanmar (two members of ASEAN) to form a sub-regional group are to expand regional trade with the fastest-growing nations of East Asia and to attract FDI from these nations. As mentioned earlier, through trade reform, a nation expects to achieve two key objectives: to create a market for its exports and to attract foreign investment (Rodrik 1992). In practice, this was the lesson learnt from East Asian experiences. Following the notable success of the Asian tiger development model in the 1980s in Hong Kong, Singapore, South Korea, and Taiwan, most of the East Asian nations embarked on an international trade-based economic development path where China, Malaysia, Thailand, and the Philippines were also commonly known as newly industrialized countries (NICs). Therefore, these countries demonstrated a high level of openness for inter-regional and intra-regional trade with the South Asian nations. Consequently, the East Asian nations have grown much faster. The only NIC in the South Asian region is India.

It is also evident that the East Asian nations were more successful than South Asian nations in attracting FDI, for example (see Table 9.15). All South Asian countries, except for India, have been able to attract a much lower level of FDI compared to Southeast Asian countries. Japan was the major FDI donor country for Southeast Asian countries in the 1980s and 1990s. This suggests that a stronger sub-regional integration had taken place in the East Asian region.

In recent years, the coastal belt of southeastern China has been successful in attracting FDI from South Korea, Taiwan (province of China), and Hong Kong through trade liberalization measures (see Map 9.2). In addition, location-specific advantage is one of the driving forces behind FDI flows. China's southeastern coastal belt has sufficiently satisfied foreign investors' demand on such an advantage. One can make a parallel of China's coastal belt with the coastal regions of southeastern India, southern Bangladesh, and eastern Sri Lanka (see Map 9.2). It is expected that in the future, with the encouragement of the newly formed sub-regional grouping, the coastal regions of India, Bangladesh, and Sri Lanka are likely to attract East Asian investment. These three countries are currently well placed to attract FDI due to their commitment to developing new infrastructure. For example, Bangladesh, being a delta and having numerous and complex river systems, has constructed bridges over its major rivers to connect northern regions with the coastal belt over the past few years. Additionally, an eight-kilometre-long

TABLE 9.15 FDI inflows to Southeast and South Asia 2990–2022 (US$ million)

Region	*1990*	*2000*	*2010*	*2022*
Southeast Asia				
Malaysia	2,332.5	3,787.6	10,885.8	14726.0
The Philippines	530.0	1,487.0	1,070.4	9199.9
Thailand	2,443.5	3,366.0	14,746.7	10196.1
Vietnam	180	1,298	8,000	17900
South Asia				
Bangladesh	3.2	280.4	1232.3	1555.4
India	236.7	3,584.2	27,396.9	49940.3
Pakistan	245.3	308.0	2,022.0	1339.0
Sri Lanka	43.4	172.9	477.6	898.3

Source: World Bank (2023)

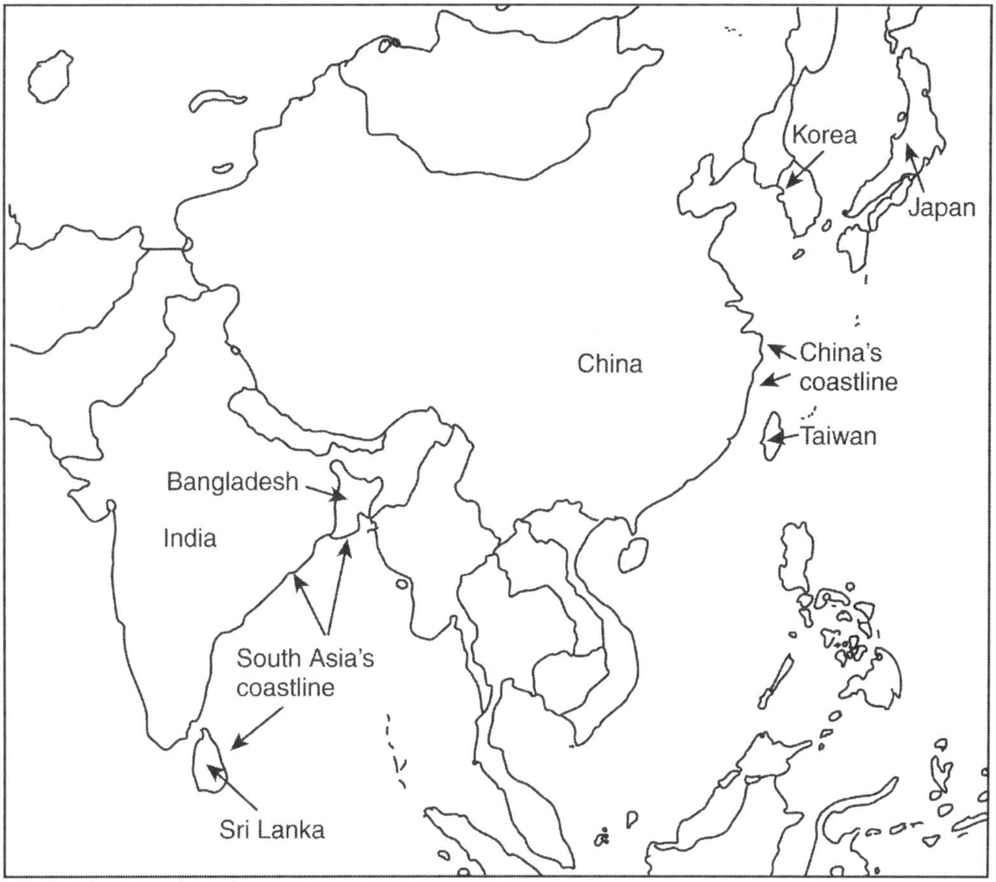

MAP 9.2 China's and South Asia's coastal belt

bridge was built over the river Jamuna in 1998. It was built with support from Japan and ADB to link northern and southern Bangladesh. It has been playing a pivotal role in connecting the nation with India in the west and with Myanmar and China in the southeast. It is expected that this multipurpose bridge (road, rail, and gas pipelines) will make Bangladesh a bridge between two Asias (East and South). It is likely to attract further investment from the east. In addition, recently found natural gas reserves (expected to be 50 trillion cu. ft. compared to current 10.5 trillion cu. ft. and believed to be larger than the North Sea reserve) in the Bay of Bengal started to attract further foreign investment from the world's largest oil companies.

Bangladesh's infrastructure building and establishment of improved transport networks in the future will create opportunities to satisfy the long-term demand by both India and Nepal to provide them with inland transit facilities through Bangladesh's territories. To achieve further integration at a sub-regional level, it will be hard for Bangladesh to reject such a proposition, which will be economically beneficial for all three nations. It appears that, on the issue of providing transit facilities, particularly to India, Bangladesh has divided opinions. The present government seems sympathetic towards such a move, not only for the sake of further regional integration but also for economic benefits, which will come to the nation through revenue generation. The opposition seems undecided on this issue. To address any opposition to transit issues from any corner of the political spectrum, the government should start mobilizing public opinion in its favour without delay.

Industrialization, trade prospects, and growth in South Asian nations will be influenced not only by their attempts at globalization and open economy policies but also by the changes they face in the internal trade environment and their policy adjustments to those changes. The principal internal environment of the region, which needs to be watched closely, is transit facilities extended to the landlocked SAARC member nations. The issues of road transit, intra-regional trade, and economic integration must be taken seriously at this stage of economic development in South Asia.

South Asian economies have undergone considerable levels of economic structural changes over the last several decades. Nevertheless, the region has remained inward-looking. In particular, trade among South Asian countries has remained much below potential, mainly owing to tariff and non-tariff barriers. According to the World Bank's Services Trade Restriction Index (2017), increasing trade within the region will require the elimination of tariff and non-tariff barriers, leveraging of private and interregional investment, investment in efficient connectivity and border crossings, and liberalizing services: logistics, shipping, air travel, etc. (World Bank 2017). These factors need further and deeper attention and policy interventions to facilitate South Asian regional development and economic integration.

The objective must be to show what prospects the SAARC nations have for expanding their current trade and to integrate the region further with a provision of a road transit system to the neighbouring landlocked member nations. In particular, the road transit should include the southeast sub-region of the SAARC: India (the states of Assam, Meghalaya, Tripura, Nagaland, Mizoram, Manipur, and Arunachal), Bhutan, and Nepal.

The United Nations Conference on Trade and Development (UNCTAD) conducted a study on this subject in 2001. This study concludes that current approaches to alleviating transit problems should concentrate on the following:

- Nepal should operationalize its ICD at Birgunj as a dry port and establish a significant alternative transit route through the JNPT port on India's west coast, using railways for hauling containers.
- Bhutan should construct and establish a dry port at Phuentsholing to stimulate its external trade sector.

The nations of this sub-region will need to establish a road transport system. This road transit facility will ultimately work as a bridge between the fastest-growing nations of East Asia and the emerging nations of South Asia.

The issue of transit is going to be the litmus test for the South Asian region in regard to its genuine desire in achieving economic integration. The experience in the last 30 years has been very disappointing. It gave birth to fear, suspicion, and lack of trust. Genuine effort will be needed in these nations to remove such a hostile environment and work towards generating meaningful co-operation among these nations in the future. It is essential now to start rebuilding political trust, economic infrastructure, and capacity building of human resources towards transit facility, economic integration, and growth under the auspices of the SAARC.

Bibliography

ADB (2004) *Asian Development Outlook 2004*, Oxford: Oxford University Press.

Anderson, K. and Blackhurst R. (1992) *The Greening of World Trade Issues*, London: Harvester Wheatsheaf.

Ahmad, Q. K. (1994) "Anatomy of economic liberalization efforts and results in Bangladesh", Paper presented to the Conference on Economic Liberalisation in South Asia, Australia South Asia Research Centre, Australian National University, Canberra.

Balassa, B. (1962) *The Theory of Economic Integration*, London: Allen and Unwin.

Bhagwati, J. N. and Desai, P. (1970) *India Planning for Industrialization: Industrialization and Trade Policies Since 1951*, London: Oxford University Press.

Bhagwati, J. N. and Srinivasan, T. N. (1993) *India's Economic Reform*, New Delhi: Ministry of Finance.

Carbough, R. J. (2009) *International Economics*, 12th Edition, Mason: South-Western Cangage Learning.

de Melo, J. and Panagariya, A. (1993) "Introduction", in J. de Melo and A. Panagariya (eds.), *New Dimensions in Regional Integration*, Cambridge: University Press.

Dean, J. M., Desai, S. and Reidel, J. (1994) "Trade policy reform in developing countries since 1985", World Bank Discussion Paper 267, Washington, DC: The World Bank.

Dunham, D. and Kelegama, S. (1994a) "The second wave of liberalisation in Sri Lanka 1989–93: Reform and governance", Paper presented to the Conference on Economic Liberalisation in South Asia, Australia South Asia Research Centre, Australian National University, Canberra.

Hossain, M. and Chaterjee, S. (1996) "India's liberalisation in communications: Some preliminary observations", Conference Proceedings of the Asian Studies Association of Australia Inc., La Trobe University, Melbourne.

Hossain, M. and Maswood, S. (2005) *WTO Agriculture Negotiations: An Assessment of Australian Position in Doha Round*, Joypur: CUTS, Electronic.

Hossain, M. and Mukhpadhyay, H. (2001) "Currency crisis: A South Asian perspective", *The Review of Asian and Pacific Studies*, 21: 15–34.

Hossain, M., Nurun Nabi, A. K. M. and Islam, I. (eds.) (2003) *Bangladesh's Development Agenda and Vision 2021: Rhetoric or Reality?* Dhaka: University Press Ltd.

IMF (2023) https://data.imf.org, Washington, DC.

Krueger, A. (1986) "General issues in economic liberalisation", in Choksi and Pappageorge (eds.), *Economic Liberalisation in Developing Countries*, Oxford: Basil Blackwell.

Madan, D. K. (1996) *Indo-Bangladesh Economic Relations and SAARC*, Dhaka: Tyk Prokason.

OECD (2023) *Agricultural Financial Support*. https://www.oecd.org/en/data/indicators/agricultural-financial-support.html#indicator-chart

Rodrik, D. (1992) "The limits of trade policy reform in developing countries", *Journal of Economic Perspectives*, 6, 1: 87–105.

Salvator, D. (1995) *International Economics*, Englewood Cliffs: Prentice Hall Inc.

Srinivasan, T. N. and Canonero, G. (1995) "Preferential trading arrangements in South Asia: Theory, empires and policy", IED seminar paper presented in May, International Institute for Economic Development, Boston University, Boston.

UNIDO (1995) *Industrial Development: Global Report 1995*, United Nations Industrial Development Organisation, Oxford: Oxford University Press.

World Bank (1993) *'Regionalism and South Asia's Trade', South Asia Division*, Washington, DC: World Bank.

World Bank (1995) *Global Economic Prospects and the Developing Countries 1995*, Washington, DC: World Bank.

World Bank (2005) *World development indicators 2005 (English)*. Washington, DC: World Bank Group. http://documents.worldbank.org/curated/en/947951468140975423/World-development-indicators-2005

World Bank (2017) World Bank's Services Trade Restriction Index. Washington, DC.

World Bank (2023) *World Integrated Trade Solution Data*, Washington, DC. https://Wits.WorldBank.Org/

World Trade Organization. www.wto.org, several articles accessed on 2008.

WTO (2010) *Global Financial Crisis (2008–2009)*. www.wto.org, accessed on 2010.

WTO (2023) Trends in South Asia and East Asian's Trade Integration, World Trade Organization.

10

AGRICULTURE AND RURAL DEVELOPMENT

Eliyathamby A. Selvanathan, Saroja Selvanathan, and Maneka Jayasinghe

Introduction

Immediately after the Second World War, countries in Asia, Africa, and Latin America emerged from centuries of colonial rule and became independent, but they were essentially underdeveloped. The primary concerns of the economists during those days were to achieve rapid economic growth and development in those countries. To achieve these, it was essential to address the problems in the production process of the underdeveloped nations. In order to bring about a change in the method of production, which was expected to add to profits, Schumpeter (1951) stressed new machines, new processes, new markets, and sources of inputs. In other words, the application of scientific technology to production was emphasized.

Lewis (1955) contends that growth of output per head depends basically on two sources: available natural resources and human behaviour of the country concerned. Lewis concentrates on the second source and identifies three major causes of growth:

> First, there is the effort to economize, either by reducing cost of any given product or by increasing the yield from any given input . . .; second, there is the increase of knowledge and its application . . . and third, growth depends upon increasing the amount of capital per head.
>
> *(Lewis 1955: 11)*

Lewis' prescription on growth theory, in the meantime, has been found impractical due to the huge population boom in the less developed countries (LDCs) in the 1950s and 1960s and their dependency on the agricultural sector. Fei and Ranis (1964), however, developed a surplus labour model for LDCs' economic growth. Fei and Ranis indicate that it is essential to formulate a theory of growth for a particular type of underdeveloped economy that has a supply of surplus labour and functions within the framework of the capitalist system. They emphasize the capitalist system because, during the 1950s and 1960s in some LDCs, in both Asia and Africa,

DOI: 10.4324/9781032716244-12

there was a wave of forming (former) Soviet-style economies. According to Fei and Ranis, the majority of newly independent nations

> are characterized by the coexistence of two sectors: a relatively large and overwhelmingly stagnant subsistence agricultural sector in which institutional forces determine the wage rate, and a relatively small but growing commercialized industrial sector in which competitive conditions obtain in the input markets.
>
> *(Fei and Ranis 1964: 3)*

The thesis of Fei and Ranis further argues that:

> it is the agricultural sector which is called upon to supply the manpower as well as substantial portion of the savings fund to fuel the development process. The major contribution to the savings fund is in the nature of a marketable agricultural surplus which may be viewed as agricultural output in excess of agriculture's own consumption requirements. The emergence of such an agricultural surplus thus obviously depends, on the one hand, on the change in agricultural productivity . . . and, on the other hand, on the growth of the rural population.
>
> *(Fei and Ranis 1964: 8)*

Fei and Ranis' prescription for growth was mainly adopted by South Korea, Taiwan, Pakistan, and India. With the application of the Fei and Ranis model, all these countries' agricultures have developed strongly since the 1970s, but South Korea and Taiwan were successful in channelling savings from agriculture to the industrial sector and have been successful in developing a strong industrial base.

Following the Schumpeterian line, in the 1960s, economists and agricultural economists in the United States published numerous theoretical and empirical studies on transforming LDCs' (traditional) agriculture through technological change (Johnston and Mellor 1961). An outstanding study was done by Schultz (1964), where he hypothesized that there are 'few significant inefficiencies in the allocation of factors of production in traditional agriculture.' This hypothesis has been widely tested by researchers and generally found to be true. It has been maintained so far by others that the most promising means of increasing the output and income of peasant farmers is the introduction of new technologies as extra factors of production (Southworth and Johnston 1967; Hayami and Ruttan 1971). In real terms, these technologies have high-yielding variety seeds, better breeds of livestock, more efficient implements and machines, fertilizers, pesticides, and insecticides.

Coincidentally, during the 1960s there were 12 international research institutions (e.g. IRRI and CYMMIT) established to develop high-yielding seed varieties for grains and other cash crops. Numerous inorganic fertilizer factories were built to sustain the additional supply of fertilizers in demand in LDCs. Similarly, facilities of irrigation and credit availability to innovative farmers of modernized agriculture were provided either by encouraging them to form co-operatives or through individual contact with the supplying agencies.

Almost all developing countries have introduced modern technology into agricultural production during the last quarter of a century. There are two main reasons for this. First, to attain food self-sufficiency for the growing population. Second, to increase the supply of raw materials for the newly established industrial sector. The countries representing South Asia, Indonesia, and the Philippines are commonly identified as the cases for the former, and South Korea, Taiwan, Thailand, and Malaysia are regarded as the cases for the latter.

Agricultural technology, however, has been classified into two categories: mechanical technology and biological (or biological-chemical) technology. In general, the mechanical technology involves lumpy machinery capital, which has labour-saving effects. In contrast, the biological technology depends on divisible inputs, such as seeds and fertilizer, and is usually geared to increase output per unit of land (Hayami 1982).

The introduction of these technologies revolutionized agriculture in the 1970s and 1980s. It was regarded as the 'Green Revolution.' Numerous studies have explained the impact of the Green Revolution in South Asian countries. The intention here is not to survey such a vast amount of literature; however, it has been claimed in the literature that additional production of food grains, wheat, and rice are the main successes for the Green Revolution. In the next section, a brief survey of this success story is attempted for the countries studied.

Growth in food grain production

Cropping contributes more than 80 per cent of value added in agriculture in South Asia. In the cropping sub-sector's progress, rice and wheat account for more than three-quarters of value-adding in cropping. Therefore, the increase in food grain production is the major source of agricultural growth in the four countries studied. Table 10.1 presents, in particular, the growth in the production of cereals and rice over selected years: 1990, 2000, 2010, and 2022. The figures suggest that despite Bangladesh experiencing a marginal negative growth rate in cereal production recorded during 2000–2010, cereal production increased notably, with almost 200 per cent growth during 2010–2022. Rice production also grew marginally throughout the last

TABLE 10.1 Cereals and rice production in 1985–1994 (five-year averages), ('000 tonne)

Country	*1990*	*2000*	*2010*	*2022*	*1990–2000*	*2000–2010*	*2010–2022*
Cereals (excluding rice)							
Bangladesh	969	1,876	1,801	5,360	93.6	−3.9	197.5
India	82,402	107,466	123,875	158,843	30.4	15.3	28.2
Pakistan	160,66	23,257	27,576	36,735	44.8	18.6	33.2
Sri Lanka	41	36	169	259	−11.6	368.0	53.4
Rice							
Bangladesh	26,778	37,628	50,061	57,189	40.5	33.0	14.2
India	111,517	127,465	143,963	196,246	14.3	12.9	36.3
Pakistan	4,891	7,204	7,235	10,983	47.3	0.4	51.8
Sri Lanka	2,538	2,860	4,301	3,393	12.7	50.4	−21.1

Source: FAO (2023)

Note: Cereal includes wheat, maize, barley, oats, rye, millet, sorghum, buckwheat, and mixed grain.

three decades in Bangladesh. In India, cereal production saw a greater than 25 per cent growth during 1990–2000 and 2010–2022, and rice production experienced a notable growth from less than 15 per cent growth during 1990–2000 and 2000–2010 to more than 35 per cent growth during 2010–2022. Pakistan experienced moderate growth in cereal and rice production during 1990–2000 and 2010–2022 and a notable fall in both products during 2000–2010. Cereal and rice production in Sri Lanka experienced substantial fluctuations, where 1990–2000, cereal production recorded a negative growth followed by an incredible 350 per cent growth during 2000–2010. During 2010–2022, cereal production further grew by 53 per cent. Although the rice production in Sri Lanka showed a marginal growth in 1990–2000 and 2000–2010, in 2010–2022 it recorded a negative growth greater than 20 per cent. This could be highly associated with the government policy shift towards organic farming, which resulted in a substantial drop in yield.

Table 10.2, in particular, shows the productivity performance in cereal production in four countries for selected years: 2105, 2018, and 2021. Of these countries, during 2018–2021, India has achieved the highest productivity growth, followed by Pakistan. However, India's notable growth in productivity in 2018–2021 was followed by a substantial drop in productivity (13 per cent) during 2015–2018. Sri Lanka has also experienced a marginal growth in productivity during the period. Bangladesh has the lowest productivity growth in the 2018–2021 period.

Agricultural productivity in value-added terms is presented in Table 10.3 for the four countries. It refers to the ratio of agricultural value added, measured in 2000 in US dollars, to the number of workers in agriculture. Although Bangladesh enjoyed the highest productivity in agriculture among the countries in the region during 1995–2015, the productivity in Bangladesh in the 2015–2019 period is lower than that of India and Sri Lanka. During the 2005–2015 period, all countries, except Pakistan, had a notable productivity growth. Nevertheless, the productivity growth of all countries declined in the 2015–2019 period.

TABLE 10.2 Yield of cereal (including rice) 2015–2021 (kg/ha)

Country	*2015*	*2018*	*2021*	*2015–2018*	*2018–2021*
Bangladesh	4,791	4,560	4,965	−4.8	8.9
India	3,278	2,856	3,479	−12.9	21.8
Pakistan	2,887	2,942	3,565	1.9	21.2
Sri Lanka	3,777	3,849	4,557	1.9	18.4

Source: FAO (2023)

TABLE 10.3 Agriculture value-added per worker 1995–2019 (US$)

Country	*1995*	*2005*	*2015*	*2019*	*1995–2005*	*2005–2015*	*2015–2019*
Bangladesh	497	731	1,109	1,284	47.1	51.7	15.8
India	927	1,072	1,668	2,076	15.6	55.6	24.5
Pakistan	2,328	2,427	2,405	2,634	4.3	−0.9	9.5
Sri Lanka	1,525	1,455	2,790	3,248	−4.6	91.8	16.4

Source: World Bank (2023)

Agricultural transformation: deficits to surpluses of food grains

It is claimed in the literature that, in the South Asian region, food shortages were unheard of until the Second World War (Chaudhry 1991). The great famine of Bengal, which struck in 1943, was recorded as a major food-related human disaster. Even at the time of independence in 1947, there was hardly any country in the region that could truly be regarded as a food-deficit area (Pakistan 1983 cited in Chaudhry 1991). The deficit started to emerge only in the 1950s and early 1960s due to rapid growth in population and stagnating agricultural and cereal production. The shortages in food grain production made the countries in South Asia spend huge foreign exchange on food imports and also made them dependent on the food aid programmes, mainly from the United States (e.g. PL480, a 1970s aid programme). It is in the wake of these developments that food self-sufficiency became a prime objective in South Asia in the late 1960s and early 1970s. South Asia's planning departments regard the term 'self-sufficiency' as the overall fulfilment of food grain requirements from domestic production. It has nothing to do with the fulfilment of adequate food requirements at household levels.

The agenda of gaining food self-sufficiency at national levels has been intensely pursued by adopting new technology in agriculture. As a result, net cereal imports began to taper off as early as 1967–1968 in India, Pakistan (Bangladesh was then the eastern wing of Pakistan), and Sri Lanka. Pakistan became self-sufficient in the mid-1970s, and India reached self-sufficiency in the late 1980s. As can be seen in Table 10.4, this trend continued in India and Pakistan to date, where both countries show negative net import values, suggesting that their export quantity of wheat and rice exceeds that of imports. However, Bangladesh and Sri Lanka remained import-dependent for some rice and wheat during this period. Bangladesh's deficit has been unpredictable since this country's vulnerability in cereal production is due to flood, cyclone, drought, and other natural calamities.

Production of export crops and allied products

As can be seen in Table 10.5, much of the export crop sector in the region has an indifferent performance during 2010–2020.

Bangladesh's tea and frozen fish and shrimp exports have remained stagnant during the period under consideration. Table 10.5 further suggests that India has a strong level of export for all products. In particular, coffee, spices, fish and fish preparations, and fruit and vegetable exports recorded notable growth during 2010–2020.

During 2010–2020, the food and vegetable export growth in Pakistan has seen strong growth while rice production has remained the major export cash crop in Pakistan despite a marginal fall in quantity exported in 2020.

TABLE 10.4 Net imports of wheat and rice ('000 tonnes)

Country	*2010*	*2015*	*2016*	*2017*	*2018*	*2019*	*2020*	*2021*
Bangladesh	4,268	5,525	5,551	9,830	6,369	4,734	7,970	12,409
India	−3,313	−17,100	−13,537	−13,336	−17,825	−15,148	−2,3026	−38,343
Pakistan	−6,040	−7,141	−6,526	−4,969	−8,014	−7,555	−3,334	−3,308
Sri Lanka	806	1,536	917	2,282	1,642	941	1,334	1,442

Source: FAO (2023)

TABLE 10.5 Export quantity of cash crops and allied products 2010–2020 ('000 tonnes)

Crop	*2010*	*2015*	*2020*
Bangladesh			
Tea	2	1	2
Frozen fish and shrimps	29.7	16.3	29.5
India			
Coffee	312	367	399
Tea and mate	238	240	218
Nuts and products	351	414	263
Spices	558	693	1146
Fish and fish preparations	523	595	744
Fruits and vegetables	3,053	3,172	4299
Pakistan			
Fruits and vegetables	859	1,117	1164
Rice	6,236	6,040	5824
Sri Lanka			
Tea	314	307	288
Coconuts	183	225	213

Source: FAO (2023)

Tea and coconuts have been the main export crops in Sri Lanka. While tea export volume has seen a drop during 2010–2020, that of coconuts has seen a growth during 2010–2015 before declining slightly in 2020.

In sum, the above analysis provides some clear indications that the region has achieved, to a large extent, the objectives of food self-sufficiency. To achieve this objective, all countries have been following a uniform policy instrument, providing adequate seed, fertilizer, and irrigation technology to farmers, including small farmers. It is unlikely that in the near future any government will attempt a shift from such a policy until there are genuine indications that the population growth rate has been neutralized with agriculture's rate of growth.

Sri Lanka's organic farming disaster

In April 2021, the Sri Lankan government imposed a ban on the import of agrochemicals. This policy is aimed at providing a toxin-free diet for all citizens by promoting organic agriculture and utilizing $400 million spent annually on fertilizer imports towards other essential imports. This policy change resulted in rice production dropping 20 per cent in the six months after it was implemented, leading a country that had been self-sufficient in rice production to spend $450 million on rice imports.

Similarly, the production of tea, Sri Lanka's only cash crop, declined by 18 per cent following the policy change. The reduction in crop yield of major export goods and the import of rice, the staple food in Sri Lanka, made the foreign reserves crisis even worse, further aggravating the economic crisis. The fertilizer ban was revoked in November 2021, having only been in force for six months.

Many argue that the policy towards transition to organic farming is not the culprit of a series of economic and political issues that took place in Sri Lanka during 2021–2022. It was the other important factors, such as the speed at which the policy was implemented, the lack of support to transition to organic farming, and the lack of knowledge and skills of farmers to implement organic farming practices, that resulted in the policy failure and subsequent negative implications. The Sri Lankan experience clearly demonstrates how (not) to implement policy changes abruptly.

Is the second 'Green Revolution' in the offing?

It has been shown that South Asia, until the 1990s, enjoyed phenomenal growth in food grain production by adopting new seed, fertilizer, and irrigation technology. The increase in productivity and bringing more and more land under irrigation were universally known as the 'Green Revolution.' In recent years, international food grain production, according to the Food and Agriculture Organization estimates, has taken a downward trend (Mittal 2008). There are many reasons for this. Most importantly, global climate change has been regarded as the major cause of crop failures in several parts of both developed and developing regions. In the past, there were warnings that if the two giants, India and China, started buying food grains on a large scale from food-surplus western nations, which has been the case in recent years, the world price of food grains would rise instantly. In 2008, this is what happened. The world has witnessed a phenomenal increase in the prices of rice and wheat.

This resulted in making extra efforts for policies that would contribute towards creating a second Green Revolution in South Asia. This is illustrated in Table 10.6, which shows how the use of new technology recently expanded further in South Asia (over 1992 and 2021). In all countries under consideration, the land under irrigation, land under cereal cultivation, and fertilizer use increased over this period.

Inter-country comparison suggests that in 2021, Bangladesh has the highest rate of irrigated land (79 per cent), followed by Pakistan (53 per cent), while India has the lowest. Bangladesh, India, and Sri Lanka have more opportunities in investing further in building irrigation infrastructure in the future. In all the nations, there are opportunities to bring more and more land under cereal production, particularly in Sri Lanka. Fertilizer use has further scope for expansion in India and Pakistan. Sri Lanka has been using the highest amount, and Bangladesh has been using the second highest amount in the 1990s, while by 2021, Bangladesh used the highest amount of fertilizer kilogram per hectare, followed by India and Pakistan. Sri Lanka used the lowest amount of fertilizer, and this could be partly associated with the fertilizer ban during May-November 2021.

TABLE 10.6 Adoption of seed-fertilizer-irrigation technology, selected years, 1990–2021

Country	*Irrigated land (% of crop land)*				*Land under cereal ('000 hectares)*				*Fertilizer use (kg/hectare of arable land)*			
	1990	*2005*	*2015*	*2021*	*1990*	*2005*	*2015*	*2021*	*1990*	*2005*	*2015*	*2021*
Bangladesh	33.8	51.1	57.7	78.9	10,683	11,176	12,156	12,519	99	198	299	384
India	28.3	32.9	38.1	42.3	99,451	99,519	100,101	102,435	74	128	171	193
Pakistan	n/q	52.8	51.7	52.7	12,211	12,810	13,962	14,703	64	124	138	157
Sri Lanka	28	34.5	n/a	n/a	934	950	1312	1234	190	255	190	154

Source: World Bank (2023)

The expansion of agricultural technology over the last decade certainly suggests that a second Green Revolution is in the offing in South Asia. It is now well established that food grain production due to the expansion of seed, fertilizer, and irrigation technology will take an upward turn soon. The next section illustrates India's food grain production and consumption gap in recent years and projections until 2026 studied by the Indian Council for Research on International Economic Relations.

Demand and supply trends and projected food grain in India

In population count, it is well known that India has one-sixth of the world's population and is the largest nation (keeping China the second largest of the world), with now more than 1.4 billion people. Among South Asian nations, India carries more than two-thirds of the population in the region. Thus, it is appropriate here to investigate the present and future food grain production and consumption gap for India. Since India has the largest number of producers and consumers of food grains in South Asia, any reduction in production affects the region adversely. Let us see below how India is going to perform in the future as far as the food grain gap is concerned.

Table 10.7 presents the estimates of the supply and demand gap of cereals in India to 2026. A negative gap indicates that the country will be in deficit in cereals from 2020, after enjoying a strong surplus during the preceding quarter century. The deficit will even further deteriorate in 2026, and this will hit a deficit of almost 17 million tonnes.

The Indian policymakers and government have taken these projections seriously and have started directing investment to building irrigation infrastructure. As mentioned earlier (see Table 10.6), India has only one-third of its arable land under irrigation. This nation also has the lowest rate of use of fertilizer among the nations of South Asia. Thus, it has further scope to increase fertilizer use and increase productivity to meet the deficit of cereals in 2020.

Concluding comments

The introduction of agricultural technology revolutionized South Asian agriculture in the 1960s, 1970s, and 1980s. This was called the 'Green Revolution.' The major elements of the Green Revolution have been the huge increase in food grain production (i.e. wheat and rice). One estimate suggests that the cropping sub-sector contributes more than 80 per cent of value added in agriculture in South Asia. Within the cropping category, rice and wheat account for more than three-quarters and, therefore, the increase in grain production was the major source of agricultural growth in the region. The growth pattern of cereals between 1990 and 2022 was highest in Bangladesh (except during 2000–2010) and was second highest in Sri Lanka (except during 1990–2000). In terms of rice production, Pakistan showed the highest growth during the period under consideration.

TABLE 10.7 Supply-demand gap projection for rice and wheat in India, 2005–2026 (million metric tonnes)

Food item	*2005*	*2011*	*2021*	*2026*
Total cereals	25.00	21.19	−2.94	−16.97

Source: Mittal (2008)

Note: The projections considered a GDP growth rate of 9 per cent and a negative sign indicates a supply-demand deficit.

With this record increase in the production of food grains in the two relatively densely populated nations of South Asia, the region has avoided the major food deficits of the past. Until the mid-1980s, all the countries studied except Pakistan were in deficit in food grain production. In 1985, India joined Pakistan as a food-surplus nation. In more recent times, these two countries have been enjoying a surplus in food grains. Sri Lanka and Bangladesh have been struggling to maintain their deficits at as low a level as possible.

South Asia was the test case of UN agencies in the field of rural development in the 1960s and 1970s. However, since the early 1980s, the NGOs of both domestic and foreign origins have been the major partners in carrying out rural development activities in the region. It appears that the NGO movement has been successful in bringing some meaningful changes to the millions of poor households by reducing poverty and providing them basic support in the areas of health, education, and housing.

Bibliography

Chaudhry, M. G. (1991) "Agricultural transformation in South Asia: Self-sufficiency to surplus", Paper presented to the conference held in New Delhi on the Future of Asia-Pacific Economies, 11–13 March, Asian and Pacific Development Centre, Kuala Lumpur.

FAO (Food and Agriculture Organization of the United Nations) (2023) *FAOSTAT-Crops and Livestock Products*. www.fao.org/faostat/en/#data/QCL, accessed on 24 March 2024.

Fei, J. and Ranis, G. (1964) *Development of the Labour Surplus Economy*, New Haven: Economic Growth Centre, Yale University.

Hayami, Y. and Ruttan, V. (1971) *Agricultural Development: An International Perspective*, Baltimore: Johns Hopkins University Press.

Johnston, B. F. and Mellor, J. W. (1961) "The role of agriculture in economic development", *The American Economic Review*, 51, 4: 566–593.

Lewis, W. A. (1955) "Economic development with unlimited supplies of labour", Paper presented at The Manchester School, May, 139–191.

Mittal, S. (2008) "Demand-supply trends and projections of food in India", Working Paper No. 209, New Delhi: ICRIER.

Schultz, T. W. (1964) *Transforming Traditional Agriculture*, New Haven: Yale University Press.

Schumpeter, J. (1951) *The Theory of Economic Development: An Inquiry into Profits, Capital, Credit, Interest and the Business Cycle*, Cambridge, MA: Harvard University Press.

Southworth, H. and Johnston, B. (1967) *Agricultural Development and Economic Growth*, Ithaca: Cornell University Press.

World Bank (2023). *World Development Indicators*, Washington, DC: The World Bank.

11

CLIMATE DISASTER-RELATED DISPLACEMENT AND RESILIENCE

Moazzem Hossain

Introduction

In simple words, as the atmosphere becomes richer in the greenhouse gases, it becomes a better insulator, retaining more of the heat provided to the planet by the sun. Climate scientists use elaborate computer models of temperature circulation to study global warming. On the basis of these models, they have made several predictions about how global warming will affect weather, sea levels, coastlines, agriculture, wildlife, and human health (Mia 2008). According to the World Bank, South Asia's poorest of the poor are most at risk due to global warming. Almost 40–50 million people of the coastal belt of the Bay of Bengal will suffer from inundation by 2030. According to Sir Nicholas Stern (2007), even a moderate rise in temperature could cause serious changes to the environment in South Asia. Stern led the 'Stern Report on the Economics of Climate Change.' It was commissioned by the UK Treasury and released in October 2006. Despite the controversy surrounding the report regarding some of the assumptions and the choice of the social discount rate, it would be irresponsible to ignore the call for urgent global action to fight climate change (World Bank 2008).

In a study by the Norwegian Red Cross, NRC (2015), Community Resilience and Disaster-Related Displacement in South Asia studied eight countries, including four countries this volume analysed: Bangladesh, India, Pakistan, and Sri Lanka. This chapter tries to summarize the NRC's study below, with the Bangladesh case first. This nation is considered the worst case as far as the global warming hazards in years to come.

Bangladesh

It is now widely recognized that the South Asia region, in general, and Bangladesh, in particular, would suffer heavily in both economic and social terms from global warming. Moreover, according to Oxford University climatologist Mark New, over the past 30 years, snow cover and ice cover may have reduced by 30 per cent in the eastern Himalayas. There is now a real risk that these glaciers might disappear altogether in the coming decades. If this happens, Bangladesh's mighty rivers originating from the eastern part of the Himalayas would severely affect

DOI: 10.4324/9781032716244-13

the availability of freshwater, and as a result, drought and lack of water for irrigation would become permanent features for a nation that had, for hundreds and thousands of years in the past, abundant freshwater.

In 2008, the President of Iceland visited Bangladesh and suggested some adaptation measures for climate change. For example, the President suggested the creation of a Himalaya council replicating the Arctic Council for countries surrounding the Himalayas, including Bangladesh, Nepal, and India, to conduct research and co-operate on combating the accelerating effects of climate change in this region. Taking note of the President's warning that environmental challenges such as water shortages and soil erosion might spawn the seeds of future conflict, Bangladesh could possibly tap its abundant water resource and preserve it through the adoption of scientific means to augment food production. The grim warning that came from President Grímsson was that global warming is now several decades ahead of schedule because of the melting of ice sheets in the Arctic and Greenland region. These were projected to occur in the middle of this century, but they have already begun (Khan 2007).

Grímsson said:

> Iceland could possibly serve as an inspiration for switching to clean energy resources, with 100 per cent of the country's electricity now produced by clean energy sources compared to 80 per cent of it produced from coal and oil half a century ago.
>
> *(Khan 2007)*

In short, the ultimate outcome of climate change for Bangladesh can be summarized as follows:

> Bangladesh will receive a heavier rainfall during the monsoon because the rate of evaporation is expected to increase by up to 12 per cent. Mean monthly rainfall may significantly change over current variability. Monsoon rainfall may increase by 11 per cent by 2030 and 27 per cent by 2070. Due to global warming, over the past 100 years temperature has increased by 0.50°C but in the next 50 years that is, by 2050, the temperature in Bangladesh is projected to rise by 1.5 to 2.00°C.
>
> *(Hossain 2008)*

Table 11.1 presents daily actual temperature readings for four days in the middle of April for 10, 15, 20, 22, 25, and 26 April 2024. The 20 April temperature suggests a very high, 38 degrees, one of the highest temperature readings in the history of Dhaka, the capital city of Bangladesh. The lowest temperature readings show 32 degrees on 10 April, which is also a record for 2024.

A recent study by the World Bank (2023) entitled 'Building Back a Greener Bangladesh' has investigated various aspects of green growth, development pathways, the exposers to environmental health risk factors, and how environmental pollution factors limit the country's human

TABLE 11.1 Daily actual temperature readings over 10-15-22 April 2024 for Dhaka, capital of Bangladesh

10 April	*15 April =*	*20 April*	*22 April*	*25 April*	*26 April*
Hi 35, Lo 32	Hi 37, Lo 30	Hi 38, Lo 30	Hi 35, Lo 27	Hi 36, Lo 28	Hi 35, Lo 27

Source: Weather Bureau, Dhaka, 27 April 2024

Note: High—Hi, Lo—Low.

capital formation. The report has concluded that Bangladesh faces other major environmental and natural resources issues, for example, river pollution and salinity intrusions, soil degradation, biodiversity loss, high exposure to mercury and heavy metals, and noise pollution. The country has in hand a huge challenge in plastic waste management too (World Bank (2023).

A few studies in the past found that high temperatures would reduce the yields of high-yielding variety (HYV) rice during all the seasons throughout Bangladesh. An important study reveals that a 60 per cent moisture stress on top of other effects might cause as high as a 32 per cent decline in boro rice yield. One-quarter of the country's land mass is currently flood-prone in a normal hydrological year. This may increase to 39 per cent, and prolonged flooding can effectively reduce overall potential for HYV Aman rice production. Global warming will make tropical cyclones and tornadoes in Bangladesh stronger and more frequent. The category five cyclone 'Sidr,' which hit Bangladesh on 15 November 2007, and 'Nargis,' with a similar force, which hit southern Myanmar in 2008, have already drawn attention to the devastation and frequency of such a calamity (Hossain 2008).

Water-related impacts due to climate change and sea level rises are likely to be some of the most critical issues for Bangladesh, not only in relation to coastal and river flooding but also in relation to the enhanced possibility of winter drought in certain areas. In the dry season, river flow will be reduced. Consequently, salinity will penetrate along the coastal rivers. It will cause an increase in evapo-transpiration, which is detrimental to crop growth. It will also result in the release of more carbon from the topsoil (Hossain 2008).

Rises in temperature will favour pest and pathogen activities, and human health will be at higher risk, that is, increased risk of some infectious diseases like malaria, diarrhoea, and dengue. Rising temperatures may jeopardize the forest succession processes. It may result in low productivity and poor vegetative cover of the forest and affect its rich biodiversity. One-quarter of a million hectares of land will become affected by salinity, on top of the three million hectares already affected. Farmers will be forced to grow crops with economically lower returns (Hossain 2008).

It has been noticed that in recent years riverbank erosion has taken a serious turn. The farmers have been losing their cultivable land to erosion, without warning, and have become destitute overnight. There being no rehabilitation plan on the part of the government for these vulnerable and naturally evicted farmers, they have no alternative but to migrate to the large cities in search of food, jobs, and livelihood after losing farmlands forever. This has resulted in overcrowded cities with ever-growing slums and an itinerant population.

For example, Dhaka, the capital of Bangladesh, presently has a population of almost 20 million, which is about 17 per cent of the nation's total population. The population in Dhaka has doubled over a period of only 20 years, while the nation's population doubled over 40 years. A similar story of population influx to other regional cities can be found. The cities have been mushrooming with slum dwellers in recent years. This resulted in inviting major catastrophe in food security, housing, transport, education, and the health of millions of city dwellers.

As far as the prices of food grains are concerned, there seem to be imbalances in the marketplace (on demand and supply fronts) in the post-COVID-19 period. On the demand side, population growth has been the major source of additional demand. However, the supply side effects have been most daunting due to the global uncertainties since COVID-19 in 2020. For example, lack of agricultural land, alternative uses of land, and increased costs in inputs are the major problems on the supply side.

Of Bangladesh's 180 million people, more than 40 million are likely to be directly affected by climate change, according to the World Bank, in the next 20 years. Thus, it is appropriate here to investigate more closely the climate change, growth, and poverty issues of Bangladesh and the lessons for other nations in the region. Before attempting this, let us look at the global and other South Asian countries that were recently conducted on these issues.

India

NRC (2015) studied India, the world's largest country population-wise and the sixth largest country in the world in terms of land area. Among the four nations studied in this volume, India borders Pakistan to the west; it all but surrounds Bangladesh, with which it shares the Indo-Gangetic plain. Sri Lanka, on the other hand, is located south of India on the Bay of Bengal, a stone's throw from India. The two largest rivers, the Ganges and the Brahmaputra, run through most of northern, central, and eastern India in Arunachal Pradesh and pass through Assam before flowing into Bangladesh. The Ganges is the longest river in India and enters Bangladesh through the northwestern border of India and Bangladesh. In the summer, the Ganges carries a huge water system that originates from the Himalayas in the Nepal and Tibet region.

NRC (2015) further argues that India's geographical diversity makes it particularly prone to the effects of climate change. It has been a record for India of how the country is suffering from various climate-related disasters and other disasters in the recent years. For example, 68 per cent of India is vulnerable to drought, 57 per cent to earthquakes caused by tectonic activity in the Himalayas region, 12 per cent to floods, and 8 per cent to cyclones. Moreover, the IPCC predicted a rise in global temperatures between 0.3 and 4.8 centigrade. As temperatures rise and glacial melt increases, this is likely to contribute to glacial lake outbursts, and the riverbanks give up due to an increase in water flows; consequently, farm areas are flooded, destroying crops, and the number of waterborne diseases increases in rural areas during the monsoon season. It has also been predicted by the IPCC that the sea level will rise by up to 82 cm in the vast coastal areas of India by the late 21st century, which risks parts of the southern region being inundated by saline water, affecting cropland. It has been predicted that some 17 million people could be displaced by 2050 due to inundation (NRC 2015).

Pakistan

Pakistan is the second largest country in South Asia, in terms of both land and population. It borders Afghanistan, Iran, India, and China and opens out onto the Arabian Sea to the south. The transboundary Indus River is Pakistan's longest and flows from north to south from Kashmir to the Arabian Sea (NRC 2015). The Indus delta in the south is vulnerable to marine intrusion and sea level rises. It is the 67th most vulnerable country in the world from a climate change point of view.

A climate change policy adopted in 2012 aims to 'mainstream climate change into economically and socially vulnerable sectors and steer Pakistan towards climate resilient development' (National Climate Change Policy 2011, p. 3). The Ministry of Climate Change was established in 2012. However, in 2013, the ministry has been reduced to a division and drastically reduced its budget. The Ministry of Climate Change was restored again in 2015 and appointed a federal minister immediately before COP 21 of the UN Framework Convention on Climate Change. This suggests Pakistan cares less about the issues of various types of natural disasters due to the global alarming threat to 2050. On the political front, Pakistan has been in turmoil since 2022. A report from the PTI below shows the gravity of the problem. At this point of global warming emergency, Pakistan's political turmoil is unwarranted to say the least.

Press Trust of India (PTI) reports on 15 September 2022 Shehbaz Sharif, the Pakistan Muslim League-Nawaz (PML-N) president, was elected unopposed as the new prime minister of Pakistan by parliament on Monday after rival candidate Shah Mahmood Qureshi announced that his PTI party would boycott the voting and staged a walkout. Shehbaz, 70, was the only candidate left in the race after Qureshi's boycott of the election in the National Assembly. In the House of 342, the winning candidate requires the support of at least 172 lawmakers. Shehbaz, the younger brother of former three-time prime minister Nawaz Sharif, received 174 votes—two more than the simple majority of 172. He is the 23rd prime minister of Pakistan. He has served as chief minister of the country's most populous and politically crucial Punjab province thrice. Former president and Pakistan People's Party (PPP) co-chair Asif Ali Zardari had proposed Shehbaz's name for the prime minister's position in a joint opposition meeting to replace Imran Khan through a no-confidence motion.

The process of electing the new leader of the House began on Sunday after Prime Minister Imran Khan was removed from office through the no-confidence vote, becoming the first premier in the country's history to be sent home after losing the trust of the House. In the 2023 general election, the coalition of the Muslim League (PML-N) and PPP won the election and formed the government with PML-N President Shehbaz Sharif elected as PM and the co-chair of the PPP, Asif Ali Zardari, made President. It remains to be seen if the present government can bring stability to Pakistani politics, which is very crucial for the development of Pakistan in the future.

Sri Lanka

Sri Lanka is an Indian Ocean island off the southern tip of India made up of coastal plains and a mountainous area in its south-central region. It has a tropical climate and two monsoon seasons, maha from December to March and *yala* from June to October. It was once almost entirely forested, but today less than a third has tree cover. The country has 103 major river basins covering 90 per cent of the island and ten major rivers (NRC 2015). Sri Lanka suffering from intense monsoon rains associated with climate change means that floods are now a regular occurrence, made worse in some cases by deforestation and erosion, which also contribute to landslides. The main natural hazards for this nation are cyclones and tornados, and the risks associated with these hazards are increased by factors including deforestation, soil erosion, coastal degradation, and increased pollution. Also, other climate hazards like storms and floods cause most damage and loss of life, but drought causes most agricultural losses.

The seeds of Sri Lanka's crisis were laid around 2005, when its government (led by then President Mahinda Rajapaksa) started bingeing on several mega infrastructure projects, often of dubious economic value. This trend accelerated after the end of the Civil War in 2009. Growth did increase for a few years, but the path was unsustainable. In addition, since the early 2000s, an increasingly complicated and non-transparent labyrinth of tariffs and hidden tariffs has been levied on imports, increasing the policy bias against exports, with renewed impetus since 2019, when the Rajapaksas came back to power after a four-year hiatus.

Total trade as a share of Sri Lanka's GDP fell from 89 per cent in 2000 to 46 per cent in 2010, a decline of perhaps unprecedented magnitude in a modern economy. In 2019, it was 52 per cent. The need to fund large trade deficits and the debt overhang meant that external debt kept growing and external reserves shrinking, leading eventually to the sovereign debt default announced on 12 April 2022. Moreover, high domestic spending, coupled with low tax collections, resulted in high fiscal deficits and borrowing needs and a total debt stock as high as 119 per cent of GDP in 2021, up from 70 per cent in 2012.

To compound all this, the overall investment climate favours entrenched business, with negative implications for exports and economic growth. Finally, while the Easter bombings and COVID-19 did exacerbate the shortage of foreign currency earnings in an economy highly dependent on tourism, it should be noted that the economy was already on an unsustainable path prior to the onset of the pandemic.

Climate change studies from first decade of 21st century

Fighting climate change: human solidarity in a divided world

The UNDP dedicated its 2007–2008 Human Development Report to the issues of climate change globally (UNDP 2007). This study has four chapters. They examine: first, the challenges of climate change in the 21st century; second, risk and vulnerability due to climate shocks in an unequal world; third, the possible strategies for mitigation of climate change dangers; and fourth, adaptation to climate change through national action and international co-operation.

The study makes it clear that there are no 'ifs' or 'buts' about climate change and its aftermath in the 21st century, in both developed and developing countries alike. The time has come for a decision to be made on how to mitigate such a disastrous and dangerous manmade menace, which has generally been created over the last century. Mitigation must seriously consider how to bring both the developed and the developing worlds closer in making future strategies. Collective action is needed to face disaster globally.

The study has identified five transmission ways by which climate change could stall and then reverse human development. These are

- agricultural production and food security
- water stress and water insecurity
- rising sea levels and exposure to climate disasters
- ecosystems and biodiversity
- human health.

(UNDP 2007)

Due to the increases in global temperature, 3–4°C could result in 330 million people (5 per cent of the world population) being permanently or temporarily displaced through flooding.

To avoid such a calamity in our lifetime, unparalleled collective action and international co-operation in the time ahead are needed because none of the above mechanisms will operate in isolation. There should be some meaningful strategies devised for mitigation. Most importantly, carbon markets are a necessary condition for the transition to a low-carbon economy; however, these are not sufficient conditions. Why carbon markets? It is now established without a doubt that a sustainable global carbon emissions strategy will be the major pathway of mitigation.

The Intergovernmental Panel on Climate Change (IPCC): sixth technical paper on climate change and water

The IPCC's sixth technical paper (Bates et al. 2008) was released in June 2008. This chapter deals with the issue of freshwater. Sea level rise has been dealt with only insofar as it can lead to impacts on freshwater in coastal areas and beyond. Freshwater is not only related to climate and biophysical systems, but it is also interconnected with socio-economic systems, which encompass multi-country and multi-origin regional networks. Hence, the study makes it clear that the relationship between climate change and freshwater resources is of primary concern to human society, and it also has implications for all living species.

The study found abundant evidence that freshwater resources are vulnerable and have the potential to be strongly impacted by climate change, with wide-ranging consequences for human societies and ecosystems. Following are the major conclusions of the study:

- Observing warming over several decades, it has been found that there is a link between warming and change in the large-scale hydrological cycle.
- By the middle of the 21st century, annual average river runoff and water availability are projected to increase as a result of climate change at high latitudes and in some wet tropical areas and decrease over some dry regions at mid-latitudes and in the dry tropics.
- Increased precipitation intensity and variability are projected to increase the risks of flooding and drought in many areas.
- Water supply stored in glaciers and snow cover is projected to decline in the century.
- Higher water temperatures and changes in extremes, including floods and droughts, are projected to affect water quality and exacerbate many forms of water pollution.
- Globally, the negative impacts of climate change on freshwater systems are expected to outweigh the benefits.
- Changes in water quantity and quality due to climate change are expected to affect food availability, stability, access, and utilization.
- Climate change affects the function and operation of existing water infrastructure—including hydropower, structural flood defences, drainage, and irrigation systems—as well as water management practices.
- Current water management practices may not be robust enough to cope with the impacts of climate change.
- Climate change challenges the traditional assumption that past hydrological experience provides a good guide to future conditions.
- Adaptation options designed to ensure water supply during average and drought conditions require integrated demand-side as well as supply-side strategies.
- Water resources management clearly impacts many other policy areas.

(Bates et al. 2008: 3)

Climate change, growth, and poverty in South Asia

In Part I, it has been demonstrated that the countries studied have been enjoying high to moderate growth over the last decade and that there have been significant achievements in alleviating poverty along the lines of MDGs (except for some setbacks due to the unprecedented natural disasters that hit Bangladesh and India over the last two years). The global financial meltdown and recession, together with fuel price and food price increases, in 2008 also took their toll on poverty alleviation in the region. For example, Bangladesh's poverty in US$1-a-day per capita terms nosedived from 35 per cent of the total population in 2006 to 40 per cent in 2008. In India, it is feared that poverty has increased from 30 to 36 per cent in US$1-a-day per capita over 2006 and 2008. A similar reverse trend can be witnessed in Pakistan and Sri Lanka. These two nations, moreover, have the added burdens of terrorism and civil war contributing towards the economic downturn and the reversal of whatever achievements have been made in the areas of MDGs.

With such a background, the present section demonstrates how the region copes with climate change challenges with respect to growth and poverty alleviation. On the impact of climate change on South Asia's poor, the World Bank (2008) concludes the following:

- Decreased water availability and water quality in many arid and semi-arid regions
- An increased risk of floods and droughts in many regions
- Reduction in water regulation in mountain habitats
- Decreases in reliability of hydropower and biomass production
- Increased incidence of waterborne diseases such as malaria and dengue
- Increased damages and death caused by extreme weather events
- Decreased agricultural productivity
- Adverse impacts on fisheries
- Adverse effects on many ecological systems

In the past, the World Bank carried out several country-level studies on large South Asian nations to investigate the impact of climate change and how to adapt in the future. For ready reference, lists are provided below for Bangladesh, India, and Pakistan.

Bangladesh

- Health impact of air and water pollution in Bangladesh
- Management of water quality in Dhaka
- Expanding renewable energy in Bangladesh

India

- Country water resources assistance strategy
- Unlocking opportunities for forest-dependent people in India
- For a breath of fresh air: ten years of progress and challenges
- Better crops, higher incomes for farmers of the Karnataka watershed

Pakistan

- Pakistan: country water resources assistance strategy
- Pakistan water economy
- Household use of commercial energy in Pakistan

Other reports of interest

- An investment framework for clean energy and development
- Building country capacity to combat climate change.
- Managing climate risk: integrating adaptation.
- Will markets direct investments under the Kyoto Protocol?

(www.worldbank.org)

It was mentioned at the start of this chapter that, according to the World Bank, Bangladesh is among the South Asian nations most affected by and vulnerable to the impacts of the climate change menace. The nation has the world's largest delta, and its neighbours, southern India and Myanmar, have large deltas as well, which are areas also vulnerable in this regard. The World Bank has estimated that by 2050, Bangladesh will have almost 30–40 million people directly affected by sea level rise presently affecting southern Bangladesh in the mouth of the Bay of Bengal delta. Because of Bangladesh's extreme vulnerability in the region to the climate change impacts, in this study it is appropriate to look at the consequences of climate change on one of the most populous nations of South Asia. This is attempted below.

The case of Bangladesh

Bangladesh is situated on the largest delta plain in the world at the confluence of the Ganges, Brahmaputra, and Meghna River systems (see Map 11.1), which collect water from the Himalayas and northeastern hills of India. Metcalfe (2003: 301) states that '[T]he Bangladesh landscape is a flat to gently undulating delta flood plain with a network of river systems. Half of the delta plain is at elevations less than 10m above sea level.'

As Map 11.1 shows, the southern coastal region forms part of the largest mangrove forest complex, called Shundor Bon (listed as a world heritage area), in the world. Natural resources

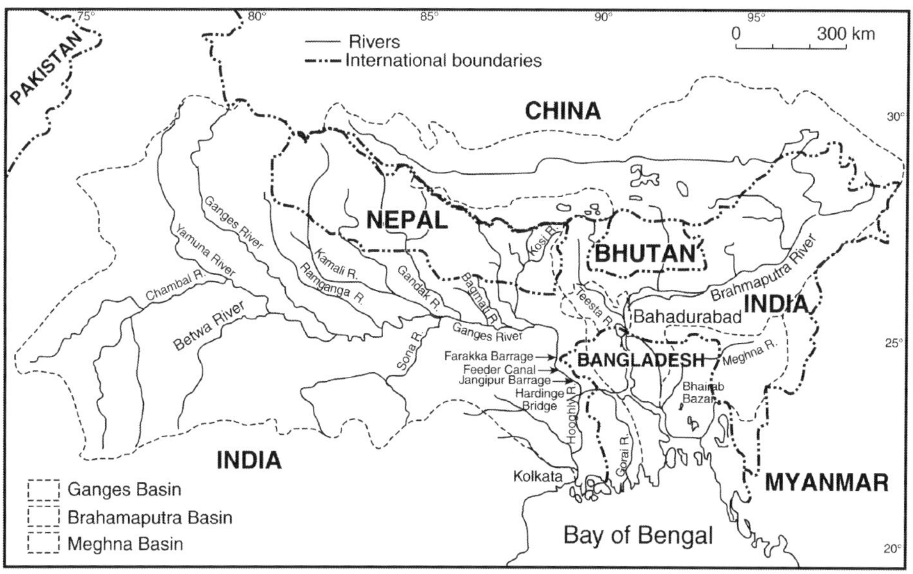

MAP 11.1 The Ganges, Brahmaputra, and Meghna river basins

of Bangladesh include abundant summer freshwater, alluvial land, sweet water and sea fisheries, forests, and wildlife. The huge population of 150 million is rapidly expanding, placing immense pressure on the country's natural resources and the environment (see basic facts about Bangladesh in Table 11.1).

Climate change and natural hazards

According to Metcalfe (2003), Bangladesh is extremely vulnerable to the effects of global warming and climate change due to its low elevation on a giant delta floodplain. The major concerns are listed as follows:

- Drainage congestion
- Reduced freshwater availability in the dry winter months
- Increased intensity and frequency of major floods
- Rising sea level.

While Bangladesh cannot have a major role in the mitigation of human greenhouse gas emissions, it remains very much on the receiving end and suffers from the consequences of climate change. Global surface temperature has increased significantly (by about 0.6°C) since direct measurements began in 1860 (see Figure 11.1). The IPCC's projections on global warming suggest a temperature rise of between 1.4 and 5.8°C from 1990 to 2010, which may cause a rise in sea level through polar ice melt and thermal expansion of between 8 and 88 cm (Watson 2001 cited by Metcalfe 2003).

Sea level along the Bangladesh coast is currently rising by 3 mm per year. Catastrophic monsoons, which previously occurred only every half a century on average, are likely, due to global warming, to occur every decade or more frequently by the latter half of this century (Palmer and Raisanen 2002 cited in Metcalfe 2003). Metcalfe (2003: 305) maintains that 'During the winters, it is expected that reduced river flow will lead to reduced freshwater availability, drainage congestion due to over silting, and more pronounced saltwater incursion along the coastal zones.' Increasing devastation from cyclones is also likely with a rise in sea level. It would also have impacts on the availability of coastal resources (World Bank 2000). Bangladesh was also subject to recurrent droughts in recent times. Between 1960 and 1991, droughts occurred 19 times, with extreme severity in 1961, 1975, 1981, 1982, 1984, and 1989. In recent years, almost annually, some parts of the nation, particularly the north, have been subject to drought from a moderate to severe range (Metcalfe 2003).

With projected future climate change in Bangladesh (see Table 11.2), droughts will become more frequent and more severe and will have significant detrimental effects on agricultural production in the country.

Ecological footprint

The ecological footprint of a country estimates the population's consumption of energy, food, and materials in terms of the area of biologically productive land required to produce those natural resources or absorb corresponding carbon dioxide emissions. Wackernagel et al. (1997) define the ecological footprint as 'the biologically productive area required to continuously provide resource supplies and absorb wastes of a particular population given prevailing technology' (cited in Metcalfe 2003: 314).

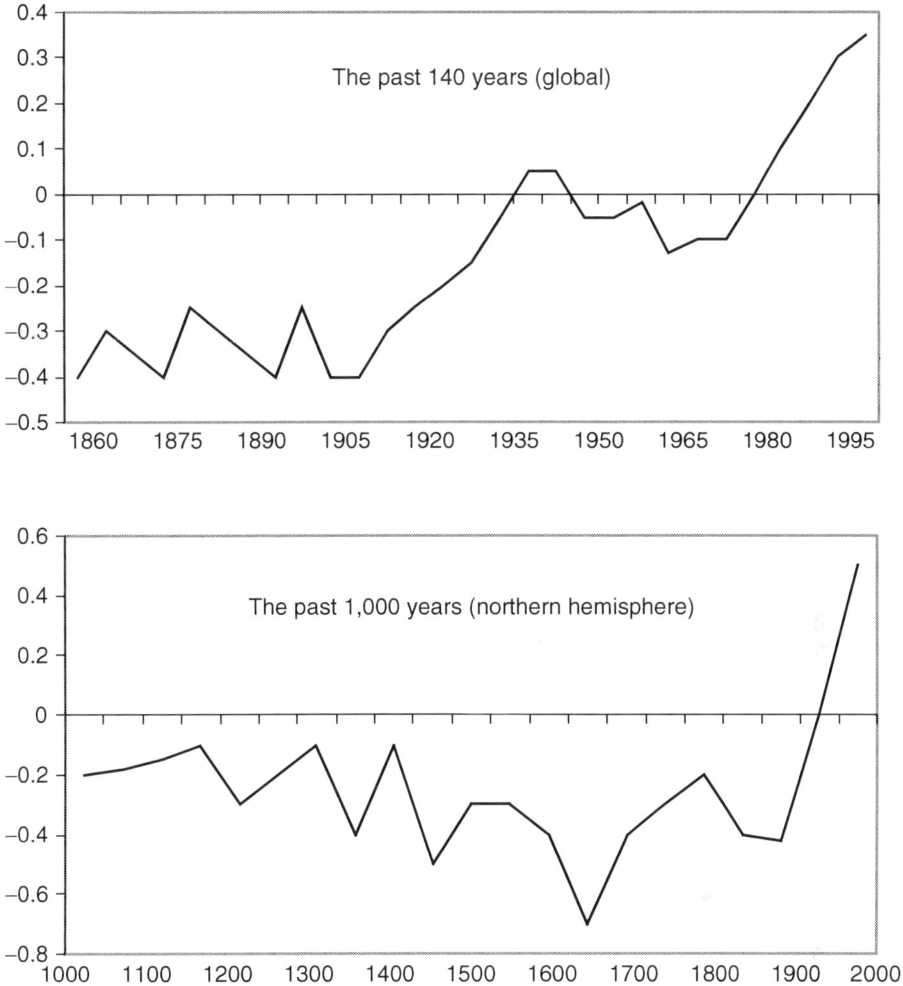

FIGURE 11.1 Departures in temperatures in °C for the past 140 years (globally) and the past 1,000 years (northern hemisphere)

TABLE 11.2 Basic facts about Bangladesh

Official name	People's Republic of Bangladesh
Territorial borders with	India (west, east, and north)
	Myanmar (east), Bay of Bengal (south)
Area	144,000 sq. km
Capital	Dhaka
Second city	Chittagong (sea port)
Population	150 million
Urban population	30 per cent
Ecological footprint (area units/person)	0.53 (1999)

Source: Metcalfe (2003)

Table 11.3 presents climate scenarios over 2030 and 2050. Of course, the temperature increases between these two periods have been presented for two broad seasons only: Monsoon and Winter. In Monsoon, the temperature increase has been predicted to be 0.4 degrees between the two periods of monsoon. While in winter this is about 0.5 degrees. Within 20-year period the temperature increases certainly showing very significant. It remains to be seen how temperature differences over monsoon and winter changes between rural and urban areas.

Figure 11.2 presents the ecological footprint of selected developed and developing countries, including Bangladesh. The figures on footprint suggest that overconsumption is more of a major problem for sustainable development than poverty issues. Bangladesh's figure suggests almost four times less of a footprint than the world average. With the dual impact of climate change (sea-level rise in particular) and population growth, Bangladesh, in 2050, will be more

TABLE 11.3 Climate scenarios for Bangladesh in 2030 and 2050

Year	*Sea level rise (cm)*	*Temperature increase (°C)*	*Precipitation fluctuations compared to 1990 (%)*
2030		+0.7 in monsoon +1.3 in winter	−3 in winter +11 in monsoon
2050		+1.1 in monsoon +1.8 in winter	−37 in winter +28 in monsoon

Source: Metcalfe (2003)

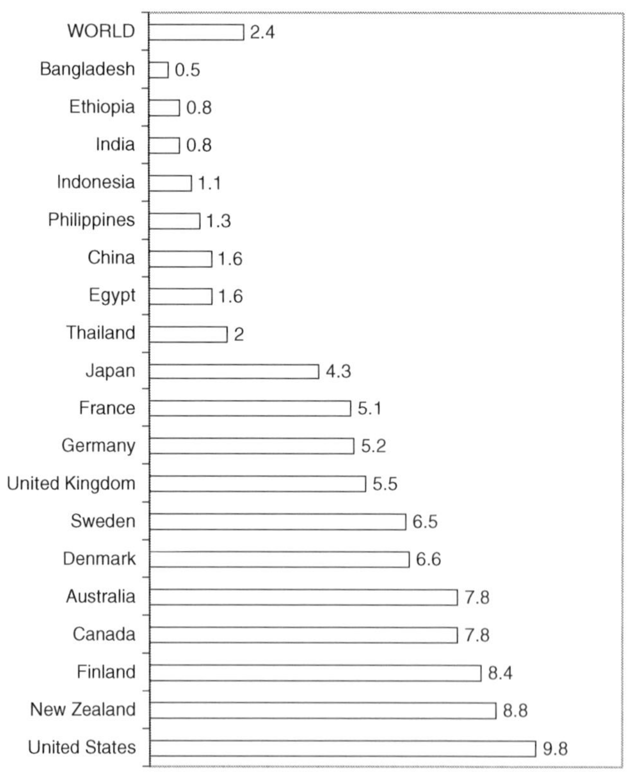

FIGURE 11.2 Ecological footprints of selected developed and developing countries (hectares per capita)

vulnerable as a nation. By that time, almost 20 per cent of its 250 million people will likely become climate refugees and will look for livelihoods in the highlands or overseas.

Concluding comments

It is true that the extent of achievements South Asian nations enjoy in growth terms has never been witnessed before. However, in per capita terms, the region remains dismally poor when compared with others (e.g. Southeast Asia and China). Almost 300 million people in India and almost 60 million people in Bangladesh live on less than US$1 a day. Indeed, development remains elusive to the poor people of these nations, which have been growing at a very high rate by historical standards. Moreover, it remains to be seen what further deterioration of quality of life will take place in South Asian populous nations due to the climate change and its aftermath. The effect of climate change has no bounds. Hence, this chapter has demonstrated that, although it is late, climate change is at the top of the agenda of the neighbouring regions of South Asia, Southeast Asia, and China. One may conclude, however, that, while South Asia has been growing on the back of globalization and exports (see earlier chapters) in recent years, it is now a reality that climate change could take away the entire growth opportunity in the future. It is now time the governments of South Asian nations take initiatives, like China and Southeast Asia, and make a comprehensive plan to fight climate change in the years to come.

Bibliography

Bates, B., Kundzewicz, Z., Wu, S. and Palutikof, J. (eds.) (2008) *Climate Change and Water*, IPCC, Geneva: WMO and UNEP.

Hossain, M., Ahmad, Q. K. and Islam, M. (2020) *Climate Adaptation for a Sustainable Economy, Lessons from Bangladesh, an Emerging Tiger of Asia*, NY: Nova Publisher.

Hossain, M. S. (2008) "Global warming, local impact", *The Daily Star*, Dhaka, 13 September.

Hossain, M. and Howard, P. (2014) "The sanitation access to developing Asia", *India's Development*, 11, 2: 93–101.

Hossain, M., Nabi, N. and Islam, I. (2003) *Bangladesh's Development Agenda and Vision 2021: Rhetoric or Reality?* University Press Limited (UPL), Dhaka. www. Conversations.com, Methews J, Macquarie University SydneyBank.

Khan, A. (2007) *Drying up of a Riverine Delta*, New York: UNEP.

Metcalfe, I. (2003) "Long term environmental issues for Bangladesh", in M. Hossain, A. K. M. Nabi and I. Islam (eds.), *Bangladesh's Development Agenda and Vision 2020: Rhetoric or Reality?* Dhaka: University Press Ltd.

Mia (2008) "Greenhouse gases", in US EPA, https://www.epa.gov/

National Climate Change Policy (2011) Government of Pakistan, *Ministry of Climate Change*, Islamabad.

NRC (2015) *Norwegian Refugee Council, works to protect the rights of displaced people during crisis all over the world*, Norway.

Stern Nicholas (2007) *The Economics of Climate Change: The Stern Review*, Commission by the UK Treasury, London.

UNDP (2007) *Human Development Report 2007*, United Nations Development Programme, Oxford: Oxford University Press.

Wackernagel, M. et al. (1997) Ecological Footprints of Nations: How Much Nature Do They Use? How Much Native Do They Have? *Commissioned by the Growth Council for the Rio+5 Forum, International Council for Local Environmental Initiatives*, Toronto.

Watson, R. T. (ed.) (2001) *Climate Change 2001: Synthesis Report*, IPCC, Cambridge: Cambridge University Press.

World Bank (2000) *World Development Indicators*. Washington, DC: The World Bank.

World Bank (2008) *The Impact of Climate Change on South Asia's Poor*. www.worldbank.org, accessed on 23 January 2009.

World Bank (2023) *World Development Indicators*. Washington, DC: The World.

12

THE DIGITAL CONNECTIVITY AND DEVELOPMENT

The case of India

Rajat Kathuria

Introduction

India's digital transformation has been a subject of interest for many years now, and COVID-19 added to this appeal. As social distancing and business lockdowns began to impact the economy, several businesses, including the beleaguered micro, small, and medium enterprises (MSME) sector, looked towards digital connectivity and platforms to overcome constraints due to COVID-19. While there is some evidence on the role of digital connectivity in overcoming constraints due to the lack of physical and social infrastructure at the individual sector level, such as in education, health, and even for MSMEs, there is, however, a lack of robust empirical evidence on what it achieved for MSMEs during COVID-19. This chapter is an attempt to construct empirical evidence on digital progress using an extremely heterogeneous cohort of firms and enterprises that together constitute the MSME sector in India. The reason for choosing MSMEs is because these are the backbone of the economy. There are 63 million MSMEs in India that employ over 111 million workers and contribute around 40 per cent to output produced, approximately 30 per cent to GDP, and account for roughly 50 per cent of all exports from India. It is therefore appropriate to provide policy support to this sector to achieve balanced, sustainable, and inclusive growth. A one-size-fits-all approach for MSMEs is destined to fail.

Growth dividends in the data

A key component of the digital economy in India is the dominance of mobile telephony, for both voice and data. From 100,000 fixed-line phones for a population of 340 million in August 1947, India had over a billion mobiles in December 2022. Tele density, that is, the number of phones per 100 population, has increased from one-third of 1 per cent to more than 84 per cent, underscoring a mobile-first development trajectory. By the end of December 2022, mobiles accounted for 96 per cent of all access lines in India. In 1999, mobiles constituted just 5 per cent of all telephones. This is truly remarkable since no other digital indicator comes close to mobile in penetration or rate of growth. Several studies have shown that tele density and per capita GDP are positively correlated. What's more, for many small businesses and sole proprietorships, including MSMEs, the mobile

DOI: 10.4324/9781032716244-14

TABLE 12.1 Wireline, wireless, and total telecom subscribers (millions)

Year	*Total subscribers*	*Fixed*	*Mobile*	*Tele-Density*
1995	14.58	14.54	0.03	1.29
2000	45.08	38.54	6.54	2.86
2005	206.82	40.77	166.05	8.95
2010	846.32	34.73	811.59	52.74
2011	951.34	32.17	919.17	70.89
2012	898.01	30.21	867.80	78.66
2013	933.01	28.50	904.51	73.32
2014	970.97	27.00	943.97	75.23
2015	1,036.41	25.52	1,010.89	79.38
2016	1,151.77	24.40	1,127.37	89.9
2017	1,190.67	23.23	1,167.44	91.9
2018	1,197.87	21.87	1,176.00	91.45
2019	1,172.44	21.00	1,151.44	88.56
2020	1,173.83	20.05	1,153.77	86.38
2021	1,178.41	23.79	1,154.62	85.91
2022	1,170.38	27.45	1,142.93	84.56
2023	1,172.34	28.41	1,143.93	84.51
Dec-23	1,190.33	31.84	1,158.49	85.23

Source: Compiled by authors from TRAI performance indicator reports, various years

phone pays for itself. On the other hand, fixed-line penetration has declined as its value proposition worsened due, *inter alia,* to poor quality of service and limited functionality (see Table 12.1).

Total investment in telecom infrastructure varies significantly among the 19 Indian states in the sample. According to our calculations, Maharashtra and Tamil Nadu have made the highest contributions with telecom investments exceeding US$5 billion. On the other hand, the least investments are observed in Jammu and Kashmir and the Northeast. Delhi stands out with a tele density of 271.97; on the contrary, Bihar and Uttar Pradesh demonstrate lower tele densities of 55.18 and 66.53, respectively, in December 2022. Uttar Pradesh, however, leads in total subscribers with an impressive 164.28 million, which reflects its huge population (see Table 12.2).

Interestingly, there's no straightforward correlation between investment and tele density. While Maharashtra, Gujarat, and Tamil Nadu have made huge investments, their tele density remains relatively moderate; whereas Delhi's high tele density contrasts with its comparatively lower investment. Northeast, despite having lower investments, exhibits decent tele density and the number of subscribers. Bihar, with low investment, presents a promising prospect for future growth. Similarly, Haryana, with moderate investment and subscriber count, has potential for further expansion. The diversity among Indian states in economic indicators and in telecom outcomes makes for a compelling case to estimate the digital growth dividend.

Explaining sources of GDP growth has been a preoccupation among economists since the time of John Maynard Keynes. He argued that the economic impact of investment is not limited to just the direct effect of the investment. Investment in public works such as road building and construction of hospitals and the more modern investments in broadband will have substantial indirect effects, especially if the economy is operating within the production possibilities frontier or below potential. Jointly, the direct and indirect effects will tend to raise income and demand and help 'crowd in' more investment.

TABLE 12.2 State-wise investments and tele density, 2022

State/service area	*Cumulative investment in telecom 2001–2022 ($m)*	*Tele density (December 2023)*	*Total subscribers (million) (December 2023)*
Andhra Pradesh	3,053	94.34	86.46
Assam	564	72.38	26.05
Bihar	143	55.23	94.9
Delhi	253	273.67	60.35
Gujarat	4,569	92.58	67.86
Haryana	2,185	89.61	27.18
Himachal Pradesh	627	119.69	9.01
Jammu and Kashmir	199	88.94	12.55
Karnataka	2,785	101.91	69.48
Kerala	879	122.13	43.98
Madhya Pradesh	1,233	66.73	79.96
Maharashtra	5,046	101.96	94.94
North East	36	79.71	12.72
Orissa	790	75.74	33.73
Punjab	1,651	115.31	36.56
Rajasthan	1,457	79.45	63.99
Tamil Nadu (incl. Chennai)	5,077	103.46	81.03
UP	3,193	66.12	166.3
West Bengal	1,558	81.95	57.79

Source: TRAI performance indicator report and ASI

A key component of the digital economy is thus the use of the Internet, especially broadband. For effective broadband usage, both parties engaged in the transaction activity need access, implying that basic connectivity between markets and firms is a necessary starting point. In addition, the speed and quality of the connection can limit the types of activities that can occur. For example, if MSMEs have access to only a 2G mobile connection, they may be unable to access many online services that involve images and video. Meanwhile, users with access to high-bandwidth, direct fibre-optic cable connections are able to engage in a greater number of data-intensive activities with minimal delay. The rapid expansion of Internet access via mobile devices in India has resulted in a 'digital determinism,' that is, a belief that digital technology is the principal method that can help overcome societal problems like jobs, growth, and distribution, to name a few. Accordingly, a substantial policy emphasis has been placed on digital infrastructure and connectivity.

For digital investments, the most noticeable direct effect is the increase in demand for cables, switches, and other components of the telecom network. Besides, network construction, digging trenches, and installing towers also result in job creation. These are examples of the direct effects. The indirect effects are a consequence of the innovation triggered by greater digital diffusion in the economy, generated as a result of network externalities in other sectors. These are the indirect and induced effects and also result in expanded job opportunities. The rise of the gig economy and online freelancing showcases the role of the Internet in generating new jobs, particularly in digitally connected remote areas.

It is, however, access to digital technology that promises to enhance the efficiency of user sectors, or the so-called indirect effects, that have received the most policy attention in India, especially for the MSME sector. These are likely to be much more pronounced than the returns to the sector itself (Roller and Waverman (2001). The indirect benefits include better access to backward and forward markets and information that enables informed decision-making, which in turn yields improvements in productivity (Khuong 2011). As communication systems improve, the costs of doing business fall, and output increases for individual firms across several sectors of the economy. In 1980, Andrew Hardy claimed, 'If the telephone does have an impact on a nation's economy, it will be through the improvement of the capabilities of managers to communicate with each other rapidly over increased distances' (Hardy 1980). The seminal study by Jensen (2007) on Kerala's fisher-folk on the availability of simple price information via a mobile is now interpreted to be hackneyed. And yet it was a novelty then. The study immutably showed that between 1996 and 2001, immediately before and after the introduction of mobile phones in Kerala, the prices of fish dropped significantly and yet increased both consumer and producer welfare. The benefits of faster dissemination of information and dis-intermediation through digital connectivity are well and truly embedded in the literature. The efficiency improvements are pervasive as better digital access allows expansion of opportunities (Wellenius 1977).

Theoretically, there are clear linkages between digital infrastructure and macroeconomic growth. By reducing information asymmetries and transaction costs that often cause markets to fail, connectivity drives efficiencies in the economic system. Empirically, while estimates vary by geography and time, the available evidence unequivocally suggests that substantial benefits accrue to investment in digital infrastructure. In 2009, a World Bank study using a sample of 120 countries found the relative magnitudes of growth dividends of communication technologies to be higher for developing countries than that for high-income countries (Table 12.3).

There is a strong degree of correlation between broadband penetration and per capita income across Indian states at a point in time (see Figure 12.1). The same property is exhibited in the data over time. The positive correlation indicates the presence of network externalities that drive growth in other sectors along with growth in the digital economy itself.

Digitalization of MSMEs and the promise of increased connectivity

Digital connectivity in India is profoundly impressive at the national level. There are over a billion points of connectivity and over 800 million broadband connections, of which 96 per cent are mobile. India's strength in numbers also masks some stark drawbacks. Broadband has been biased in favour of urban areas. More than 35 per cent of broadband subscribers are in the top ten metros, and more than 60 per cent of connections are in the top 30 cities. Only 35 per cent of the broadband connections and 44 per cent of total mobile phones are in rural areas, which

TABLE 12.3 Economic effects of fixed, mobile, internet, and broadband

	High income	*Low income and middle income*
Fixed	0.43	0.73
Mobile	0.6	0.81
Internet	0.77	1.12
Broadband	1.21	1.38

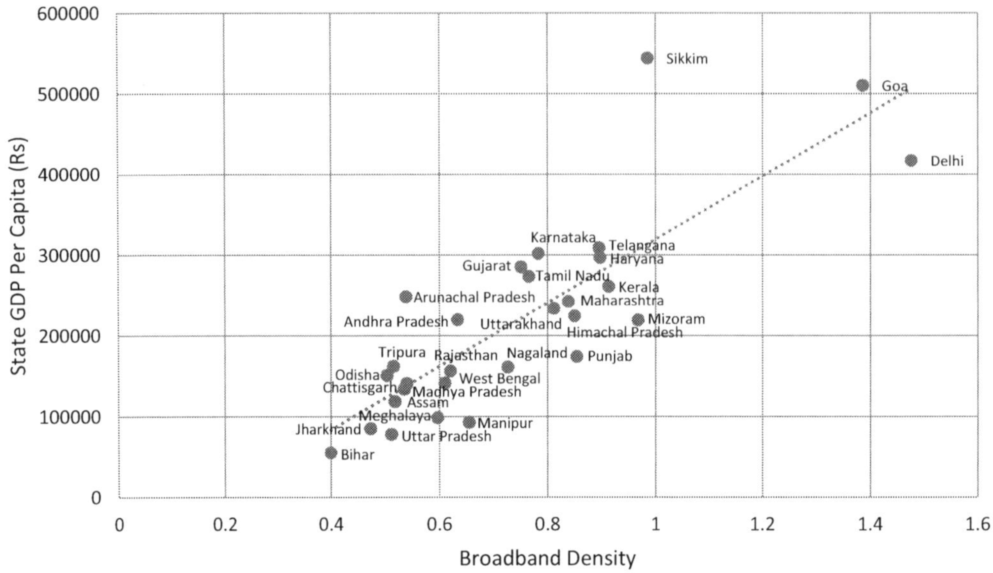

FIGURE 12.1 Scatterplot for broadband penetration and state per capita GDP

Source: Author's compilation based on data from TRAI and MoSPI

covers two-thirds of the total population, creating a rural-urban imbalance. Further, the benefits of connectivity are also unevenly distributed across Indian states (see Table 12.2), reflecting that some states have taken advantage of digital access more than others.

We examine the unrealized potential of MSMEs in India, including the impact and the strategic response to the COVID-19 shock. The reason we isolate MSMEs is because of their critical role in creating jobs, fostering entrepreneurship and innovation, supporting rural development, and their vast contributions to GDP. Accordingly, MSMEs are strong contenders for a focused industrial policy in the aftermath of the pandemic. For the record, there are 63 million MSMEs in India that employ over 111 million workers and contribute around 40 per cent to output produced, approximately 30 per cent to GDP, and account for roughly 50 per cent of all the exports from India.

Despite this remarkable feat, MSMEs face several hurdles in day-to-day operations, such as in marketing products, accessing finance, retaining customers, finding the right employees, among others, which prevents them from reaching their full potential. The government of India has implemented several policies targeted towards nurturing the growth of MSMEs in areas such as credit provision, skill improvement, infrastructure development, marketing aid, and technology advancement. A registration portal for MSMEs, called Udyam, was launched in 2020 that is integrated with the Central Board of Direct Tax and Goods and Services Tax networks to ease tax compliance. According to recently available data, the Udyam portal has registered close to 25 million MSMEs, of which almost 96 per cent are micro-enterprises. Globally too, lockdowns were used to reduce risks associated with the pandemic, but it had many undesirable side effects. Lockdowns caused unemployment, a reduction of output, and disruption in supply chains as non-essential production was forced to close. This persuaded many MSMEs to hasten and some reluctant ones to consider the adoption of digital services to ensure business continuity. Digital connectivity, as demonstrated carefully, is akin to a GPT that drives economic growth, impacting agriculture, manufacturing, and service industries. The government expects much from the digital economy and has projected it to grow to $1 trillion in two years. The expectation is that deployment of digital tools and applications in firms and in their processes would help boost competitiveness, especially of MSMEs that operate well within the frontier. It is a global occurrence that MSMEs face several constraints, like delay in revenue realization, product marketing, procurement, access to credit, and lack of scale, and in such circumstances, digital tools possess the ability to act as a solution to many, if not all, factors that limit growth.

The available evidence is encouraging. Firms using the Internet and digital technologies for various aspects of their business operations have brought in twice as much revenue through exports in comparison to MSMEs using the Internet sparingly. Firms have also reported increases in profit margins and revenue, better inventory management, broader market reach, enhancements in productivity, cost reduction, and retention of customers. In India, digitalization is reported to generate $158–$216 billion by 2024.

MSMEs have begun using social media marketing and integration with e-commerce to grow sales. A survey conducted by CRISIL found that the use of digital technology has gone up significantly among MSMES, from around 29 per cent pre-pandemic to 47 per cent and 53 per cent for micro and small enterprises, respectively, in 2020. It is recognized that digital adoption by MSMEs is not a one-time event but a process that occurs in stages, progressing from basic digital tools like email, WhatsApp, and computers to establishing an online presence through websites, social media, and e-commerce and finally using more advanced digital tools for core business tasks such as automating data and using CRM systems.

But as envisaged, there are trade-offs. The digital makeover poses obstacles due to a lack of digital know-how, the need and costs of upskilling their workers, the risk of digital fraud, and capital constraints. *A priori* MSMEs believe that integrating with e-commerce is expensive and that the potential benefits are uncertain. The government has implemented a range measure to enable small businesses to compete with large e-commerce entities that enjoy significant market power and hence the ability to squeeze MSMEs. These initiatives include the launch of platforms like MSME 'Champions Portal,' which is a technology-driven grievance management and information platform; Government e-Marketplace; Trade Receivables Discounting System; and msmemart.com, which is a B2B web portal that helps MSMEs in market access through online presence. Most recently, the Open Network for Digital Commerce was introduced as an open protocol based on open-source specifications to reduce barriers to e-commerce. The initiative is expected to facilitate rapid adoption of e-commerce and boost and strengthen the growth of start-ups in India.

Conclusion

MSMEs were particularly hard hit during the pandemic and in the aftermath of demonetization in 2016. It is well known that MSMEs in India employ contract labour, deal in cash, and are vulnerable to shocks such as the COVID-19 pandemic and demonetization. Targeting economic relief for small businesses has been a critical component of policy interventions in APEC economies. These interventions have included a range of fiscal and monetary policies, as well as initiatives promoting digital adoption. In the past too, economic crises have prompted governments to take countercyclical policy measures. The 2008 global financial crisis (GFC) was widespread, but there were better-coordinated responses then because of the learnings from the Great Depression. In a similar vein, one could argue that during COVID-19, relief packages were informed by the revealed efficacy of countercyclical fiscal stimulus packages designed to increase demand, create jobs, and expand production implemented during and immediately after the GFC. Investing in digital infrastructure, specifically broadband and next-generation networks, became a standard counter-cyclical tool to create jobs and provide the foundation for economic recovery and long-term sustained growth. The multiplier impacts and growth dividends of digital technologies presented in this study are a befitting reflection of that intelligence. As one would have thought, our research also reveals that MSMEs that integrate with digital technologies and e-commerce marketplaces experienced increases in turnover and profit margins and employed more workers. Embracing digital technologies into normal business operations made MSMEs more efficient and increased their resilience to an economic shock like COVID-19. Moreover, firms that integrated with e-commerce were able to scale by increased investments in plant and machinery and, to an extent, in R&D. Although, various initiatives have been taken by the Indian government to empower MSMEs, unfortunately, the level of awareness about these schemes stays low.

Bibliography

Hardy, A. (1980) "The role of telephone in economic development", *Telecommunications Policy*, 5, 4: 278–286.

Jensen, R. (2007) "The digital provide: Information (technology), market performance, and welfare in the South Indian fisheries sector", *The Quarterly Journal of Economics*, 122, 3: 879–924.

Khuong, M. Vu. (2011) "ICT as a source of economic growth in the information age: Empirical evidence from the 1996–2005 period", *Telecommunications Policy*, 35: 357–372.

Roller, L. H. and Waverman, L. (2001) "Telecommunications infrastructure and economic development: A simultaneous approach", *The American Economic Review*, 91, 4: 909–923.

Wellenius, B. (1977) "Telecommunications in developing countries", *Telecommunications Policy*, 1, 4: 269–297.

PART III

South Asia in the 21st century

13

ARTIFICIAL INTELLIGENCE (AI) AND SOUTH ASIAN ECONOMIES

Navigating opportunities and facing challenges

Vishal Rana and Govand Khalid

Introduction

The speedy advancement of artificial intelligence (AI) is transforming economies and societies worldwide, promising unprecedented opportunities for growth, innovation, and social progress. AI, intersecting with IoT, big data analytics, cloud computing, etc., has become increasingly sophisticated and ubiquitous. The hegemonic view is that AI has the potential to drive productivity gains, create new industries, and help solve some of the world's most pressing challenges (Bughin et al. 2018). Yet, as Yuval Noah Harari (2017) warns in his book *Homo Deus*, the AI revolution also raises profound contradictions and questions, even fear, about the future of work, political institutions, inequality, and what it means to be human in an age of intelligent machines.

These AI-related questions today become especially pertinent for South Asia. As the likes of Khanna (2019) in his book *The Future Is Asian* correctly affirm, Asia is a region known for its vast geography, growing and dynamic economies, a large, young, increasingly educated workforce, abundant raw resources, and rapid technological adoption. It is also a region where, Khanna argues, not a single person of the five billion Asians wakes up to aspire for their country or culture to be like those of the United Kingdom or the United States (Khanna 2019). AI then makes an appearance in this cultural, geopolitical, and technical context. It is a technological system that presents both immense opportunities and complex challenges. On the one hand, AI could be a game changer for economic development in the region, enabling countries to leapfrog traditional growth models and move up the value chain into knowledge-intensive digital industries (Chitturu et al. 2017). Khanna is partly right. With its young, tech-savvy population and growing digital infrastructure, South Asia is well-positioned to harness AI for innovation, competitiveness, and social good.

However, realizing the full potential of AI in South Asia will also require navigating a complex web of historical variables, factors, and conditions. The region is haunted by economic, social, political, cultural, and ethical dilemmas and challenges mostly inherited from its colonial past. As the likes of Marx, Max Horkheimer, Theodor Adorno, and Herbert Marcuse remind us, technological innovation, production, application, and accessibility are not socially neutral,

DOI: 10.4324/9781032716244-16

one-directional processes where social forces have total control over them. Rather, technological devices and systems, techniques, and scientific knowledge are always a set of genealogically evolutionary processes and politically directed tools often designed to reaffirm private ownership, large capital monopolies, and centralized power formations Marx Karl (1867). This technological pattern has been the case from the plough and watermill to the steam engine and cotton gin. AI is no exception. As Harari (2018) argues, the AI revolution could exacerbate existing inequalities and power imbalances. It could intensify inequality, exploitation, and repression within countries among classes, ethnicities, genders, etc. But it can also magnify structural inequalities between states. It could reaffirm the structural power that core states have had over periphery. In other words, AI, like steam power and engines, can also replicate the same colonial and capitalist relations. In other words, if its benefits are captured primarily by a small elite of states, corporations, and individuals, and if they can monopolize its use, then it may create an even more dangerous hierarchy and uneven relations.

This raises critical questions about the political economy of AI in South Asia. Will AI be harnessed as a tool for inclusive growth and shared prosperity, or will it entrench a new substratum of digital divide over the existing unequal relations between the haves and have-nots, the exploiter and exploited? Will AI empower local communities and national economies to own, innovate, and compete, or will it lead to a concentration of power and profits in the hands of a small comprador force and the few global Western AI superpowers? As dependency theorists like Marini (1973) and Amin (1974) have long argued, these are not just simply developmental issues, but they are also structural economic questions and processes, like super-exploitation of labour and extraction of resources, that unravel the historically unequal yet combined nature of the global system.

In this context, South Asian policymakers, sociologists, policymakers, and civil society organizations face a monumental geopolitical, economic, and even existential question. How to steer the design, production, and deployment of AI in a way that maximizes its benefits for economic development and social welfare, for enhancing the life of the working masses? All of these while aiming to minimize its internal absolute contradictions, structural risks, and negative externalities. This will require not only strategic thinking and policy making but also state investments in AI infrastructure, research, and skills development. Proactive governance frameworks and social policies that prioritise transparency, accountability, privacy, and ethics. This, of course, we contend, is not possible without making the process a native, democratic, participative, and inclusive project where the working populations and masses are able to contribute to these developments.

The AI will also require setting up national institutions and frameworks and academic-expert committees to grapple with the broader philosophical and existential questions that AI raises about the nature of intelligence, consciousness, work, social relations, and the future of humanity (Boden 2016). As AI systems become increasingly autonomous, self-generative, and capable of matching or surpassing human performance on a wide range of cognitive tasks, they challenge long-held assumptions about the uniqueness and superiority of human intelligence or even institutions (Kurzweil 2005). At the same time, they raise concerns about the erosion of human subjectivity, creativity, and purpose, as well as civil society, law, collective agency, and voice. After all, we are entering a world where machines can do many things better, faster, and cheaper than humans (Brynjolfsson and McAfee 2014).

For South Asia, these questions take on urgency given the region's historical and colonial past. AI applications raise questions of possible loss of sovereignty and autonomy at the state level. It could lead to dissymmetry with the diverse cultural and religious traditions, which have historically placed a strong emphasis on communal values, social harmony, and spiritual fulfilment (Mahbubani 2018). As AI reshapes the nature of work, education, and social interaction, it could disrupt these traditional ways of life and create new forms of cultural and psychological displacement and alienation. On the other hand, if harnessed effectively, AI could also help to empower its economies and political institutions. It could preserve and promote South Asia's rich and heterogeneous cultural heritage by enabling new forms of native creative expression, language preservation, and community engagement, but now available even in a digitalized and virtual form.

The stakes are high, and the questions are difficult. As Harari (2018) argues, the AI revolution is not just a technological shift but also a politico-economic, philosophical, and existential one. This technological tsunami will reshape the very foundations of social relations, institutions, and even human civilization. For South Asia, the challenge will be even greater. The task is to think and organize this AI imposition and develop underdeveloped economies, help the region flourish, while at the same time preserve the region's unique cultural, social, and ecological diversity.

This chapter explores these issues in depth, drawing on insights from political economy, philosophy, history, science and technology studies, and other disciplines to analyse the opportunities and challenges of AI for economic development in Southeast Asia. It is structured as follows: section one provides an overview of the current state of AI development and adoption in South Asia, highlighting key trends, drivers, and barriers. Section two examines the potential economic impacts of AI in South Asia, including its effects on productivity, employment, and structural transformation. It also analyses the distributional implications of AI across different sectors, skill levels, and social groups. Section three explores the social and political dimensions of AI in South Asia, including its implications for citizenship, societal relations, and fair governance. It also examines the role of different stakeholders, including governments, market forces, civil society organizations, and international organizations, in shaping the development and governance of AI in the region.

Section four delves into a politico-economic analysis of the structures of the global capitalist system that creates a relation of dependency and subjugation for South Asia. We highlight apropos the likes of Samir Amin and Mauro Marini the historical patterns organized between core and periphery. Following from the fourth section, we conclude by highlighting that the region's underdevelopment is developed via the core states extracting raw mineral resources, cheap super-exploited labour, and a primitive agrarian economy. This heavily shapes not only the region's AI but also technological infrastructure, projects, and capacity. We conclude with a call to action for South Asian policymakers and civil society organizations to proactively push for the complete native ownership, production, and governance of AI in the region. South Asia, we argue, can not only harness the transformative potential of AI for economic development but also contribute to a more egalitarian, rational, inclusive, sustainable, and human-centric future for all.

AI in South Asia: current state and key trends

South Asia is a region of immense diversity. It consists of heterogeneous social systems and singular politico-economic circuits and structures. Each of these states and societies has its own unique history, culture, and socio-economic context (World Bank 2019). Despite this diversity and historical difficulties, the region for the likes of Khanna, Krugman, and Pezzini has experienced rapid economic growth and technological transformation in recent decades, driven by factors such as rising middle-class consumption, growing global trade and investment, and increasing digital connectivity (Pezzini 2019). While David Harvey demonstrates that a large part of this 'prosperity' is built upon foreign production and capital turning to the cheap resources and labour in the region, there is no doubt that the region has still seen some economic advances. Albeit largely unequal. Accordingly, it is plausible to state that at a macro-economic level, the region's economy is nationally healthier than large parts of Europe, even the United States—admittedly, as Prabhat Patnaik shows, this growth in the last five decades has come with the region 'delinking from imperialism' (Patnaik 1999).

In this context, AI has emerged as a key strategic priority for many Southeast Asian countries, as they seek to leverage the technology for economic development, social welfare, and national competitiveness. According to a recent report by Guterres (2021), South Asia is one of the fastest-growing regions for AI adoption, with the market for AI products and services expected to reach more than $13 billion by 2025.

Direct and forceful government support or intervention has been fundamental when it comes to the AI success in the region. Many Southeast Asian countries, in opposition to the neoliberal spirit of our moment, have developed national AI strategies and policies to promote the development and adoption of AI, including Singapore's National AI Strategy, Indonesia's National AI Strategy, and Vietnam's National Strategy for AI Research, Development, and Application. Almost all the states are also pushing for a national policy framework to oversee the entire process of AI development. Take Indonesia's 2020 Stranas KA (*Strategi Nasional Kecerdasan Artifisial*) as an example. Building on Jokowi's digital roadmap named Making Indonesia 4.0 (2014), this new AI strategy pushes for technological sovereignty, autonomy, and native ownership. It outlines the use of AI in five sectors and domains: health security, digital citizenship-public services, education and schooling, food security and smart agriculture, fisheries and management of natural resources, and smart infrastructure and cities. In 'supporting the implementation of these five national priority areas, the National AI Strategy also identifies four key focus areas: (1) ethics and policy; (2) talent development; (3) infrastructure and data; and (4) industrial research and innovation' (Asia Society Policy Institute 2024).

This is not unique to Indonesia. The strategies throughout Southeast Asia typically include investments in AI research and development, skills training, and infrastructure, as well as measures to promote responsible and ethical AI governance. There is also the expanding digital infrastructure throughout the region. Some pockets of the region have seen rapid growth in digital connectivity and infrastructure in recent years (i.e. Hyderabad, India; pockets of Colombo, Srilanka; and Jakarta, Indonesia), with the number of Internet users in the region expected to reach 480 million by 2025 (Davis et al. 2019). This has created a fertile environment for the development and deployment of AI applications, particularly in areas such as e-commerce, fintech, and digital services.

The large, young, and tech-savvy population is another point of strength when it comes to AI production in the region. South Asia has a relatively young and tech-savvy population, with a median age of 30.2 years (World Bank 2021). This demographic dividend has created a large and growing market for digital products and services, as well as a pool of talent for the development of AI technologies and applications. It is not unusual for tech and AI companies in the West to hire large teams of South Asian engineers, data analysts, and experts. This is also supported with the emergence of a vibrant start-up ecosystem that often co-produces AI products and systems. This ecosystem is expanding as a network within the region and has close relations with foreign companies and firms. One can say that South and Southeast Asia have a thriving start-up ecosystem, with more than 10,000 start-ups across the region (Khoeng 2023). Many of these start-ups are focused on developing AI-powered products and services, particularly in areas such as fintech, healthtech, and edtech. Some notable examples include Grab, a ride-hailing and delivery platform that uses AI for demand forecasting and route optimization, and Kata.ai, an Indonesian start-up that develops AI-powered chatbots and virtual assistants.

Yet one must be careful in not generalizing the above conditions. Despite these positive trends, the adoption and development of AI in Southeast Asia on account of its place within the international division of labour, the transnational system of production and exchange tends to face significant challenges and barriers. These challenges are not just technical but also economic and social. The first and most important of these issues is the unequal and largely class-stratified civil societies that impact the state's efficiency, society's harmony, and the market's operations. Often this translates to the system not investing in human capital, hence creating a gap in the skilled and talented professionals. The pool of professionals and experts is large but nowhere near enough for large-scale production of these technologies at home.

AI systems also require large and diverse datasets to train and operate effectively. However, many Southeast Asian countries face challenges not only in shortage of labour but also in collecting, managing, and sharing data, due to factors such as limited digital infrastructure, data privacy concerns, and lack of standardization (Chitturu et al. 2017). It is why these countries often begin with having a large digital roadmap plan, that is, Indonesia's Making Indonesia 4.0 or Digital India (2015) and Digital Bangladesh (2009). Despite the effort to digitalize governance, to foster e-commerce and online services, and to enhance education and infrastructure, the progress has been slow. The small and mostly unequal representation of datasets (middle class ran and oriented) can limit the accuracy and effectiveness of AI applications, particularly in areas such as healthcare, education, and public services.

Accompanying the above shortcomings are the general ethical and social concerns regarding data and AI. The development and deployment of AI in South Asia also raise important ethical and social concerns, particularly around issues such as data privacy, the digital divide, algorithmic bias, military and police repression, and job displacement (Ariffin 2018). For example, the use of AI-powered surveillance technologies by some South and Southeast Asian governments has raised concerns about civil liberties and human rights (discrimination based on religion and race, lack of transparency and accountability, etc.), while the automation of jobs in sectors such as manufacturing and services could exacerbate existing class inequalities and social tensions.

To address these socio-technical challenges and fully realize the potential of AI for economic development in South Asia, the state, through national frameworks and strategies, would need to manage the private sector and support the labour force. The state, functioning on behest of civil society and the community, would need to develop and implement comprehensive and inclusive AI strategies and policies. This will require not only greater investment in AI research, development, and skills training but also the creation of enabling environments for responsible and ethical AI innovation, including robust data governance frameworks, transparency and accountability measures, and multi-stakeholder collaboration and dialogue.

Economic impacts of AI in South Asia

AI has the potential to significantly impact economic development in South Asia, in terms of both driving productivity and economic growth, as well as shaping the nature and distribution of work and income. According to a recent study by McKinsey Global Institute (2020), AI could add up to $1 trillion to South and Southeast Asia's GDP by 2030, equivalent to a 10–18 per cent boost, depending on the speed and scale of adoption. This growth is expected to be driven by a range of factors, including:

Productivity gains: AI has the potential to significantly boost productivity across a wide range of sectors and industries in South Asia by automating routine tasks, optimizing processes, and enabling new products and services (Mulgan 2017). For example, in the manufacturing sector, AI-powered robotics and predictive maintenance systems could reduce downtime and increase output, while in the agriculture sector, AI-powered precision farming and supply chain optimization could increase yields and reduce waste. The other factor could be the new industries and business models. Technological optimists have argued that AI has the potential to produce new industries and business models in Southeast Asia, particularly in areas such as e-commerce, fintech, and digital services (Guterres 2021). For example, the rise of AI-powered chatbots and virtual assistants is enabling new forms of citizen and consumer engagement and support. Examples of such AI-powered chatbots in the region include *Veronika* and *Jakarta Kini* (Jaki, which includes JakWarta, JakLapor, JakRespons, and JakSurvei) in Indonesia (Sulianta et al. 2021), *IRCTC* in India, and *Amar Sarkar* (Bangladesh) *Artificial Intelligence Virtual Assistant* (AVA in Malaysia). The growth of the AI industry in South and Southeast Asia is also creating new opportunities for human capital development and skills training, as workers seek to acquire the knowledge and skills needed to work with and alongside AI systems (WEF 2020). This could have positive spillover effects on the broader economy, as a more skilled and productive workforce drives innovation and competitiveness across sectors.

In saying all this, there is the adverse and negative aspect of the AI wave. The economic impacts of AI in South and Southeast Asia may replicate the existing socio-economic, regional, and national inequalities. The concern is that these inequalities will be reproduced and digitalized, even more exacerbated by AI. We know from existing scholarship and case studies that AI can lead to job displacement, income inequality, a digital divide, unevenness in skills and training, etc. In sectors such as manufacturing, agriculture, and services, even finance AI could replace low-skilled workers, leading to increased unemployment and a widening skills gap (Tran et al. 2019). While AI may create new jobs in data science and software engineering, these opportunities may not be accessible to physical labourers or marginalized communities without the necessary reskilling, upskilling, or education. This divide and inequality in social, cultural, and economic capital could reinforce existing social hierarchies and power structures. The owners of algorithms and developers of AI technologies, as well as the upper echelon of society, capturing a disproportionate share of the economic benefits, while workers and communities bear the costs of job displacement and economic disruption (Nguyen and Chen 2021).

Moreover, the adoption of AI in South and Southeast Asia may widen the digital divide, as those without access to the market, digital infrastructure, devices, and skills are left behind (Zhao and Yu 2021). This could result in new forms of social and economic exclusion, particularly in barrios, rural and remote areas, and among marginalized communities such as working people, women, ethnic minorities, and people with disabilities. The lack of digital infrastructure and skills in countries like Myanmar or India has hindered the adoption of AI in rural areas, leaving many communities behind and perpetuating existing inequalities. This highlights also the fundamental structural inequality between core industrial cosmopolitan centres and the rural agricultural and underdeveloped parts of these countries.

To challenge these power imbalances and create a more inclusive AI-driven future, policymakers in South and Southeast Asia must develop comprehensive strategies that prioritize human capital development, social protection, and digital inclusion. This could include investing in skills training and education programmes that equip workers with the knowledge and skills needed to work with and alongside AI systems, particularly in areas such as data science, software engineering, and digital literacy (ILO 2019). Additionally, governments could strengthen social protection systems and safety nets, such as unemployment insurance, retraining programmes, and basic income schemes, to support workers and communities affected by job displacement and economic disruption (ESCAP 2020). This, however, often clashes with global powers and transnational institutions like the IMF, WB, and WTO, which demand of the global south states to do the exact opposite (privatize, deregulate, austerity measures, etc.) (Harvey 2005).

Furthermore, investing in digital infrastructure and access initiatives is crucial to ensure that all segments of society have access to the tools and resources needed to participate in the AI economy, including affordable Internet access, digital devices, and public Wi-Fi hotspots (ASEAN 2024). By taking a critical approach to AI development and adoption and implementing inclusive policies and strategies, Southeast Asian countries can work towards dismantling existing power structures and creating a more equitable and just AI-driven future that is often driven and enforced by European and US private interests.

Ultimately, the economic impacts of AI in Southeast Asia will depend not only on the speed and scale of technological change but also on the policies, choices, and actions of key stakeholders in shaping the direction and governance of AI. By developing and implementing comprehensive and inclusive native AI systems and policies and strategies that prioritize human capital development, social protection, and digital inclusion, South and Southeast Asian countries can harness the transformative potential of AI for economic development while mitigating its risks and negative externalities.

Social and political dimensions of AI in South and Southeast Asia

The social and political dimensions of AI in South and Southeast Asia are complex and multifaceted, presenting significant challenges and opportunities for the regions. As AI technologies continue to advance and become more widely adopted, it is imperative to critically analyse their implications for society, politics, and governance. The development and deployment of AI in South and Southeast Asia have far-reaching social and political implications that extend beyond economic considerations, and failing to address these issues could lead to severe consequences for the region's future.

One of the most pressing concerns is the potential for AI to exacerbate existing social and economic inequalities in Southeast Asian countries. Arora (2019) argues that the benefits of AI may accrue disproportionately to those who already possess the necessary skills, resources, and access to technology, while those who are already marginalized may be left further behind.

This raises critical questions about the distribution of power and resources in the region. If left unchecked, the unequal distribution of AI's benefits could lead to a widening digital divide and create new forms of social and economic exclusion, further entrenching poverty and inequality in a region already grappling with these issues (Seah et al. 2021). Moreover, as AI systems become more pervasive, they have the potential to perpetuate biases and discrimination and concentrate power in the hands of dominant actors. Marcuse (1964) warns of the dangers of technological rationality, arguing that 'technology serves to institute new, more effective, and more pleasant forms of social control and social cohesion' (p. xlvi). This is particularly alarming in Southeast Asia, where many countries have a history of social and political exclusion and where democratic institutions may be weak or underdeveloped (Haerpfer et al. 2020). The uncritical adoption of AI could lead to the further erosion of democratic freedoms and the consolidation of power by authoritarian regimes.

The development of AI in South and Southeast Asia also raises important questions about cultural identity and diversity. While AI-powered language tools could help preserve the region's linguistic diversity, the dominance of global cultural values in AI systems could lead to the erosion of local knowledge and traditions (Gómez-Baggethun 2022). This raises critical questions about the role of AI in shaping cultural identity and the potential for AI to be used as a tool for cultural homogenization. To mitigate these risks, policymakers must prioritize the development of culturally and linguistically inclusive AI systems and promote participatory governance frameworks that involve a wide range of stakeholders (Daly et al. 2019). Failure to do so could result in the loss of cultural diversity and the imposition of a global monoculture.

The political dimensions of AI in South and Southeast Asia are also significant, particularly in relation to surveillance and social control. As AI systems become more powerful and autonomous, there are concerns about their potential to be used for surveillance, manipulation, and control by authoritarian governments in the region (Lee 2018). The use of AI-powered surveillance technologies could further entrench existing power structures and limit democratic freedoms (Feldstein 2019). This raises critical questions about the role of AI in shaping the political landscape of the region and the potential for AI to be used as a tool for political oppression. Moreover, the role of foreign corporations in shaping the development and governance of AI in the region raises concerns about the prioritization of economic and geopolitical interests over local needs and values (Hoadley and Lucas 2018). This raises important questions about the autonomy and sovereignty of South and Southeast Asian countries in the face of global corporate and political interests.

While AI presents significant opportunities for South and Southeast Asian countries to address pressing social and economic challenges, realizing these benefits will require a critical and nuanced approach to AI governance. South Asian countries must develop AI governance frameworks that emphasize transparency, accountability, and public participation, and that prioritize the needs and values of local communities. This could include implementing AI ethics and human rights frameworks, promoting multi-stakeholder collaboration and dialogue, investing in public education and awareness, and strengthening regional co-operation and coordination (ITU 2021; UNESCO 2021; ASEAN 2024). However, these efforts must be grounded in a critical analysis of the power dynamics and political interests that shape the development and deployment of AI in the region.

One key challenge in developing effective AI governance frameworks in South and Southeast Asia is the diversity of political systems and levels of economic development in the region. While some countries, such as Singapore and Malaysia, have relatively advanced AI ecosystems and well-developed governance frameworks, others, such as Cambodia and Laos, and the likes of Sri Lanka and Bangladesh, are still in the early stages of AI adoption and may lack the necessary institutional capacity and resources to effectively regulate AI (Chitturu et al. 2017). This diversity highlights the need for a context-specific approach to AI governance that takes into account the unique challenges and opportunities facing each country in the region.

Another important consideration is the role of public-private partnerships in shaping the development and governance of AI in South and Southeast Asia. Given the significant investments required to develop and deploy AI technologies, governments in the region will need to work closely with the private sector to promote innovation and economic growth. However, these partnerships must be carefully managed to ensure that they prioritize the public interest and do not lead to the capture of AI governance by corporate interests. This will require the development of clear guidelines and principles for public-private collaboration, as well as mechanisms for public oversight and accountability (Daly et al. 2019).

The development of AI in South and Southeast Asia also has significant implications for the region's geopolitical landscape. As AI becomes increasingly central to economic and military power, the region is likely to become a key battleground in the global competition for AI dominance (Lee 2018). This raises important questions about the role of South and Southeast Asian countries in shaping the global AI landscape and the potential for AI to be used as a tool for geopolitical influence and coercion. To navigate these challenges, Southeast Asian countries will need to develop a clear and coordinated strategy for engaging with global AI powers while also working to strengthen regional co-operation and collaboration on AI governance (ASEAN 2024).

Ultimately, the social and political dimensions of AI in South and Southeast Asia are deeply intertwined with broader questions of power, inequality, and social justice. Addressing these issues will require a fundamental rethinking of the role of technology in society and a commitment to developing AI systems that prioritize the needs and values of local communities. This will require a sustained effort by policymakers, researchers, civil society actors, and the private sector to engage in critical and inclusive dialogue about the future of AI in the region.

In conclusion, the social and political dimensions of AI in South and Southeast Asia are complex and multifaceted, presenting both significant challenges and opportunities for the region. Addressing these issues will require a critical and nuanced approach that goes beyond technical considerations and considers the broader social, political, and cultural context in which AI is developed and deployed. This will require the development of context-specific AI governance frameworks that prioritize transparency, accountability, and public participation, as well as a commitment to promoting social justice and reducing inequalities. Only by critically examining the implications of AI and taking proactive steps to shape its development and governance can South and Southeast Asian countries harness its potential benefits while navigating the complex social and political landscape of the regions. Failure to do so could lead to severe consequences for the region's future, including the entrenchment of social and economic inequalities, the erosion of democratic freedoms, and the loss of cultural diversity.

The challenges of economic dependence and pursuing development

As AI technologies are predominantly developed and controlled by a few dominant powers, particularly Western states, and big capital firms (Lee 2018), the importation and adoption of AI in South and Southeast Asian countries raise critical questions about technological dependence, economic autonomy, and the ability to shape the direction and impact of these transformative technologies in line with local values, priorities, and developmental goals (Cath et al. 2018; Smith and Neupane 2018).

The concentration of AI power in the hands of a few core-owned tech giants and the uneven distribution of AI's benefits and risks across different states, regions, and social groups (Crawford 2021) pose significant threats to the sovereignty and independence of South and Southeast Asian nations. One should remind themselves that the technical and scientific issues are always operating within a socio-technical and property regime. The triad of technology, state, and the market cannot be divorced from one another. Marcuse in his One-Dimensional Man (1964) was aware of this. For him, 'the productive apparatus tends to become totalitarian to the extent to which it determines not only the socially needed occupations, skills, and attitudes, but also individual needs and aspirations' (p. 4). The reliance on imported AI technologies, without adequate local ownership, control, and governance, could perpetuate new forms of colonialism and dependence that are not only technological but also material and concrete like previous phases (Couldry and Mejias 2019). Technological regimes without native ownership and control undermine the ability of Southeast Asian countries to chart their own developmental paths and protect their national interests.

However, the adoption of AI also presents significant opportunities for economic development and prosperity in South and Southeast Asia. AI has the potential to drive productivity gains, innovation, and competitiveness across various sectors, from manufacturing and agriculture to healthcare and financial services (Bughin et al. 2018). To harness these benefits while mitigating the risks of technological dependence, South and Southeast Asian countries must prioritize the development of local AI capabilities, infrastructure, and governance frameworks (Smith and Neupane 2018). This requires significant investments in AI research and development, skills training, and digital infrastructure, as well as the cultivation of local AI ecosystems and partnerships (Lee 2018).

Moreover, to ensure that the benefits of AI are broadly shared and aligned with local developmental priorities, South Asian countries must actively shape the governance and regulation of AI technologies. This involves developing inclusive and participatory governance frameworks that engage diverse stakeholders, including government, industry, academia, civil society, and marginalized communities, in the design, deployment, and oversight of AI systems (Moon 2023). It also requires the establishment of ethical guidelines, standards, and accountability mechanisms to ensure that AI is developed and used in ways that respect human rights, promote social justice, and advance the public good (Floridi et al. 2018). By taking a proactive and inclusive approach to AI governance, South Asian nations can work towards ensuring that the transformative potential of AI is harnessed for the benefit of all while safeguarding their sovereignty, independence, and developmental aspirations.

Conclusion

The AI revolution brings forth immense opportunities and complex challenges for South Asia, a region known for its geographic and demographic diversity, dynamic economies, young workforce, and cultural heterogeneity. While AI has the potential to drive economic growth and innovation, it also raises critical questions about development in the region. There is the spectre of economic inequality, power imbalances, and the erosion of traditional values and ways of life whenever western technologies and institutions penetrate the region. As demonstrated, the adoption and utilization of AI in South Asia is not a neutral process but one that is shaped by historical, political, and economic factors, including the region's colonial past and its position within the global capitalist system. To harness the benefits of AI while mitigating its risks, South Asian policymakers and civil society organizations must navigate a complex web of technological, social, and ethical challenges and develop proactive governance frameworks that prioritize transparency, accountability, and inclusion.

It is important for all to understand that the AI question is not just a technical, ahistorical, and apolitical question. In fact, it is through South Asia's position in the global economic hierarchy as a semi-peripheral region ripe for extraction and exploitation that one may really understand the phenomenon. The core hegemonic industrialized states that dominate the world economy and their large multi-national corporations may leverage their technological superiority in AI to maintain and extend their economic and political dominance over the periphery and semi-periphery, including South Asia. This could lead to a new form of technological and economic dependency, where South Asian nations rely on imported AI technologies and expertise from the core countries, potentially further undermining their economic sovereignty and developmental autonomy. To mitigate these risks and navigate the AI revolution successfully, Southeast Asian countries would need to intensify investment, nationalize infrastructure, and develop robust governance frameworks and regulations that ensure the responsible and ethical development and deployment of AI technologies while also investing in, boosting, and even building local AI capabilities and infrastructure to reduce technological dependence on foreign powers and firms.

At the same time, in the global arena, the South Asian countries would need to actively shape the global governance of AI, working together with other peripheral and semi-peripheral countries (especially populous nations) to challenge the technological dominance of the core and promote a more equitable and inclusive global economic order (Cox 1994). This could involve pushing for technological transfer and capacity-building programmes, advocating for more balanced intellectual property regimes, and building alternative regional and sub-regional AI co-operation frameworks that prioritize the interests and values of the global south. Ultimately, the success of South Asia's AI-driven development, like in Africa and Latin America, will depend on its ability to resist the pressures of global capitalist control, the global dictatorship and tyranny of big capital, and chart a more native, localized, autonomous, and self-determined path in the face of the AI revolution.

Bibliography

Amin, S. (1974) "Accumulation and development: A theoretical model", *Review of African Political Economy*, 1, 1: 9–26.

Ariffin, E. (2018) "The role of AI in Southeast Asia", *The ASEAN Post*. https://theaseanpost.com/article/prospect-ai-southeast-asia-0

Arora, P. (2019) *The Next Billion Users: Digital Life beyond the West*, Harvard University Press.

ASEAN (2024) *The 4th ASEAN Digital Ministers' Meeting and Related Meetings*. Asean.org

Asia Society Policy Institute (n.d.) *Indonesia. Asia Society*. Retrieved May 24, 2024, from https://asiasociety.org/policy-institute/raising-standards-data-ai-southeast-asia/ai/indonesia

Boden, M. (2016) *AI: Its Nature and Future*, Oxford University Press.

Brynjolfsson, E. and McAfee, A. (2014) *The Second Machine Age: Work, Progress, and Prosperity in a Time of Brilliant Technologies*. W. W. Norton & Company.

Bughin, J., Hazan, E., Lund, S., Dahlström, P., Wiesinger, A. and Subramaniam, A. (2018) "Skill shift: Automation and the future of the workforce", *McKinsey Global Institute*, 1: 3–84.

Cath, C., Wachter, S., Mittelstadt, B., Taddeo, M. and Floridi, L. (2018) "Artificial intelligence and the 'good society': The US, EU, and UK approach", *Science and Engineering Ethics*, 24: 505–528.

Chitturu, S., Lin, D. Y., Sneader, K., Tonby, O. and Woetzel, J. (2017) "Artificial Intelligence and Southeast Asia's future", Singapore Summit, McKinsey Global Institute.
Couldry, N. and Mejias, U. A. (2019) "Data colonialism: Rethinking big data's relation to the contemporary subject", *Television & New Media*, 20, 4: 336–349.
Cox, R. W. (1994) "The crisis in world order and the challenge to international organization", *Cooperation and Conflict*, 29, 2: 99–113.
Crawford, K. (2021) *The Atlas of AI: Power, Politics, and the Planetary Costs of Artificial Intelligence.* Yale University Press.
Daly, A., Hagendorff, T., Hui, L., Mann, M., Marda, V., Wagner, B., . . . and Witteborn, S. (2019) Artificial Intelligence Governance and Ethics: Global Perspectives. arXiv preprint arXiv:1907.03848.
Davis, S., Sipahimalani, R., Hoppe, F., Lee, W., Girona, I. M., Choi, C. and Smittinet, W. (2019) *e-Conomy SEA 2019: Swipe Up and to the Right: Southeast Asia's $100 Billion Internet Economy.* www.thinkwithgoogle.com/intl/en-apac/tools-resources/research-studies/e-conomy-sea-2019-swipe-up-and-to-the-right-southeast-asias-100-billion-internet-economy/
Digital India (2015) https://www.gov.in
Digital Bangladesh (2009) https://thedailystar.net
ESCAP (2020) *Social Outlook for Asia and the Pacific: Poorly Protected*, United Nations Publication. www.unescap.org/sites/default/d8files/knowledge-products/SDD-SP-Social-Outlook-v14-1-E.pdf
Feldstein, S. (2019) "The global expansion of AI surveillance", *Carnegie Endowment for International Peace*. https://carnegieendowment.org/2019/09/17/global-expansion-of-ai-surveillance-pub-79847
Floridi, L., Cowls, J., Beltrametti, M., Chatila, R., Chazerand, P., Dignum, V., . . . and Vayena, E. (2018) "AI4People—an ethical framework for a good AI society: Opportunities, risks, principles, and recommendations", *Minds and Machines*, 28: 689–707.
Gómez-Baggethun, E. (2022) "Is there a future for indigenous and local knowledge?", *The Journal of Peasant Studies*, 49, 6: 1139–1157.
Guterres, A. (2021) "Technology and innovation report 2021", *United Nations Conference on Trade and Development*. https://unctad.org/webflyer/technology-and-innovation-report-2021
Haerpfer, C., Inglehart, R., Moreno, A., Welzel, C., Kizilova, K., Diez-Medrano, J., Lagos, M., Norris, P., Ponarin, E. and Puranen, B. et al. (eds.) (2020) *World Values Survey: Round Seven—Country-Pooled Datafile*, Madrid and Vienna: JD Systems Institute & WVSA Secretariat.
Harari, Y. N. (2017) *Homo Deus: A Brief History of Tomorrow*, Harper.
Harari, Y. N. (2018) *21 Lessons for the 21st Century*, Spiegel & Grau.
Harvey, D. (2005) *A Brief History of Neoliberalism*, Oxford University Press.
Hoadley, D. S. and Lucas, N. J. (2018) *Artificial Intelligence and National Security, Congressional Research Service*. https://a51.nl/sites/default/files/pdf/R45178.pdf
ILO (2019) *ILO: Future of Work Strategies in Asia-Pacific Should Focus More on People Than Technologies*. www.ilo.org/resource/news/ilo-future-work-strategies-asia-pacific-should-focus-more-people
ITU (2021) *AI for Good Global Summit 2021*, International Telecommunication Union. https://aiforgood.itu.int/
Khanna, P. (2019) *The Future is Asian: Commerce, Conflict, and Culture in the 21st Century*, Simon & Schuster.
Khoeng, G. (2023) "Southeast Asia's startup ecosystem: Hopeful utopia or reality check?", *Tatler*. www.tatlerasia.com/gen-t/leadership/the-startup-ecosystem-in-southeast-asia
Kurzweil, R. (2005) *The Singularity Is Near: When Humans Transcend Biology*, Viking.
Lee, K. F. (2018) *AI Superpowers: China, Silicon Valley, and the New World Order*, Houghton Mifflin Harcourt.
Mahbubani, K. (2018) *Has the West Lost It? A Provocation*, Penguin.
Marcuse, H. (1964) *One Dimensional Man: Studies in the Ideology of Advanced Industrial Society*, Boston: Beacon Press.
Marini, R. M. (1973) *The Dialectics of Dependency*, NYU Press.
Marx, K. (1867, 2019) *Capital: Volume I: A Critique of Political Economy*, Dover Publications.
McKinsey Global Institute (2020) *How Artificial Intelligence Will Impact Southeast Asia's Growth.* www.mckinsey.com/featured-insights/artificial-intelligence/how-artificial-intelligence-will-impact-southeast-asias-growth
Moon, M. J. (2023) "Searching for inclusive Artificial Intelligence for social good: Participatory governance and policy recommendations for making AI more inclusive and benign for society", *Public Administration Review*, 83, 6: 1496–1505.

Mulgan, G. (2017) *Big Mind: How Collective Intelligence Can Change Our World*, Princeton University Press.
Nguyen, D. D. and Chen, C.-T. (2021) "The impacts of Artificial Intelligence on the labor market and income distribution: An evidence from ASEAN countries", *Asian Economic and Financial Review*, 11, 2: 169–189. https://doi.org/10.18488/journal.aefr.2021.112.169.189
OECD (2019) *Artificial Intelligence in Society*, OECD Publishing. www.oecd-ilibrary.org/science-and-technology/artificial-intelligence-in-society_eedfee77-en
Patnaik, P. (1999) "Capitalism in Asia at the end of the millennium", *Monthly Review*, 51, 3: 53–70. https://monthlyreview.org/1999/07/01/capitalism-in-asia-at-the-end-of-the-millennium/
Pezzini, M. (2019) "An emerging middle class", *OECD Observer*. http://oecdobserver.org/news/fullstory.php/aid/3681/An_emerging_middle_class.html
Seah, S., Ha, H. T., Martinus, M. and Thao, P. T. P. (2021) The State of Southeast Asia: 2021 Survey Report, ISEAS–Yusof Ishak Institute.
Smith, M. and Neupane, S. (2018) Artificial Intelligence and Human Development: Toward A Research Agenda, International Development Research Centre, Canada.
Stanford University (2021) *Human-Centered Artificial Intelligence*. https://hai.stanford.edu/
Sulianta, F., Laksana, E. A., Rosita, A., Rumaisa, F., Yuliani, S. and Zulpratita, U. S. (2021) "Tools of digital learning scheme in the era of pandemic Covid 19", *Turkish Journal of Computer and Mathematics Education*, 12, 8: 327–332.
Tran, D. N., Pham, T. T., Nguyen, T. T. T. and Do, H. T. (2019) "Impacts of technology 4.0 on the labor market in Vietnam", *Journal of Asian Finance, Economics and Business*, 6, 2: 173–180. https://doi.org/10.13106/jafeb.2019.vol6.no2.173
UNESCO (2021) "Recommendation on the Ethics of Artificial Intelligence", *United Nations Educational, Scientific and Cultural Organization*. https://unesdoc.unesco.org/ark:/48223/pf0000380455
US (2021) "The national artificial intelligence research and development strategic plan: 2019 update", *Subcommittee on Machine Learning and Artificial Intelligence, Committee on Technology*, National Science and Technology Council. www.nitrd.gov/pubs/National-AI-RD-Strategy-2019.pdf
WEF (2020) "The future of jobs report 2020", *World Economic Forum*. www.weforum.org/reports/the-future-of-jobs-report-2020
World Bank (2019) The Digital Economy in Southeast Asia: Strengthening the Foundations for Future Growth, International Bank for Reconstruction and Development, World Bank.
World Bank (2021) *The World Bank Open Knowledge Repository*, https://openknowledge.worldbank.org
Zhao, J. and Yu, X. (2021) "Digital divide in Southeast Asia: Evidence from Vietnam, Myanmar, and Thailand", *Telecommunications Policy*, 45, 10: 102201.

14

IMPROVEMENT OF SANITATION FACILITIES IN SOUTHEAST AND SOUTH ASIA DURING UN MDGS PERIOD (2000–2015)

Paul Howard

Introduction

Certainly, the inclusion of sanitation in both the MDGs (and the subsequent Sustainable Development Goals) was hugely important, both symbolically and in terms of the need for pragmatic solutions to address the need for adequate universal sanitation access. As is evidenced by the data in this chapter, sanitation access throughout South and Southeast Asia varies greatly by country. This variance extends also to qualitative aspects of sanitation access and sanitation delivery. Consequently, there is a need to also consider those qualitative aspects of the sanitation picture. In that regard, even the definition of the descriptors used is important. For example, the use of terms like 'basic' or 'safely managed' invokes an understanding of the definition and parameters of such terms.

The understanding of what constitutes these terms will vary regionally and by country or even locality. There is also great variation in respect to the working environment that sanitation workers in certain parts of the service supply chain must endure. This is highlighted by the analysis of the plight of some sanitation workers later in this chapter. It is first necessary to provide a broad overview of some data pertaining to the respective countries, which will then be followed by more specific analysis of relevant quantitative and qualitative aspects of sanitation delivery within the respective countries.

Brief comparative analysis

It is challenging to retrospectively aggregate data pertaining specifically to this period. Nevertheless, there are some useful insights provided by the data and descriptors. Note, for example, the substantial variation between the figures for access to 'basic' sanitation facilities and the figure for access to 'safely managed' sanitation facilities. It must be noted that due to the limitation of available data, the countries represented differ for those two categories slightly. The point is clear, though, that is, that the World Bank's data for safely managed facilities is far lower than that of the general access figure in all cases (Table 14.1).

DOI: 10.4324/9781032716244-17

TABLE 14.1 Percentage of population with access to *basic* sanitation services (2000–2015)

Country	*2000*	*2013*	*2014*	*2015*
Malaysia	93.1	95.2	95.3	95.4
The Philippines	64.2	74.4	75.5	76.6
Thailand	92.4	96.4	96.8	97.1
India	14.1	51.7	54.7	57.8
Pakistan	30.9	54.9	56.7	58.4
Bangladesh	24.5	45.5	47.1	48.7

Source: World Bank 2024a

TABLE 14.2 Using managed sanitation services (% of total population)

People using safely managed sanitation services % of population		
	2000	*2022*
Malaysia	76.1	86
The Philippines	45.5	62.7
Thailand	19.9	26.3
Viet Nam	31.7	43.7
South Asia (averages of four nations)	7.6	48.7

Source: World Bank 2024b

However, it is noteworthy that the figures for 'South Asia' improved significantly in the period from just 7.6 per cent of the population using safely managed sanitation services in 2000 to 48.7 per cent (Table 14.2) using safely managed sanitation services in 2022 (World Bank 2024b)

Clearly, drawing the distinction between 'basic' and 'safely managed' sanitation facilities is important, and it leads to vastly different numerical outcomes in terms of overall levels of 'sanitation' for some countries. However, another point to make is that while differences in levels of access to even 'basic' sanitation vary throughout the Asian region, one commonality throughout the countries of the region is the differential between levels of rural and urban access. Table 14.2 illustrates this disparity. It also shows, though, that some countries made substantial progress towards bridging this disparity (see Bangladesh, e.g. where rural levels of sanitation access showed great improvement in the period).

Vietnam: exceeding targets but disparities remain

At a country level, Vietnam made 'dramatic' improvements in access to sanitation facilities during the MDG period. By 2011, for example, Tuyet-Hanh et al. (2016) note that household access to both water and sanitation access improved, with 90 per cent of households having access to a water supply and 77 per cent of households having access to improved sanitation facilities. The authors point out that this saw the 2015 MDG targets met, which were set at 88 and 75 per cent

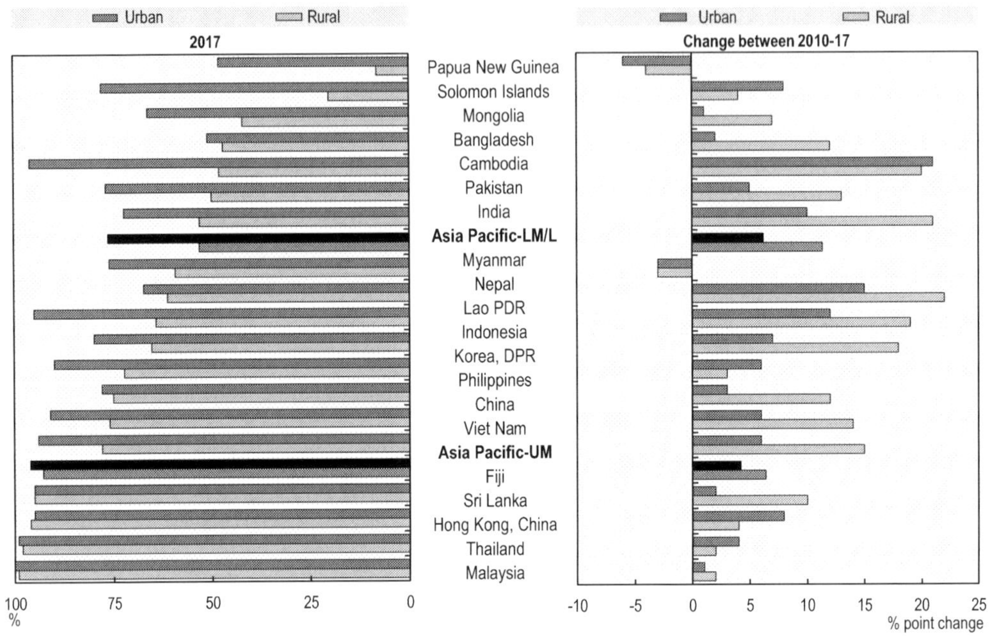

FIGURE 14.1 Access to basic sanitation, 2017 and change between 2010 and 2017

Source: OECD 2020

of households having access to water and sanitation, respectively (Tuyet-Hanh et al. 2016). This certainly represents great progress. However, there were still disparities both on a rural-urban basis and on a regional basis.

For example, in terms of the regional disparity, the authors noted that while the Red River Delta saw 95 per cent of households with access to both improved water and sanitation facilities (as of 2011). In contrast, just 47 per cent of households in the Mekong River Delta had access to both improved water and sanitation facilities (Tuyet-Hanh et al. 2016). Similarly, in terms of the rural-urban disparity, urban households were 'twice as likely to' have access to improved water and sanitation facilities (Tuyet-Hanh et al. 2016).

Thailand and Malaysia: a qualitative distinction

As is evidenced by the data, Thailand and Malaysia had the highest rates of access to 'basic' sanitation in their respective populations such that both were approaching universal access to sanitation by 2015. This was in stark contrast to the selected South Asian countries and significantly higher than the figure for the Philippines (although it may be added that the Philippines figure was still vastly higher than those of the South Asian countries).

Thailand already had a relatively high rate of sanitation access nationwide, with 92.4 per cent of people having access to an improved sanitation facility (World Bank 2024a). However, this rate grew further to more than 97 per cent of people having sanitation access by 2015 (World Bank 2024a), the end of the MDG target period. On the face of it, this represents a significant outcome in that it was approaching universal access to sanitation, the sanitation access goal of the UN.

However there remains the question of how the targets were reached and whether the process and systems for waste management were of acceptable standards. In respect to this, one study identified certain adverse outcomes. The resultant article was pointedly titled 'The Inconvenient Truth: Unsafely Managed Fecal Sludge After Achieving MDG for Decades in Thailand' (Koottatep et al. 2021). The authors summarized the methodology and findings as follows:

> 'Based on data collected from 20 cities located in the north and northeastern regions of Thailand during the period of 2015–2020, the sanitation facilities data on conventional centralized systems and FS management facilities that affect the prevalence of diarrhea and liver infections were analysed and interpreted using statistical and response surface methodology techniques. The findings showed that most of the surveyed cities have achieved the MDG7c targets, but 70% of the FS generated from on-site sanitation systems are still unsafely managed, caused by limited expansion of sewage systems for wastewater collection and conveyance (with inadequate operation and maintenance) as well as the financial constraints, especially in areas outside of urban neighbourhoods.'
>
> *(Koottatep et al. 2021: 1062)*

It must be noted that there are shortcomings to taking figures for access to sanitation at face value. For example, Koottatep et al. (2021: 1063) argue that a focus on merely attaining a headline figure for sanitation access may mean that there is inadequate focus on the 'safe containment, collection, and treatment of FS' (i.e. Fecal Sludge).

It is beyond the scope or ability of this chapter to analyse in any depth the disconnect between headline access figures and the outcomes of poor infrastructure planning. Nevertheless, it is pertinent to simply note that one cannot extrapolate a headline figure to imply ultimate success in health outcomes. As a case in point in Southeast Asia, Malaysia's headline figure for basic sanitation access (95.4 per cent), which was marginally below that of Thailand's in 2015 at the end of the MDG period (World Bank 2024a). However, the achievements of Malaysia in developing the sanitation service sector and corresponding high rates of sanitation access in the population were noted in a 2020 Asian Development Bank Institute Policy Brief Case study of sanitation service delivery in Malaysia. Indeed, that report ultimately concluded that

> Malaysia stands out as a success story in ensuring that the majority of its people enjoy safely managed sanitation. Strong points of its philosophy of integrity are seen at every level of government, as well as good governance, management, and coordination of resource allocation.
>
> *(Narayana and ADBI 2020: 12)*

The Philippines: a complex picture

While the Philippines does have a higher rate of sanitation access than the South Asian countries, it still performs poorly relative to more advanced economies in Southeast Asia, such as Thailand and the Philippines. As UNICEF (2020) pointed out, more than 50 million Filipinos still didn't have access to 'safely managed' sanitation facilities (as of 2020). Again, there is a need to clarify that data for access to 'basic' sanitation facilities may be substantially higher than that regarding access to 'safely managed' sanitation facilities (as defined by the UN).

More pertinent to the end of the MDGs period, though, are earlier observations by UNICEF (2017) regarding the large variation in water and sanitation access in the Philippines based on socioeconomic and regional factors. For example, as of 2017, 91 per cent of the population did have 'access to at least basic water services' (UNICEF 2017). However, UNICEF (2017) made the point that such access is highly variable in regional terms, with the figure for people with access to basic water supply being 100 per cent in some locations but dropping to as low as 62 per cent in others. However, there was a clear correlation between wealth and access to a water supply. For example, of the top 20 per cent of households in terms of household wealth, 99 per cent of those households had access to a 'basic' water supply. In contrast, of the poorest 20 per cent of households, only 80 per cent had access to a 'basic' water supply.

Regarding access to sanitation facilities, there was also a great regional variance. Indeed, access to 'basic' sanitation facilities ranged between 22 and 86 per cent on a regional basis (UNICEF 2017). Furthermore, over six million Filipinos still had no access to any sort of sanitation facility (basic or otherwise) and therefore practiced open defecation (UNICEF 2017). The correlation between open defecation and poorer health outcomes and the spread of related disease is well documented. Clearly, for both water and sanitation access, both regional inequality and wealth inequality remained significant hurdles at the end of the MDG period to achieving the goal of universal access to safe and clean water and sanitation facilities.

The plight of sewer workers: India and Pakistan

While not an issue of sanitation access as such, the plight of sewer workers is an important issue as part of the delivery of sanitation. In South Asia, many sewer workers face danger in performing their work, the pay is low, and they are often marginalized and discriminated against within the broader society. WaterAid (2020) conducted studies into the working conditions of frontline sanitation workers in Bangladesh, India, Pakistan, and Nepal during the COVID-19 pandemic. Those studies highlighted many aspects specifically related to the period of the COVID-19 lockdowns when public fear was greatest. In this respect, the studies noted that attitudes towards sanitation workers generally became worse, largely due to people's fear of the virus and the vulnerability of sanitation to infection (WaterAid 2020).

However, there were also general findings about the nature of sanitation work and outcomes for the frontline sanitation workers. For example, the informal nature of sanitation work left workers highly vulnerable to exploitation. Employment in informal sanitation work was, according to the studies, highest among women, leaving them disproportionately vulnerable to exploitation (WaterAid 2020). However, informal employment was common among sanitation workers regardless of gender. There are multiple implications with such arrangements. Workers employed informally are generally relatively lowly paid, are not covered by insurance, and have no real employment protections. Regarding the pandemic period specifically, the studies found that many worked without personal protective equipment (PPE) (WaterAid), something that placed them at greater risk.

The percentages of sanitation workers employed in an informal capacity varied according to the specific task they were performing. The studies collated data quantifying the nature of the engagement of sanitation workers in India for various types of sanitation work. For waste collectors and cleaners employed in hospitals and quarantine centres (QCs), the study found no informal employment, although 85 per cent of 'cleaners' employed in the hospitals and QCs were employed on a contractual basis, with only 15 per cent being employed as permanent staff (WaterAid 2020). All other categories of frontline sanitation workers had some rate of informal employment, with 100 per cent of both 'waste rag pickers' and 'dry latrine cleaners' being employed informally (WaterAid 2020). Other categories experienced varying rates of informal employment, with the next highest rates of informal employment being 'sweepers' at 38 per cent and 'drain cleaners' at 20 per cent informally employed (Water Aid 2020).

Health risks

Apart from the issues surrounding insecure employment and poor sanitary conditions, there is also a very real risk to some frontline sanitation workers posed by noxious gases and lack of oxygen in confined spaces. For example, one such case in Tamil Nadu, India, Moses died of asphyxiation in a sewer factory (Chhara 2023). Highlighting the correlation between economic vulnerability, insecure employment, and unsafe work conditions, the man's wife, Annamma, was unaware that he even cleaned sewers, as he had told her he worked in a canteen and sometimes worked for daily wages in other jobs. Another man, Umesh Bamaniya, died while 'cleaning a blocked sewer,' a task for which he may earn around 2000 Rupees or around US$24 at the time of writing (Chhara 2023).

The ILO provides a personal account of the working conditions of a sanitation worker in Lahore, Pakistan, Shafique Massih, who is Chair of the Punjab Sanitation Workers Union:

> I am a sewer worker in Lahore, Pakistan. I clear sewer system blockages. Every time I enter a sewer I don't know if I will get out alive. I risk getting cut by blades and broken glass. Getting injured is a normal part of my job. The most frightening thing is the gases that can be released. Some sewer gases can't be assessed from the outside. It's only when you're in and move your feet in the sludge that those gases rise. They can be so toxic that a person can die within seconds.
>
> *(Massih 2023)*

Sewer workers: implications of a rising India

The plight of India's sewer workers may well be something that can be better addressed as India's economic and political power grows for a couple of reasons. The first reason is that with greater economic prosperity, such issues tend to be addressed by the market to an extent. For example, if economic development translates to increased prosperity generally, it may well be that many workers, such as sewer workers exposed to risk and poor working conditions, will have other options. This can't be assumed, of course, but there tends to be a correlation between greater prosperity and greater choice, rather than a simple case of there being no alternate means of income.

The second reason is that commitments to economic and political organizations and groupings may require adherence to certain objectives. For example, India is a member of the G20 and even had the presidency of the organization in 2023. As a member of the G20 and as a past president of the group, India is inherently connected to the organization's explicit and implicit objectives of great inclusivity and equity. As with great economic choice prosperity, organizational imperatives cannot be assumed to be automatically translating to positive changes for sewer workers. However, membership in organizations or groupings sets firm objectives that members must adhere to; this in itself may provide a conduit for change through a form of enlightened self-interest as it were.

Conclusion

In a sense, it could be argued that success in sanitation delivery for all must extend to the safety and dignity of those performing the most difficult and dangerous tasks in their daily duties. At the same time, the analysis of core data across the region also builds a picture of the progress towards universal sanitation access. In both quantitative and qualitative terms, there has been great progress in South and Southeast Asia. At the level of the respective countries in the region, levels of access to sanitation show great variation. In that respect, it is perhaps a positive sign that change is in many cases becoming more incremental with more focus on the nuances of sanitation delivery and quality. This is only the case because of the tremendous strides that have been made in the region in terms of sanitation access and delivery.

Nevertheless, as was apparent in the analysis of certain aspects, great challenges remain. At this juncture then, it is pertinent to acknowledge the inadequacy of the analysis in this chapter of the plight of some sewer workers in certain countries in the region. Their conditions and safety are not peripheral to the ultimate achievement of sanitation for all. Rather, their dignity and safety must be integral and essential to any declaration of ultimate success. Finally, rather than sounding a negative note, what has been achieved to date should be celebrated. At the same time, along with efforts to provide adequate and safe access to sanitation for all, there remains the need to ensure that all workers in the supply of that outcome are given the support and safe working environment they both need and deserve.

Bibliography

Chhara, R. G. (2023) "Manual scavenging: The unending pain of India's sewer workers", *BBC News Gujarati*, 25 October. www.bbc.com/news/world-asia-india-67191131

Koottatep, T., Taweesan, A., Kanabkaewc, T. and Polprasert, C. (2021) "Inconvenient truth: Unsafely managed fecal sludge after achieving MDG for decades in Thailand", *Journal of Water, Sanitation and Hygiene for Development*, 11, 6. http://iwaponline.com/washdev/article-pdf/11/6/1062/966657/washdev0111062.pdf

Massih, S. (2023) "As a sewer worker, I want respect and safer working conditions", *ILO Voices*, 27 April. https://voices.ilo.org/stories/as-a-sewer-worker-i-want-respect-and-safer-working

Narayana, D. and ADBI (Asian Development Bank Institute) (2020) "Integrity in sanitation access and service delivery: A case study of Malaysia's sanitation sector", Policy Brief No. 2020-8, December.

OECD (2020) (data sources) *Health at a Glance: Asia/Pacific 2020: Measuring Progress towards Universal Health Coverage*. www.oecd-ilibrary.org/sites/f6a5d600-en/index.html?itemId=/content/component/f6a5d600-en

Tuyet-Hanh, T. T., Lee, J.-K., Oh, J., Van Minh, H., Lee, C. O., Hoan, L. T., Nam, Y.-S. and Long, T. K. (2016) "Household trends in access to improved water sources and sanitation facilities in Vietnam and associated factors: Findings from the multiple indicator cluster surveys, 2000–2011", *Glob Health Action*, 9. www.ncbi.nlm.nih.gov/pmc/articles/PMC4780076/

UNICEF (2017) *Two Billion People Lack Safe Drinking Water, More Than Twice Lack Safe Sanitation*. www.unicef.org/philippines/press-releases/two-billion-people-lack-safe-drinking-water-more-twice-lack-safe-sanitation

UNICEF (2020) *Sanitation Targets Are Off-Track: DOH, WHO and UNICEF Ask Local Governments to Invest in Sanitation* (Press Release). www.unicef.org/philippines/press-releases/sanitation-targets-are-track-doh-who-and-unicef-ask-local-governments-invest

WaterAid (2020) *Safety and Wellbeing of Sanitation Workers during COVID-19 in South Asia: A Rapid Assessment from Bangladesh, India, Pakistan and Nepal in Lockdown*. https://washmatters.wateraid.org/sites/g/files/jkxoof256/files/safety-and-wellbeing-of-sanitation-workers-during-covid-19-in-south-asia-synthesis-report.pdf

World Bank (2024a) *World Development Indicators 'People Using at Least Basic Sanitation Services'*. https://databank.worldbank.org/reports.aspx?source=2&series=SH.STA.BASS.ZS&country=MYS,PHL,THA,IND,PAK,BGD#

World Bank (2024b) *World Development Indicators: Disease Prevention Coverage and Quality* (extracted selected country and regional data). https://wdi.worldbank.org/table/2.13#

15

INDIA'S G20 PRESIDENCY

Elevating the voice of the 'Global South'

Paul Howard

Introduction

Initially, the G20 'was founded in 1999 after the Asian financial crisis as a forum for the Finance Ministers and Central Bank Governors to discuss global economic and financial issues.' (G20 2023). This focus evolved, though, in the wake of the Global Financial Crisis (2007), such that the G20 became, according to the G20, the 'premier forum for international economic cooperation' (G20 2023). In more recent times, one could argue that the G20 has begun to transform, if not so much in organizational structure, at least in terms of giving a larger voice to the emerging economies of the 'global south.'

Maria Monica Wihardja and Sharon Susan Koshy (2023) presciently observe:

> The trend of middle and emerging powers from the Global South taking the reins of the G20 to fashion a fair and equitable global governance agenda is a welcome sign. But it is equally important that in leadership roles these powers take international and domestic accountability seriously to reflect the ideas that the G20 is founded on.

The point is clear. While leadership of the G20 is an opportunity to allow emerging economies a fairer role, reflective of their collective growing contribution to global GDP, that role needs to incorporate maintenance of the core principles and aims of the G20. Of course, the same case can also be made regarding G20 leadership by developing economies.

In a 2019 article, 'Twenty years of the G20: Has it changed global economic governance?' Suman Bery, Filippo Biondi, and Sybrand Brekelmans argued that:

> The G20 played a key role during the crisis of 2008, but policy coordination has been problematic since. Our review suggests that the G20 Presidencies of the emerging economies have made considerable efforts to shape the agenda toward issues of their interest, but have not always prevailed, notably on issues of global financial governance.

DOI: 10.4324/9781032716244-18

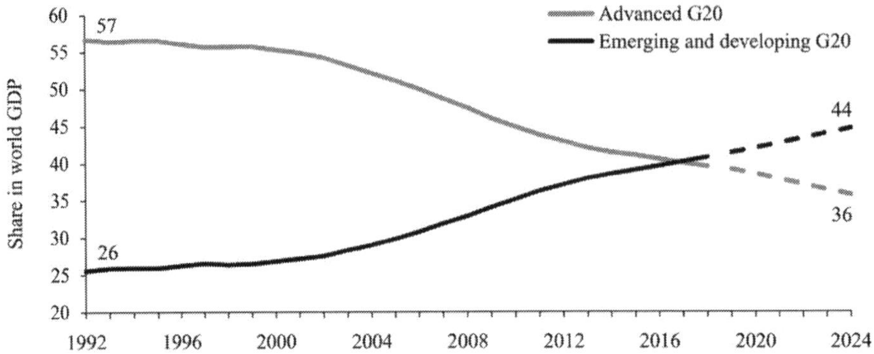

FIGURE 15.1 Emerging and developing economies compared to advanced member nations between 1992 and 2024

Source: Bery, Suman, Biondi, Filippo and Brekelmans, Sybrand, 2019

The authors also note the imminent crossover point at which the 'emerging and developing economies of the G20' would account for a greater share of GDP than the 'advanced' economies of the group (see Figure 15.1).

Notwithstanding the subsequent impact of the pandemic, the trajectory is clear. The collective might of so-called 'emerging' economies in the G20 is not only going to be substantial into the future but that growing proportional economic power will also likely become increasingly influential in terms of the G20's operation and may leverage the collective influence and reach of the major growth economies.

One caveat on that position, though, is that it cannot be assumed that the 'emerging' economies will have collective and aligned aims. Economic and political pragmatism dictates that nations will, for the most part, at least simply act in their own respective interests. At times, that may mean subordinating their immediate interests in favour of longer-term economic and political interests. In either case, though, countries acting in the interests of organizational integrity cannot be assumed.

The very nature of G20 decision-making, built on consensus rather than voting, is an intriguing and not insubstantial element in this regard. How is consensus reached? And is this process truly equitable? These are not questions that can be addressed here, but it is worth at least considering that in evaluating the success of the organization in any given period or indeed, under the presidency of a particular country, such as India's presidency in 2023.

India's year at the G20 Helm: a success?

In assessing the outcomes of the G20 summit in India (2023), the European Parliament simply noted that the collective agreement of the leaders on a final declaration was in itself a 'success' not only for the Indian presidency but also for Indian Prime Minister Modi (European Parliament 2023). This may be true, but 'success' in this sense does not necessarily imply that the best interests and integrity of the G20 are preserved. However, the Director for *OECD* Global Relations and Co-operation, Andreas Schaal (Economic Times 2023a), has similarly described some of the outcomes of India's presidency of the G20 as 'impressive,' specifically pointing to positive developments under India's presidency with respect to aspects including 'SDGs, Digital Public Infrastructure, development, climate finance.' Indian Prime Minister Modi's own assessment of India's presidency focused on the theme of inclusivity (Modi 2023):

> *Inclusive, ambitious, action-oriented, and decisive*—these four words defined our approach as G20 president, and the New Delhi Leaders' Declaration (NDLD), unanimously adopted by all G20 members, is testimony to our commitment to deliver on these principles.
>
> Inclusivity has been at the heart of our presidency. The inclusion of the African Union (AU) as a permanent member of the G20 integrated 55 African nations into the forum, expanding it to encompass 80 per cent of the global population. This proactive stance has fostered a more comprehensive dialogue on global challenges and opportunities.

Counter to these positive assessments, though, Oxfam (2023) provided a strong critique of the G20's performance regarding some major global issues stating that

> The G20 has failed to meet the huge challenges our world faces. They continue to stumble away from taking the bold actions necessary to tackle poverty, inequality, and climate change after an uninspiring and underwhelming Summit in India this weekend.

Following from that assessment, Oxfam (2023) did nevertheless see the ascension of the African Union (AU) to a permanent seat on the organization as an essential step towards greater inclusivity within the organization.

Oxfam's hope for the AU's ascension is that it will help to elevate the G20's performance in areas that impact the global south disproportionately, socially, environmentally, and economically; that is, that the AU will help to drive consensus in the body to directly address such issues as climate change and poverty. Bays (2023) has pointed to the nature of the organization being an impediment to concrete action on issues that are raised.

> The G20 was originally set up as an economic body of finance ministers in 1999. It has no permanent secretariat and there is no one to do checks on how things are being delivered. Since it is a multilateral grouping, change is slow and incremental. That, many experts fear, won't deliver the progress needed to solve the huge problems humanity faces.

Oxfam's criticisms of the G20's past inability to address global issues and Bays' assertion that the body is essentially structurally ill-equipped to tackle those issues, it is worth noting that even if one accepts those criticisms and assertions, such criticisms should not be construed as a direct criticism of India's presidency of the organization. Quite simply, the structural aspects Bays' point to were not, it seems, cultivated by a single year's presidency of the group but were inherited aspects that point more to a need to create structural reform. That, of course, is if one accepts Bay's assertions.

Making a definitive assessment of those structural issues is beyond the focus of this chapter. However, it may be more a point of future consideration for the organization to consider the validity or otherwise of the need for structural change. On balance, though, the inclusion of the AU as a permanent member under India's presidency has, arguably (and as Oxfam has suggested), been a positive development regarding the inclusivity of the group. Consequently, it is worth now giving some specific consideration to the AU's accession.

Enter Africa

The African Union (AU) was admitted as a permanent member of the G20 in September 2023 (Acharya and Singh 2023), marking the end of many years of negotiation. The ascension of the AU can be seen as logical, given its collective potential but also in terms of equity. It has been asserted by proponents of the AU's entry into the G20 that a grouping such as the G20, with such substantial global economic influence, should not function without the input of large parts of the global community. Exactly to what extent Africa benefits from its place in the G20 will become apparent over time.

However, the AU was, as Ruth Namatovu (2023) points out, 'forced to digest the decisions of outsiders, even those on matters that directly impact African nations.' While Namatovu (2023) sees Africa's ascension to the G20 as a positive development, she still points out that Africa as a collective has internal challenges. For example, along with the rising economic stars within the AU, there are also nations suffering coups and general instability, conditions not amenable to promoting economic growth and trade. Namatovu (2023) also notes that 'the continent is engulfed in terrorism and insurgencies that stretch from the Great Lakes and Eastern regions to the Horn of Africa and the Sahel' but ultimately essentially concludes that, despite these issues, Africa's collective voice will have to be heard and acknowledged within the G20. It is worth noting, though, that even as a combined entity, as of 2023, the AU only accounted for 5.07 per cent of global GDP on a purchasing power parity basis (IMF 2023). This compares to the Asia Pacific as a collective accounting for 45.58 per cent of global GDP, with China alone accounting for 18.82 per cent of global GDP (IMF 2023). The ascension of the AU occurred during the latter part of India's presidency, but of course, that does not in and of itself imply that India alone facilitated the entry. However, Prime Minister Modi certainly openly advocated for the AU to be admitted as a permanent member, and this, at another level, highlighted the growing competition between India and China for influence globally, but crucially, among the collective 'global south.'

Godbole (2023) notes that while China was 'supportive of the decision,' the China Institutes of Contemporary International Relations explicitly criticized India for the way that India, in its view, utilized its status as the rotational president of the G20 to engineer the entry and gain greater influence with emerging economies, something that clearly highlighted the China-India rivalry in respect to both the AU and emerging economies more generally.

Outcomes for India

Pant (Global Memo 2023) essentially argues that India's presidency of the G20 was a success in terms of elevating the collective voice of the 'global south' and asserts that India 'underscored its own credentials as a leading player in the global hierarchy, one that is increasingly willing and able to shape global outcomes as opposed to merely being a passive recipient of decisions made by others.' While this is true, there is a new reality that with that increased power, India will be subject to greater scrutiny globally.

A reminder of the often-difficult path to dealing constructively with counterparts was evident in the form of the tense relations between Prime Minister Trudeau of Canada and Prime Minister Modi during the G20 meeting. The tension arose from Trudeau alleging that the Indian government had a role in the assassination in Canada of a prominent Sikh separatist activist (calling for the secession of 'Khalistan') in June 2023 prior to the G20 meeting (Australian Financial

Review [AFR] 2023). As a result, there were severe tensions between the Indian and Canadian delegations and between the two leaders at the meeting.

Much of the commentary relating to the outcomes for India relates to foreign policy and global influence. In terms of domestic outcomes, specifically for the Indian people, commentary is relatively scarce. Pankaj Chaudhary, India's finance minister (The Economic Times 2023a), has asserted that India's presidency of the G20 has benefitted the country in terms of increased foreign investment. Nadadur (2023) has cited the Jaipur Call to Action as a positive outcome for small to medium business enterprises along with the final declaration's 'Financial Inclusion Action Plan.' It is worth noting, though, that this focus on financial inclusivity was reflective of the G20's commitment to achieving the UN's SDGs. It was also a path pursued by Indonesia, and, indeed, the outcome of greater financial inclusion is of great importance for the 'global south' as a whole.

Analysis and conclusion

There is little doubt that in recent years, the G20 has developed to be a far more inclusive institution. The rotating presidency passing from Indonesia to India, and then to Brazil, was of itself a clear signpost of the more prominent role afforded to major emerging economies. This, it can be argued, may in turn translate to greater input from smaller emerging economies globally. As a sidenote, that does not mean to say that the process of great inclusivity in the organization is complete, but the passing of the stewardship of the group to major economies of the 'global south' certainly evidenced a new, broader representation of the interests collectively of the emerging economies. In that regard, the inclusion of the AU as a permanent member of the G20 was an important development. That it occurred under the presidency of India emphasized the rising collective voice of the 'global south.' The ascension of the AU under the presidency of a rising India was both highly symbolic and transformational in terms of the G20's focus.

To evaluate the success or otherwise of India's year of presidency is complex, though. For along with this greater level of the group's inclusivity, there were also challenges. The tensions between India and Canada over the death of a prominent separatist in Canada would always have been problematic for Canada-Indian relations. However, the issue provided unwanted negative media attention for India and Prime Minister Modi during the 2023 G20 summit in New Delhi. Indeed, the issue was undoubtedly amplified by India's position on the world stage because of India's role as the rotational President of the organization. This highlights the path that India must now navigate as a growing power, both economically and in terms of global political influence.

Domestically, the outcomes for India are perhaps more generic, with some hailing the 'final inclusion action plan' as a beneficial economic outcome that works towards addressing economic inequality. On the same theme, at the broader global level, the G20 is an organization built on the notion of consensus, with, at least in principle, the shared goal of creating universal economic benefit. In that sense then, the single biggest achievement of India's presidency was overseeing the ascension of the AU as a permanent member. This was no merely symbolic outcome, bringing as it did the collective voice of African economies firmly into the tent. Overall, on balance, the years of the rotational presidencies of both Indonesia and India have been important for elevating the profile and voice of emerging economies within the G20 consensus process.

Bibliography

Acharya, S. and Singh, S. C. (2023) "G20 admits African Union as permanent member", *Reuters*, 10 September. www.reuters.com/world/g20-admit-african-union-permanent-member-new-delhi-summit-draft-declaration-2023-09-09/

Bays, J. (2023) "Analysis: Does an 'uninspiring' G20 have a future?", *Aljazeera*, 10 September. www.aljazeera.com/news/2023/9/10/analysis-does-an-uninspiring-g20-have-a-future

Bery, S., Biondi, F. and Brekelmans, S. (2019) "Twenty years of the G20: Has it changed global economic governance?", *Russian Journal of Economics*, 5, 4. https://rujec.org/article/49435/

The Economic Times (2023a) *India's G20 Presidency Opens Doors for Global Investment, Sustainable Economic Growth, Says MoS Finance*, 28 October. https://economictimes.indiatimes.com/news/economy/finance/indias-g20-presidency-opens-doors-for-global-investment-sustainable-economic-growth-says-mos-finance/articleshow/104785039.cms?utm_source=contentofinterest&utm_medium=text&utm_campaign=cppst

The Economic Times (2023b) *India's G20 Presidency Was Really Impressive on SDGs, Digital Public Infrastructure: OECD Sherpa*, 26 November. https://economictimes.indiatimes.com/news/india/indias-g20-presidency-was-really-impressive-on-sdgs-digital-public-infrastructure-oecd-sherpa/articleshow/105505020.cms?utm_source=contentofinterest&utm_medium=text&utm_campaign=cppst

European Parliament (2023) *Outcome of the 2023 G20 Summit in New Delhi, India*. www.europarl.europa.eu/RegData/etudes/ATAG/2023/751474/EPRS_ATA(2023)751474_EN.pdf

G20 (2023) *About G20*. www.g20.org/en/about-g20/

Global Financial Crisis (2007) https//en.wikipedia.org

Global Memo by ORF, SWP, ISS, NIIA, and IISS-PKU (2023) *Was the G20 Summit a Turning Point for the Global South?* 14 September. www.cfr.org/councilofcouncils/global-memos/was-g20-summit-turning-point-global-south

IMF (International Monetary Fund) (2023) *GDP Based on PPP, Share of World*. www.imf.org/external/datamapper/PPPSH@WEO/WEOWORLD/AFQ/WHQ/TCD

Modi, N. (2023) "India's G20 presidency heralded a new dawn of multilateralism", *Australia Financial Review*, 30 November. www.afr.com/policy/foreign-affairs/india-s-g20-presidency-heralded-a-new-dawn-of-multilateralism-20231130-p5eo1q

Nadadur, G. (2023) "A lasting legacy of India's G20: Trade opportunities for small businesses", *New Atlanticist*, 3 October. www.atlanticcouncil.org/blogs/new-atlanticist/indias-g20-presidency-increase-small-businesses-gains-from-trade/

Namatovu, R. (2023) "Africa's bargaining chip to the G20", *Wilson Center*. www.wilsoncenter.org/blog-post/africas-bargaining-chip-g20

Oxfam International (2023) *An Underwhelming G20 Skates over the Big Issues of Poverty, Inequality and Climate—Maybe the African Union Can Inject Some Urgency Ahead: Oxfam*, 9 September. www.oxfam.org/en/press-releases/underwhelming-g20-skates-over-big-issues-poverty-inequality-and-climate-maybe

Sevastopulo, D., Foy, H. and Kerr, J. (2023) "Biden raised Canadian Sikh's death with Modi at G20", *AFR (Australian Financial Review)*, 22 September. www.afr.com/policy/foreign-affairs/biden-raised-canadian-sikh-s-death-with-modi-at-g20-20230922-p5e6xb

Wihardja, M. M. and Koshy, S. S. (2023) "Indian and Indonesian G20 presidencies juggle nationalism and global cooperation", *East Asia Forum*, 7 November. www.eastasiaforum.org/2023/11/07/indian-and-indonesian-g20-presidencies-juggle-nationalism-and-global-cooperation/

16

SOUTH ASIA IN THE FIRST QUARTER OF THE 21ST CENTURY

What next?

Moazzem Hossain and Mamun Ahmed

Introduction

South Asian economies, particularly India and Bangladesh, experienced a remarkable economic transformation over the last three decades. This has resulted in a significant reduction in poverty levels in the region. Chapter 2 examined the overall economic performance of four South Asian economies compared with four Southeast Asian economies: Malaysia, Thailand, the Philippines, and Vietnam, with special reference to the impact of COVID-19. In doing so, the concluding chapter attempts to answer the frequently asked question in the literature: is South Asia catching up with the Southeast? Overall, South Asian economies demonstrated steady economic growth, despite some fluctuations, during the last three decades. However, the growth of all the countries was adversely affected by the COVID-19 pandemic, with most countries reporting negative growth. Interestingly, four South Asian countries under consideration, except Sri Lanka, bounced back and showed an even stronger economic growth rate in 2022. Over 2000–2022, the agricultural sector showed moderate growth in South Asian nations, while that of Southeast Asian growth was low. Bangladesh and India demonstrated strong growth performance in the industry and services sectors too among the four South Asian nations. The analysis also indicated that over the last two decades, Asian countries have undergone further structural changes. In particular, the contribution to GDP from the agricultural sector continued to drop in many countries while that of the industry sector showed a slow growth rate. The services sector's contribution to GDP is substantial in both South and Southeast Asian countries.

Considering domestic savings, while major macroeconomic variables of most of the South Asian nations contributed to growth, all Southeast Asian countries experienced a slight reduction in savings. Over the last two decades, all South Asian countries, except Sri Lanka, experienced strong growth in the trade sector; however, with some fluctuations. All countries have demonstrated substantial growth in terms of their integration into the global economy with respect to merchandise trade, merchandise services, and foreign direct investment (FDI) over the last two decades. During the last three decades, the burden of external debt as a percentage of gross national income from various bilateral and multilateral sources has been declining in most of the South and Southeast Asian countries, except Pakistan and Sri Lanka. With

DOI: 10.4324/9781032716244-19

respect to fiscal balance, the exchange rate movements, and the inflation rate, all countries studied provided a mixed bag over the period between 1990 and 2022. The adverse effects of the COVID-19 pandemic and the Russian-Ukrainian war on South and Southeast Asian economies were substantially visible with increasing inflation rates in many countries. Among all the countries studied, Sri Lanka and Pakistan appeared to be struggling most, with highly depreciated currencies, increased debt burdens, and problematic macroeconomic management. A resilient recovery from pandemic- and war-related economic downturns and critical domestic economic mismanagement requires a wide range of policies, including carefully thought-through fiscal and monetary policies.

The general demographic trends and the effects of population growth on economic development in South Asia are matters for concern in the long run. Overall, there has been a declining trend in population growth in South Asia, where the average annual population growth rate during 1995–2005 was 1.8 per cent, over 2005–2015 was 1.3 per cent, and between 2015 and 2022 was 1.0 per cent per annum. A similar trend is seen in Southeast Asia too over the same period. The declining fertility rates in the region are the main reason for the drop in population growth. Rapid urbanization, increased female labour force participation, increased female median age at marriage, and higher cost of raising children, as well as government policies on curbing population growth, have substantially contributed to the declining fertility rates in the region. Among the South Asian nations, Pakistan had the highest annual population growth rate between 1995 and 2022, while Sri Lanka had the lowest population growth. On the other hand, the population density has seen notable growth in all countries in South Asia. In particular, the population density increased by more than 30 per cent in Bangladesh and by 40 per cent in Pakistan over the last 30 years. Although the population density in Southeast Asian countries has also increased, the population density in South Asian countries is higher than in Southeast Asian countries. When considering the population distribution, although the proportion of children in the age group 0–14 years was very high in the early 1990s, this has substantially dropped by 2022, and currently, this age group constitutes the second largest proportion of the total population of each country. On the other hand, the proportion of the 65+ population has increased in all South and Southeast Asian nations, with Sri Lanka having the highest and Pakistan having the lowest in South Asia. The analysis also revealed that the dependency ratio declined for all the countries under consideration except Sri Lanka and Thailand, potentially owing to a higher proportion of the aged population. There have been notable structural changes in labour force participation in all the countries, but labour force participation in the agriculture sector has substantially dropped. However, participation in the service sector has been increasing in all countries. South Asian countries generally have substantially lower female labour force participation compared to Southeast Asian nations.

The Millennium Development Goals (MDGs) and South Asia's ascendancies

The achievements of South and Southeast Asian countries in meeting important targets of the Millennium Development Goals (MDGs) over the period between 2000 and 2015 have been impressive. The achievements of these countries towards satisfactory implementation of the United Nations Sustainable Development Goals (SDGs) by 2030, however, remain slow. In terms of eradicating extreme poverty, all four nations have managed to drastically reduce the proportion of the population below \$1 a day over 1990–2022, and Southeast and East Asian nations are certainly ahead of South Asia. Among the South Asian countries, the performance in

Sri Lanka is outstanding in eradicating extreme poverty before the economic crisis hit in 2022. When considering the achievements in universal primary education and the promotion of gender equality, again, in 2022, Southeast and East Asian nations were ahead and have made strong progress since the early 1990s. As far as child mortality is concerned, all countries under consideration have made significant progress, with Bangladesh, Nepal, India, China, and Thailand recording a greater than 75 per cent reduction in child mortality over 1990–2022. Outstanding performance in reducing maternal mortality rates was observed in India, Nepal, Bangladesh, and Sri Lanka. The region also demonstrated remarkable achievement in reducing the proportion of people without access to safe drinking water by half, reversing the prevalence of HIV/AIDS, and slowing the spread of tuberculosis in some countries. However, the Asia-Pacific region, the world's most populous region, still faces many challenges concerning economic development and human well-being. With increasing poverty and inequality, growing issues about sustainable development, and issues pertaining to external and internal economic stability in the post-pandemic era will continue to pose challenges in their progress towards the SDGs.

The macroeconomic management issues of the four South Asian economies in relation to an open economy trade-dependent framework need promotion. South Asian countries experienced a high to moderate level of inflation during the last three decades, although the pandemic adversely affected the level of inflation in all countries. In South Asia, historically, at least two exchange rate regimes existed between the nations. While all the nations have been governed by pegged (fixed) rates in the past, since the mid-1990s, all the nations have gradually embraced a flexible rate regime. All South Asian countries have seen a substantial level of depreciation in currency against the US$; Pakistan and Sri Lanka have seen the highest level of depreciation, particularly during the post-pandemic period. The trade deficit/surplus of all countries studied has been fluctuating wildly over time, and Pakistan has been having the highest trade deficit in the region. Out of all the nations studied, India has the highest level of debts in US$ terms, followed by Pakistan and Sri Lanka. The debt-service ratios have increased out of proportion for Pakistan and Sri Lanka, particularly after the pandemic. Over the last three decades, the region has made substantial progress on various macroeconomic performances. However, the pandemic and global demand and supply shocks linked to the Russian-Ukrainian war have adversely affected the decades of progress.

The issues pertaining to international trade and economic integration in the region were found to be working well and effective. After a notable drop in global merchandise trade during the global financial crisis in 2008–2009, global trade flows rebounded strongly since 2010. While the economic conditions continued to improve in both developed and developing economies, the recovery of both trade and output proceeded more slowly in developed countries. The trade growth in Asia was mainly driven by the fastest-growing economies in the region, such as China and India. However, a notable reduction in world merchandise trade was again witnessed during the COVID-19 pandemic before making another strong recovery in 2021. Most countries in the region have demonstrated a slower integration with the world economy. The speed of integration has substantially slowed down in the South Asian region during the pandemic, with the slowest integration seen in Bangladesh and Sri Lanka, compared to Southeast Asian countries under consideration. The trade relationships in the region have been dominated by India, with the most notable growth in trade being seen between Bangladesh and India than in any other pair of nations. The trade balance figures revealed that India is in the most advantageous position in the region with trade surpluses with all four neighbours. When considering trade between regions, all South Asian countries studied in this volume demonstrated a trade deficit with both

East Asia and Pacific countries. While India showed a trade deficit with Europe and Central Asia, all other countries experienced a trade surplus. All countries reported a trade surplus with North America and a trade deficit with the Middle East and North African and Sub-Saharan African regions. The inter-regional trade analysis reveals that regional trade within South Asia is substantially low between India and Pakistan.

Agriculture and rural development in the South Asian region have been suffering from climate change and experiencing heat waves in the summer. Cropping contributes more than 80 per cent of value added in agriculture in South Asia, with rice and wheat accounting for more than three-quarters of value added in cropping. Therefore, the increase in food grain production is the major source of agricultural growth in the four countries studied. The food crop volume and productivity experienced a high level of fluctuations during the last several decades. In all countries under consideration, the land under irrigation, land under cereal cultivation, and fertilizer use increased over this period. Sri Lankan agricultural production was adversely impacted by the ban on the import of agrochemicals in April 2021. This resulted in a reduction in major export goods and the import of rice.

The Fourth Industrial Revolution and the role of the private sector are huge issues in terms of policy contrast for developing nations since the period of the post-oil crisis of the early 1970s, the global financial crisis (GFC), and now the COVID-19 pandemic. More importantly, at present, with the UN Agenda 2030 and the role of the private sector, keeping in mind the Fourth Industrial Revolution for the industrial sector has come to the forefront. Thus, it includes the following issues that are relevant: what role does the private sector play under the SDGs 2030 framework? What motivates the private sector actors to engage with the UN 2030 agenda? Learn how sustainability can influence the future of the private sector. Learn about what the UN can do to engage the private sector under the 2030 agenda. Income inequality: what is it, and why does it matter under the 2030 agenda?

The year 2015 was the end of the MDGs launched by the United Nations under the Millennium Declaration 2000. There were eight goals of the MDGs, and the aim was to reduce each, for example, by half by 2015 from the 1990 level. It is now established that in the era of the Third Industrial Revolution, Bangladesh, among the seven member nations of the South Asian Association for Regional Cooperation, has its share of achievements, achieving the majority of the goals under MDGs by 2015. This makes Bangladesh a role model for the developing world in two MDG fronts: improved sanitation access and poverty reduction (Hossain and Islam 2019). It is important to try to investigate industrialization under the framework of the UN 2030 agenda, or SDGs, with 17 goals. In particular, the Goal 17: Partnership. More clearly, what role do private sector actors play as partners under the SDG framework? It is important to remember there is a huge difference in entrepreneurial activities between the SDGs approach and the Conglomerate approach of the miracle nations of East and Southeast Asia (NICs). Now, it is important to investigate what role the private sector plays under the SDG framework. The 2030 Agenda for Sustainable Development is a useful framework for defining a business' place in society, and the SDGs allow companies to identify areas to focus on from 'do not harm' to 'do good' (e.g., GFC and Asian Conglomerate or Winner takes all).

The major aims of India, Bangladesh, and Sri Lanka in joining Thailand and Myanmar (two members of ASEAN) to form a sub-regional group are to expand regional trade with the fastest-growing nations of East Asia and to attract FDI from these nations. As mentioned earlier, through trade reform, a nation expects to achieve two key objectives: to create a market for its exports and to attract foreign investment (Rodrick 1992). In practice, this was the lesson learnt from East Asian experiences. Following the notable success of the Asian tiger development model in the 1980s, Hong Kong, Singapore, South Korea, and Taiwan, most of the East Asian nations embarked on an international trade-based economic development path where China, Malaysia, Thailand, and the Philippines were also commonly known as newly industrialized countries (NICs). The Asian Development Bank took a major role in supporting East Asia. Therefore, these countries demonstrated a high level of openness for inter-regional and intra-regional trade in the South Asian nations. Consequently, the East Asian nations have grown much faster. The only NIC in the South Asian region is India.

It is also evident that the East Asian nations were more successful than South Asian nations in attracting FDI (see Table 16.1). All South Asian countries, except for India, have been able to attract a much lower level of FDI compared to Southeast Asian countries. Japan was the major FDI donor country for Southeast Asian countries in the 1980s and 1990s. This suggests that a stronger sub-regional integration had taken place in the East Asian region.

The introduction of agricultural technology revolutionized South Asian agriculture in the 1960s, 1970s, and 1980s. This was regarded as the 'Green Revolution.' The main aims of the Green Revolution have been to cultivate a huge increase in food grain production (i.e. wheat and rice) with the support of the International Rice Research Institute, based in Manila. One estimate supports that the cropping sub-sectors contribute more than 80 per cent of value added in agriculture in South Asia. Within the cropping category, rice and wheat account for more than 80 per cent of value added in agriculture in South Asia. With the record increase in the production of food grains in the two relatively densely populated nations of South Asia (India and Bangladesh), the region has avoided the major food deficits of the past. The staple food for the four nations of South Asia is rice and wheat; more than 80 per cent of cultivable land produces rice and wheat all year round. All the nations by now produce high-yielding varieties of rice and wheat with intensive cultivation.

The ecological footprint of a country estimates the population's consumption of energy, food, and materials in terms of the area of biologically productive land required to produce those natural resources or absorb corresponding carbon dioxide emissions. Wackernagel and Yount (1998) define the ecological footprint as 'the biologically productive area required to continuously provide resource supplies and absorb wastes of a particular population given prevailing technology' (cited in Metcalfe 2003: 314).

TABLE 16.1 FDI inflows to Southeast and South Asia 1990–2022 (US$ million)

Region	*1990*	*2000*	*2010*	*2022*
Southeast Asia				
Malaysia	2,332.5	3,787.6	10,885.8	14,726.0
The Philippines	530.0	1,487.0	1,070.4	9,199.9
Thailand	2,443.5	3,366.0	14,746.7	10,196.1
Vietnam	180	1,298	8,000	17,900
South Asia				
Bangladesh	3.2	280.4	1,232.3	1,555.4
India	236.7	3,584.2	27,396.9	49,940.3
Pakistan	245.3	308.0	2,022.0	1,339.0
Sri Lanka	43.4	172.9	477.6	898.3

Source: World Bank (2023)

TABLE 16.2 Climate scenarios for Bangladesh in 2030 and 2050

Year	*Sea level rise (cm)*	*Temperature increase (°C)*	*Precipitation fluctuations compared to 1990 (%)*
2030	30	+0.7 in monsoon +1.3 in winter	−3 in winter +11 in monsoon
2050	50	+1.1 in monsoon +1.8 in winter	−37 in winter +28 in monsoon

Source: Metcalfe (2003)

Figure 16.1 presents the ecological footprint of selected developed and developing countries, including South Asian nations. The figures on footprint suggest that overconsumption is more of a major problem for sustainable development than poverty issues. Bangladesh's figure suggests almost four times less of a footprint than the world average. With the dual impact of climate change (sea-level rise in particular) and population growth, Bangladesh, in 2050, will be more vulnerable as a nation. By that time, almost 20 per cent of its 250 million people will likely become climate refugees and will look for livelihoods in the highlands or overseas. Climate scenarios for Bangladesh to 2050 are shown in Table 16.2.

It is true that the extent of achievements the South Asian nations enjoy in growth terms has never been witnessed before. However, in per capita terms, the region remains dismally poor when compared with others (e.g. Southeast Asia and China). Almost 300 million people in development remain elusive to the poor people of these nations, which have been growing at a very high rate by historical standards. Moreover, it remains to be seen what further deterioration of quality of life will take place in South Asian populous nations due to the climate change and its aftermath. The effect of climate change has no bounds.

Hence, it has been demonstrated that, although it is late, climate change is at the top of the agenda of the neighbouring regions of South Asia, Southeast Asia, and China. One may conclude, however, that, while South Asia has been growing on the back of globalization and exports (see earlier chapters) in recent years, it is now a reality that climate change could take away the entire growth opportunity in the future. It is time now the governments of South Asian nations take initiatives, like China and Southeast Asia, and make a comprehensive plan to fight climate change in the years to come.

The UNFCCC Conference of Parties 26 (COP26) was held in Glasgow in the first week of November 2021. The last UN General Assembly (September 2021) covered extensively the agenda for Net Zero Emissions by 2050. The heads of the UN member states discussed this agenda with great optimism. It is no doubt that the Glasgow COP26 has made the agenda of net zero emissions a key issue for the recovery from CO_2 emissions. The COVID-19 pandemic made a huge dent in making progress on the COP26 agenda.

Economists are of the view that, historically, the present OECD nations took almost 200 years to reach the peak, but China and Korea took only 40–50 years and have been continuing to grow with 6 to 7 per cent per year until COVID-19 struck in 2020. Historically, the nations that had experienced industrial revolutions, for example, the second and third, witnessed two world wars during the 20th century, including the Great Depression of the 1930s, and a Global Financial Crisis (GFC) of 2007–2008. With sparing huge economic stimulus packages, the world had ultimately recovered out of these crises within a relatively short period of time.

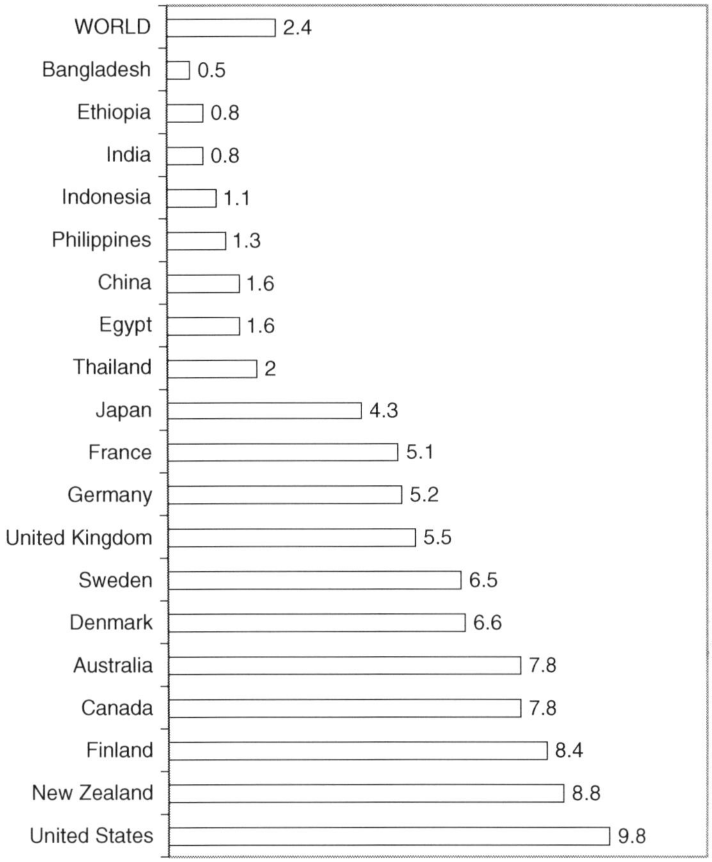

FIGURE 16.1 Ecological footprint of selected developed and developing countries (hectares per capita)

Contrary to that, the pandemic of early 2020 is having catastrophic impacts on global economic prosperity and stability over the last 18 to 22 months, and now it is uncertain again how long the impact of the pandemic will last; in turn, the recovery of growth becomes uncertain too. In the meantime, the Russian-Ukrainian war over the last 18 months has been a major catastrophe for the world, both advanced and developing nations. Moreover, from late 2023, the war between Gaza and Israel has made the political and economic crises have a new dimension in the Middle Eastern nations. On top of these present crises of cost of living and energy (oil and gas), trade contributed to the prices of goods and services at an all-time high. It looks like a new conflict is brewing in the South China Sea on the issue of Taiwan. China and the United States are exchanging fiery words and playing war games in this region at this moment. It is hard to predict what direction water flows in the world and how it changes the course in the Asia-Pacific region.

Historically, on the one hand, post-Second World War Japan and Germany, two defeated forces of the great war, took the lead in pathways to industrialization with the support of the winners, particularly the United States, introducing the Marshall Plan in 1944. On the other hand, the colonies of Asia, Africa, and Latin America at last got freedom from the clutches of centuries-old colonial rulers in the post-Second World War period. Moreover, the NICs of East and Southeast Asia went for growth with a big bang in the 1970s, 1980s, and 1990s with the support of FDI from Japan, Germany, and the United States. Within two decades the NICs hit double-digit growth by the end of the 20th century. This is indeed called prosperity in the modern world during the Third Industrial Revolution (3rd IR).

Bangladesh's ascendancy over Third Industrial Revolution

Big businesses have been talking about Fourth Industrial Revolution in the 21st century, particularly led by the South Asian nations. Let us take Bangladesh into consideration about its socio-economic achievements during the Third Industrial Revolution.

Bangladesh celebrated 50 years of independence in 2021. This nation performed extraordinarily well in economic and social terms between 2000 and 2020. Tables 16.3 and 16.4 show some facts from a recent study and other sources (Hossain et al. 2020; Hossain and Howard 2014). Bangladesh indeed achieved great prosperity between 2000 and 2020. The socio-economic indicators suggest a phenomenal improvement over the last two decades (Tables 16.3 and 16.4). The sanitation facilities with 2012 data show that Bangladesh's position was very impressive compared to India and Pakistan (Hossain and Howard 2014).

It must be acknowledged here that Bangladesh's Vision 2021, launched by PM Sheikh Hasina, has been the beginning of the nation's ascendancy between 2000 and 2021. The Third Industrial Revolution started in more developed nations in the early 1960s, particularly in OECD nations, when the world had witnessed Apollo 11 land on the Moon in 1969. The next story was well

TABLE 16.3 Bangladesh's performance in socio-economic indicators over 2000–2020

Indicators	*2000*	*2020*
GDP (US$ billion)	33	330
Growth rate (%)	5	7.8
Income (P/C US$)	378	2227
Inflation rate (%)	10	6.5
Poverty (head count %) Extreme	25	10
Poverty (head count %)*	44	21
Literacy rate (%)	65	76
Longevity (Years)	60	72

Source: Hossain et al. (2020), *Climate Adaptation for a Sustainable Economy, Lessons from Bangladesh, an Emerging Tiger of Asia*, Nova Publisher NY

TABLE 16.4 Access to sanitation facilities (in %) (Bangladesh, India, and Pakistan compared)

Nations	*2012*
Bangladesh	81
Rural	80
Urban	83
India	53
Pakistan	54

Source: Hossain M and Howard P (2014), The sanitation access to developing Asia: India's performance over 2001 and 2011, *World Journal of Science, Technology and Sustainable Development*, vol. 11, no. 2: 93–101

known about the growth and development of the West and the East Asian countries (NICs) until 2015. For example, Information Highways and Digital revolution had been taking place. Majority nations witnessed Digital Disruption and Digital Divide during the 3rd IR, particularly in less developed nations. Automation of industries made newly industrialized nations enjoy more and more gains in productivity. Labour laws and rules in industrial belts of more developed nations had been relaxed too in 2020 (Hossain and Howard 2014).

The Fourth Industrial Revolution, they say, commenced in 2015. In its fifth year of commencement, the COVID-19 pandemic stopped the 4th IR at a halt all over the world. Instead, now the Green Industrial Revolution (GIR) is the talk of the town all over the world. Why? The IPCCC expert, Woodrow Clark, and co-author Grant Cooke published their work entitled, 'The Green Industrial Revolution: Energy, Engineering and Economics' with Elsevier Press in 2015. They insist,

> [A]s fossil fuels become harder and more expensive to extract (the present condition is a recent example due to Russia and Ukraine war over last one year), and renewable energy becomes simpler and cheaper to generate, people will convert to renewable energy.

This is now happening in about 20 regions in the world, mostly in Asia, where the cost of solar is now less than Liquified Natural Gas (LNG).

According to an Australian professor, '[C]lean hydrogen revolution is a path to prosperity—but it must be powered by renewable energy,' Methews J, from Macquarie University, Sydney. He insists, '[A]s expected, the government will pursue a 'technology not taxes' approach—eschewing policies such as a carbon price in favour of technological solutions to reduce emissions. Developing Australia's fledgling hydrogen industry is a central plank in the Australian plan'—to achieve net zero emission by 2050. The burning question of development literature globally now is about net zero emissions, regardless of developing or developed nations.

Stephen O Grady (2015) published in Griffith University News in July entitled 'World prepares to recommit on climate change.' Grady writes, an International Scientific Conference was held in Paris in July 2015 on 'Our Common Future Under Climate Change.' This four-day conference was the largest forum for the scientific community to come together ahead of the 21st UNFCCC, Conference of the Parties (COP21) in December, and it addressed key issues around climate change in the broader context of global change. Griffith's Associate Professor Moazzem Hossain, who jointly convened a session in the conference on 'Asia on the Frontiers: Projected Implications, Vulnerability and Adaptation' during the conference, reflects on its outcome and implications. This conference was attended by nearly 2000 delegates from almost 100 countries to highlight the cases of adaptation and mitigation and the sustainable development solutions that are in place to address the problems all nation-states now face due to the emission of carbon dioxide and other gases from using non-renewable energy. The conference's main objective was to save the planet from self-destruction before the 21st century ends. Keeping global warming under 2°C to attain the goals of the IPCC's 5th Assessment Report (AR5) with respect to adaptation, mitigation, and sustainable development solutions was the main focus of this objective. Up to 600 oral conference papers and 800 posters dealt with both problems and solutions in this regard. The concluding statement clearly identified the following issues with 'the solution' and 'the problem spaces' (Outcome statement, CFCC15 Scientific Committee chaired by Chris Field, 10 July 2015). Let us mention, first, the issues under the problem space.

The problem space

1. Warming of the climate system is unequivocal. Human activities are to blame for much of the warming to date.
2. Impacts of climate change have affected every continent, from the Equator to the poles and mountains to the coasts. The many kinds of extremes the climate change has contributed to so far are heat waves, heavy rain, wildfires, droughts, and decreased snow and ice.
3. Vulnerability has been exposed due to climate change. Vulnerability is especially daunting where poverty, inequities, lack of infrastructure, and effective governance combine to constrain options.
4. Continued high emissions of heat-trapping gases increase the risk of impacts that are severe, pervasive, and irreversible.
5. If greenhouse gas (GHG) emissions are cut by 40–70 per cent below current levels by 2050, warming can be kept below 2 degrees Celsius at reasonable cost by 2100.
6. Near-term mitigation will determine long-term warming and risks.
7. Investments in adaptation and mitigation can provide a wide range of co-benefits to the nations;
8. Carbon pricing can support the ambitious mitigation goals of the nations.
9. Sustainable economic growth of all nations can be assured by effective implementation of the additional investment required to transition to clean energy.
10. GHG reduction is easier in some sectors than others.

All the issues mentioned earlier were presented in several plenary sessions and numerous large and small parallel sessions, including 800 posters displayed at both venues. One of the keynote speakers of the plenary session was Professor J.E. Stiglitz of Columbia University and a Nobel Laureate in Economics. He emphasized three areas related to the solution space: creating a green economy, introducing cross-border carbon taxes, and creating an environment to find a successful solution in Paris COP21. The closing plenary session was presented by the Chairman of the IPCC, UNFCCC Climate Negotiations Co-chairs, French Minister for Ecology, Sustainable Development and Energy, and French Minister of Foreign Affairs (FM) and International Development. All these top officials will play major parts in COP21 in Paris.

In his concluding remarks, the FM emphasized that the nature of the agreement in COP21 is expected to be based on the Intended Target of Carbon Reductions (INDTCs) or Intended Nationally Determined Contributions (INDCs). For example, China pledged its carbon reduction in terms of 'Carbon Intensity' while in Paris. In other words, China aims to reduce its carbon dioxide per unit of gross domestic product by at least 40 per cent by 2030 from 1990 levels. In addition, the French foreign minister emphasized financing the poor countries to reduce subsidies on fossil fuels, and the need for innovative measures to involve the local authorities, NGOs, and civil society to implement the targets of emission reduction to achieve 2-degree Celsius warming by 2100.

In the closing plenary, Scientific Committee Chair Chris Field summed up the conference with the following words: '[W]e are moving to a post-carbon era, where climate change mitigation and adaptation are combined with other goals to build a sustainable future.' He also noted the deep commitment of scientists to be part of the solution.

Conclusions on 'Net Zero' concept

Well, it was no doubt that Paris in 2015 was where the ball started rolling on the legal binding of countries to take meaningful initiatives on the target of having net zero emission by 2050. More recently, an article published online The Conversation by Ruth Morgan of Australian National University on 12 May 2024 suggests that 'Net Zero' means a 'balance' between carbon emissions and carbon sinks. It was subsequently enshrined in the IPCC's Special Report on the importance of keeping warming under 1.5 degrees, in which 195 member states agreed to get to net zero emissions by 2050 (Morgan 2024). As recent as April 2024, the leaders of the G7 declared their intentions to achieve net zero emissions by 2050. It is indeed the literature on 'Net Zero Emissions by 2050' is inundated since 2015. It is relevant here to mention a few articles on this subject in recent years. Sam et al. (2022), Stern and Valero (2021), Rogelj Joeri and others (2021), and Bataille C. G. F. (2019). Since 2015, there were numerous scientific papers published in journals, internal briefings of country assessments, and other outlets. The interest in this topic can be found as one of the largest over the period of 2015 and 2023. There is no space here to review the selected papers mentioned earlier published in recent years in prestigious journals like Nature Climate Change, Research Policy, ResearchGate, and WILEY WIRES. Having said that, indeed it is the large emitters of the world who have been taking year after year to make reasonable policy measures to achieve 'Net Zero' and having meaningful achievements over the period of almost a decade since the issue was raised in COP15 in Paris. One may ask a legitimate question: 'When would G7 and G20 nations get together in a joint meeting and take reasonable step urgently making "Net Zero" emission (Carbon Emission—Carbon Sink) a reality by 2050?'

Conclusions on emerging issues of Artificial Intelligence (AI)

Finally, another issue is the rapid advancements of Artificial Intelligence (AI), which have sparked concerns about job displacement across various industries. Chapter 13 has dealt with various aspects of AI. However, despite the potential of AI to revolutionize the workforce, there are several reasons why some argue that AI might not take the jobs as quickly as one might think.

The rules and regulations in certain industries, such as aviation and healthcare, exist for safety reasons and pose significant barriers to AI integration. For example, AI systems used in aircraft, air traffic control, and unmanned aerial vehicles must meet stringent safety and reliability standards set by aviation authorities like the Federal Aviation Administration and the European Union Aviation Safety Agency. These systems must undergo extensive testing, simulation, and certification processes to validate their performance in various flight conditions and scenarios. The high stakes involved in aviation safety necessitate a cautious approach to AI integration, which means that while AI could impact the aviation industry and many others, the regulations surrounding this industry are extremely stringent.

Similarly, in the healthcare industry, AI must meet rigorous safety standards to ensure patient safety. Regulators require extensive testing, validation, and certification of AI systems before allowing them to be used in clinical settings. There are concerns about edge cases, such as handling unexpected complications or rare medical conditions, which need to be addressed. Additionally, liability and insurance issues, as well as the need for human oversight and interpretation of AI-generated insights, pose challenges to widespread AI adoption in healthcare.

Another factor that could slow down AI's impact on jobs is the scarcity of computational resources. While companies like OpenAI and Microsoft are investing heavily in building powerful supercomputers to support the development of AI systems, computers will still be a scarce resource. Advanced AI systems, such as Artificial General Intelligence (AGI), are expected to be extremely resource-intensive and expensive to maintain due to the immense computational resources required. As a result, companies and governments are likely to prioritize allocating AGI capabilities to projects with the highest impact, such as space exploration, climate change modelling, and biomedical research. These fields will have priority access to AGI given the potential for transformative discoveries. There are still so many grey areas. Furthermore, AGI is likely to be reserved for the cases where it can readily advance areas that have the most significant economic impact and transformative nature for the society. Governments are also likely to prioritize AGI for cybersecurity defence and strategic intelligence, leaving everyday tasks to more basic systems. AGI will require robust human supervision due to ethical concerns, especially in fields like healthcare, law enforcement, and policy. In these areas, advanced AI will primarily function as an advisor rather than a decision-maker.

Energy scarcity is another bottleneck that could limit AI's impact on jobs. AI systems consume vast amounts of electricity, and as these models become more complex, the demand for servers to process them grows exponentially. For example, in January, ChatGPT consumed roughly as much electricity per month as 26,000 US households, and that's just for inference. As AI models continue to grow and become complex, the energy requirements will become challenging to meet. Last but not least, it's important to remember that humans value human interaction. If AGI becomes readily available for everyone to use, people may not embrace it as enthusiastically as anticipated. There is a growing trend of people revolting against AI, as evidenced by instances of vandalism against autonomous vehicles and backlash against companies using AI for creative tasks. Humans are likely to continue valuing human interaction in certain contexts, such as high-stakes sales interactions, restaurants, and service-oriented industries.

In conclusion, while AI has the potential to transform various industries and automate certain jobs, several factors could slow down its impact. Stringent regulations in industries like aviation and healthcare, the scarcity of computational resources, the need for human supervision in sensitive fields, energy constraints, and the inherent value placed on human interaction all contribute to the limitations of AI adoption. As AI continues to evolve, it is crucial to consider these factors and approach the integration of AI into the workforce with caution and thoughtfulness. While AI will undoubtedly bring about significant changes, it may not replace jobs as quickly or comprehensively as some have predicted (Ahmed 2024).

Bibliography

Ahmed, M. (2024) "The Human Factor: Why Artificial Intelligence (AI) Cannot Replace Everything Yet" a Commentary from Social Media, 26 May.

Bataille, C. G. F. (2019) "Physical and policy pathways to net-zero emissions industry", *WIREs Climate Change*, 11: e633.

Fankhauser, S., Smith, S. M. and others (2022) "The meaning of net zero and how to get it right", *Nature Climate Change*, 12: 15–21.

Hossain, M., Ahmad, Q. K. and Islam, M. M. (eds.) (2020) *Climate Adaptation for a Sustainable Economy: Lessons from Bangladesh, An Emerging Tiger of Asia* (p. 208), NY, USA: Nova Science Publishers.

Hossain, M., Ahmed, Q. K. and Islam, M. M. (eds.) (2023) *Towards a Sustainable Economy: The Case of Bangladesh* (p. 285), UK: Routledge.

Hossain, M., Hales, R. and Sarker, T. (eds.) (2018) *Pathways to a Sustainable Economy in the 21st Century: Bridging the Gap between COP21 Commitments and 2030 Targets of Emission Control* (p. 289), NY, USA: Springer Publishing.
Hossain, M. and Howard, P. (2014) "The sanitation access to developing Asia: India's performance over (2001–2011)", *World Journal of Science, Technology and Sustainable Development*, 11, 2: 93–101.
Hossain, M. and Islam, M. M. (eds.) (2019) *Science and Technology Innovation for a Sustainable Economy* (p. 197), Switzerland: Springer Nature.
Metcalfe (2003) *Long-term Environmental Issues for Bangladesh*, University of New England (UNE), https://rune.une.edu.au
Morgan (2024) *Climate Report 2023*, https://www.morganstanley.com
O'Grady, S. (2015) "World prepares to recommit on climate change", Griffith News, Griffith University, Brisbane.
Rodrick, D. (1992) "The limits of trade policy reform in developing countries", *Journal of Economic Perspectives*, 6, 1: 87–105.
Ruth, M. (2024) Net Zero Emission by 2050 Australian National University, Conversations, May.
Stern, N. and Valero, A. (2021) "Innovation, growth and the transition to net zero emissions", *Research Policy,* 50, 9.
Wackernagel, M. and Yount, J. D. (1998) "The ecological footprint: An indicator of progress toward regional sustainability", *Environmental Monitoring and Assessment*, 51: 511–529. https://doi.org/10.1023/A:1006094904277
World Bank (2023) *World Bank Open Knowledge Repository, World Bank FDI Inflows Data Document*, Washington, DC: World Bank.

17

THE SOUTH ASIAN MONSOON

Moazzem Hossain and Mamun Ahmed

The Arab Spring

The Arab Spring was a series of pro-democracy uprisings that enveloped several largely Muslim countries, including Tunisia, Morocco, Syria, Libya, Egypt, and Bahrain. The events in these nations generally began in the spring of 2011, which led to the name. The Arab Spring was a loosely related group of protests that ultimately resulted in regime changes in countries such as Tunisia, Egypt, and Libya. Not all the movements, however, could be deemed successful—at least the end goal was increased democracy, cultural freedom, and the end of autocracy. In fact, for many countries enveloped by the revolts of the Arab Spring, the period since has been hallmarked by increased instability and oppression. Given the significant impact of the Arab Spring throughout northern Africa and the Middle East, it's easy to forget the series of large-scale political and social movements arguably began with a single act of defiance.

Jasmine revolution: the background

The Arab Spring began in December 2010 when Tunisian street vendor Mohamed Bouazizi set himself on fire to protest the arbitrary seizing of his vegetable stand by police over failure to obtain a permit. Bouazizi's sacrificial act served as a catalyst for the so-called Jasmine Revolution in Tunisia. The street protests that ensued in Tunis, the country's capital, eventually prompted authoritarian president Zine El Abidine Ben Ali to abdicate his position and flee to Saudi Arabia. He had ruled the country with an iron fist for more than 20 years. Activists in other countries in the region were inspired by the regime change in Tunisia—the country's first democratic parliamentary elections were held in October 2011—and began to protest similar authoritarian governments in their own nations.

The participants in these grassroots movements sought increased social freedoms and greater participation in the political process. Notably, this includes the Tahrir Square uprisings in Cairo, Egypt, and similar protests in Bahrain. However, in some cases, these protests morphed into full-scale civil wars, as evidenced in countries such as Libya, Syria, and Yemen.

DOI: 10.4324/9781032716244-20

Why the name 'Arab Spring?'

The name 'Arab Spring' is a reference to the Revolutions of 1848—also known as the 'People's Spring'—when political upheavals swept Europe. Ever since, 'spring' has been used to describe movements towards democracy like Czechoslovakia's 1968 'Prague Spring.' Western media began popularizing the term 'Arab Spring' in 2011.

Arab Spring aftermath

While the uprising in Tunisia led to some improvements in the country from a human rights perspective, not all the nations that witnessed such social and political upheaval in the spring of 2011 changed for the better. Most notably, in Egypt, where early changes arising from the Arab Spring gave many hopes after the ouster of President Hosni Mubarak, authoritarian rule has apparently returned. Following the controversial election of Mohamed Morsi in 2012, a coup led by defence minister Abdel Fattah el-Sisi installed the latter as president in 2013, and he remains in power until today.

In Libya, meanwhile, authoritarian dictator Colonel Muammar Qaddafi was overthrown in October 2011, during a violent civil war, and he was tortured (literally dragged through the streets) and executed by opposition fighters. Video footage of his death was seen by millions online. However, since Qaddafi's downfall, Libya has remained in a state of civil war, and two opposing governments effectively rule separate regions of the country. Libya's civilian population has suffered significantly during the years of political upheaval, with violence in the streets and access to food, resources, and healthcare services severely limited. This has contributed, in part, to the ongoing worldwide refugee crisis, which has seen thousands flee Libya, most often by boat across the Mediterranean Sea, with hopes of new opportunities in Europe.

Similarly, the civil war in Syria that began in the aftermath of the Arab Spring lasted for several years, forcing many to leave the country to seek refuge in Turkey, Greece, and throughout Western Europe. For a time, the militant group ISIS had declared a caliphate—a nation governed by Islamic law—in northeastern Syria. The group executed thousands of people, and many others fled the region in fear of their lives. Yet, although ISIS has largely been defeated in Syria, the regime of long-time dictator Bashar al-Assad remains in power in the country. In addition, the ongoing civil war in Yemen can also be traced to the Arab Spring. The country's infrastructure has suffered significant damage, and the conflict has devolved into tribal warfare. And in Bahrain, peaceful pro-democracy protests in the capital Manama in 2011 and 2012 were violently suppressed by the government of King Hamad bin Isa Al Khalifa. Officially, the country has a constitutional monarchy form of government, but personal freedoms remain limited.

South Asia Monsoon

Sri Lanka

In 1795, the British invaded and captured the island (later they called it Ceylon) and brought for the first time two Sinhalese kingdoms and a Tamil kingdom and made three kingdoms in one country. The Sri Lankan political profile, since its independence from the British on 4 February 1948, is a mixed bag of stability and political adventurism. Among the four countries of this study, it is Sri Lanka that the British left in a sound state in both economic and political terms.

Being an island state, Sri Lanka—the British called it Ceylon—was a jewel in the British Indian crown. Sri Lanka was a home of scenic beauty and paradise in the Indian Ocean. In modern days, however, the paradise is lost due to political adventurism by successive Sri Lankan governments. Following a major government-supported riot during July 1983, several thousand Tamils were killed by Sinhalese mobs. This resulted in Tamil youths taking up arms against the Sri Lankan Sinhalese state and fighting to liberate their Tamil homeland.

After almost 25 years of civil war with the support of China, India, and the United States, the Sri Lankan government managed to end the war with the Tamil rebels surrendering in 2009. However, even after the end of the civil war against Tamils, the successive government failed to find a political solution to the ethnic problem and use that as an election-winning card; the country went into deeper economic crises after COVID-19, a major drop in tourism revenue, and low commodity prices for the major export items, such as tea, has resulted in foreign currency reserves yet to be resolved.

In the meantime, the Tamil insurgency movement intensified in the northern and eastern provinces. There was an attempt by India in 1987 to mediate the Tamil conflict. India sent its troops to northern Jaffna to put down the Tamil uprising. Indian forces were withdrawn in early 1990. The fighting between Tamil separatists and the security forces, including the army, reached a climax in mid-1991. Since 1992, military engagements have been withdrawn by both sides, and attempts are being made to reach a peaceful political solution.

Sri Lanka was put into a great crisis again on May Day in 1993 when a suicide bomber killed President Premadasa in an election rally. In the 1994 election, Chandrika Bandaranaike Kumaratunga, the younger daughter of Solomon and Sirimavo Bandaranaike, swept to power. Chandrika assumed the position of President and made her mother, Sirimavo, Prime Minister. Under the present constitution, the President is both head of state and head of government. Sri Lanka, despite fighting a civil war for the last quarter of a century, has enjoyed democratically elected governments over the last 60 years, unlike Pakistan and Bangladesh. In June 2009, the Sri Lankan government finally won the 26-year civil war against the Tamil Tigers. The separatist movement by the Tamil minority comes to a halt with the Liberation Tigers of Tamil Eelam being thrown out by the Sri Lankan army from their last stronghold.

Two years back, in 2022, Sri Lanka returned to a major crisis. A student-general public unrest over a week or two dislodged President Gotabaya Rajapakse and his brother Mahindra Rajapakse, then sitting prime minister, and both were forced to flee Sri Lanka and took shelter in India. Both have come back to Sri Lanka a few months later with some political deal made with the current President Ranil Wickremesinghe.

Pakistan

Benazir Bhutto became Prime Minister of Pakistan in 1988 but was dismissed by the President on a corruption count in 1990. Nawaz Sharif was voted to power in the next election but was also dismissed by the President in 1993 due to charges of electoral fraud and massive corruption. The Supreme Court restored the government of Nawaz, but he resigned. In the 1993 election, Benazir was swept back into power and was Prime Minister of Pakistan until November 1996, when she was sacked by the President on corruption and incompetency grounds. A general election was held in February 1997 and won by the Muslim League headed by Nawaz Sharif, who once again became Prime Minister of Pakistan. In 2000, Pakistan reverted to military rule by General Pervez Musharraf, who ruled until a general election in 2008, when he was thrown out of power. The Pakistan People's Party (PPP) of the late Benazir Bhutto won the election, and her husband, Asif Ali Zardari, became President (for five years). Since early 2009, President Zardari has become embroiled in a deadly tribal war against Taliban insurgents in Swat Valley, the northwestern province of Pakistan. Benazir Bhutto was assassinated by a Taliban insurgent. Pakistan was once again under military rule for some time.

Finally, there was an election held in 2018, and Imran Khan was elected as Prime Minister until 2024. There was an election held in 2024, and Imran Khan was barred from running in the 2024 election due to corruption charges. The 2024 election results have just been finalized. A coalition government came into power in a controversial outcome of the general election in 2024. The Pakistan Muslim League (PML) of Nawaz Sharif and the Pakistan People's Party formed the government, having the prime minister from the PML and Asif Ali Zardari from the PPP appointed as President in March 2024.

Now in August 2024, Pakistan monsoon engulfed the nation. They too are asking for corruption-free and a society uqual. Pakistan has been suffering from its independence from Britain since 1947. Presently, the immediate former Prime Minister of Pakistan, Imran Khan, is behind bars on a corruption charge, and his supporters now took to the street for his release from custody. It remains to be seen whether Imran Khan, the former Prime Minister is free from prison soon.

Bangladesh

Bangladesh was the part of Pakistan known as East Pakistan in 1947. This eastern province of Pakistan, currently called Bangladesh, severed connection from then West Pakistan out of a nine-month-long bloody liberation war in 1971. It had only 75 million people then. This country now has more than 117 million. Over the last 53 years, the population has increased by more than 43 million. Bangladesh's overwhelming problem is control of population. This vast population has created all sorts of problems for Bangladesh on all fronts: economic, political, and social. Almost 70 per cent of the total population lives in more than 100,000 villages. More than half of them have no land resource except a small homestead. For this huge number of people, the main sources of income are daily wage labour engaged in agriculture, fisheries, forestry, and occasional off-farm work.

Politically, Bangladesh has shown great instability since independence in 1971. The father of independent Bangladesh, Sheikh Mujibur Rahman, was assassinated by some disgruntled soldiers, including his entire family, killed on 15 August 1975. The army and quasi-army ruled the nation from 1975 to 1990. The democratic governments were established in 1991 when Khaleda Zia was elected as Prime Minister until 1996. Sheikh Hasina, the daughter of the father of the nation, was elected as Prime Minister in 1996–2001. Khaleda Zia returned to power once again in 2001–2006 as Prime Minister. There was a caretaker government backed by armed forces that ran the nation for two years from 2006. Sheikh Hasina came again as Prime Minister in the 2008 election and was elected for another four consecutive terms to 2029.

Prime Minister Sheikh Hasina's government fell on 5 August 2024 out of a protest march towards her official residence by students and anti-government opposition supporters in the capital Dhaka. She was immediately resigned and fled Bangladesh for Delhi, India. The US government, according to many (see below), supported protests that overthrew Sheikh Hasina. After three days an interim government was formed, endorsed by the armed forces on 8 August 2024. The interim government, led by Dr. Muhammad Yunus with 21 advisers with the status of having ministerial roles, has been sworn in to run the interim government. Ben Norton discussed the geopolitical reasons for the regime change in *Geopolitical Economy Report*, 2024.

The genesis of social business

Let us see who Dr. Mohammad Yunus is, the chief advisor. He draws from his extensive experience as the founder of Grameen Bank and articulates a vision of business that transcends the traditional profit-maximization model. He argues that this conventional approach has failed to address—and in some cases, exacerbated—societal inequalities and environmental degradation. The concept of social business emerges as a middle ground, a hybrid model that leverages market forces to tackle pressing social issues while maintaining financial sustainability.

At its core, a social business is defined as a non-dividend company designed explicitly to solve a social problem. This model diverges from traditional corporate structures in several key aspects:

1. Primacy of Social Objectives: The raison d'être of a social business is to address a specific social or environmental challenge, rather than to maximize shareholder value.
2. Financial Self-Sustainability: Unlike charities, social businesses are expected to generate sufficient revenue to cover their costs and reinvest in growth.
3. Profit Reinvestment: Any surplus generated is ploughed back into the business to enhance its social impact, rather than being distributed to investors.
4. Market-Driven Solutions: Social businesses operate within the competitive marketplace, utilizing business strategies to achieve their social goals efficiently (Guha and Majumdar 2021).

The Grameen paradigm: microcredit and beyond

Yunus' Grameen Bank serves as the archetypal example of a social business, demonstrating the model's potential to create significant social impact while maintaining financial viability. The bank's microcredit programme, which provides small, collateral-free loans to impoverished individuals—primarily women—has become a global phenomenon, challenging traditional banking norms and empowering millions to escape poverty through entrepreneurship.

The success of Grameen Bank's model is evident in its staggering statistics:

- Monthly loan disbursements of $100 million
- Average loan size of $200
- An astounding 98 per cent repayment rate

These figures not only underscore the financial viability of the model but also highlight its transformative potential. The bank's impact extends beyond mere financial transactions; it has become a catalyst for social change, education, and empowerment (Yunus 2010).

Expanding the social business ecosystem

Yunus' vision extends far beyond microfinance. The book details a plethora of social business initiatives that span various sectors:

- Grameen Telecom: Bringing telecommunication services to rural areas
- Grameen Veolia Water: Providing affordable, clean water to underserved communities
- Grameen Healthcare: A joint venture with Pfizer to establish village clinics

These ventures demonstrate the versatility of the social business model and its applicability across diverse industries and social challenges.

Critiques and challenges

While Yunus presents a compelling case for social business, the model is not without its critics and challenges:

1. Scalability Concerns: Some argue that social businesses may struggle to achieve the scale necessary to address global issues effectively.
2. Regulatory Hurdles: The hybrid nature of social businesses can create legal and regulatory ambiguities, potentially hindering their growth and operation.
3. Measuring Impact: Quantifying the social impact of these enterprises remains a complex task, making it difficult to assess their true efficacy.
4. Balancing Act: Maintaining the delicate equilibrium between social objectives and financial sustainability can be challenging, particularly in competitive markets.

The road ahead: implications for global capitalism

Yunus' concept of social business represents more than just a new organizational structure; it challenges the very foundations of modern capitalism. By demonstrating that businesses can successfully pursue social objectives without sacrificing financial viability, Yunus opens the door to a reimagining of the role of business with underclass society and economic progress.

The implications of this paradigm shift are profound:

1. Redefining Success: It encourages a broader definition of business success, one that encompasses social and environmental metrics alongside financial performance.
2. Cross-Sector Collaboration: The model promotes increased co-operation between businesses, governments, and non-profit organizations, fostering innovative solutions to complex social problems.
3. Education and Entrepreneurship: By emphasizing the potential for business to drive social change, it could inspire a new generation of socially conscious entrepreneurs.
4. Policy Implications: Governments may need to adapt regulatory frameworks to accommodate and encourage the growth of social businesses. Yunus and Weber (2010).

Conclusion: a call for action

'Building Social Business' is more than a theoretical treatise; it is a clarion call for a fundamental re-evaluation of our economic systems. Yunus challenges readers—be they entrepreneurs, policymakers, or citizens—to envision a world where business acumen is harnessed not just for profit, but for the betterment of the low-income section of society.

As we grapple with unprecedented global challenges, from climate change to income inequality, Yunus' vision of social business offers a beacon of hope. It suggests that with creativity, commitment, and a willingness to challenge entrenched paradigms, we can forge an economic system that serves both the bottom line and the greater good.

In an era marked by growing disillusionment with traditional capitalist models, 'Building Social Business' provides a roadmap for a more equitable and sustainable future. It is an essential read for anyone interested in the intersection of business, social impact, and systemic change—a guidebook for those daring to reimagine the very foundations of global economic order.

References

The *Geopolitical Economy Report* (2024), based at the University of Michigan, USA, ran the following commentaries about Sheikh Hasina's fall from power in Bangladesh over the first half of August 2024. These are mentioned as follows:

- Overthrow of Sheikh Hasina
- US military base on St. Martin Island, Bangladesh?
- Bangladesh-China relations
- US pressure to join Quad
- Russia warned about colour revolution in Bangladesh
- Was Hasina's undelivered resignation speech fabricated?
- Hasina: 'White man' demanded military base in Bay of Bengal
- Hasina: USA 'can overthrow the government in any country'
- US-backed 1975 coup against Sheikh Mujib
- US support for protests in Bangladesh
- NED funding for Bangladeshi opposition
- NED funding for opposition media outlet Netra News
- Historical context: Partition, India, Pakistan, 1971 liberation war
- Reasons for protest
- US-backed colour revolutions
- US State Department pressure on Bangladesh
- Bangladesh Nationalist Party (BNP), Jamaat-e-Islam, & extremism
- The forecast of Golam Maula Rony on student movement, Bangla TV

Bangla is a TV News and Program Based satellite TV station based in Bangladesh.

Ghua, S. and Majumdar, S. (2021) *The Search of Business Models in Social Entrepreneurships: Concepts and Cases*, Springer.

Hoyel, J. A. (2016) "A matter of framing: Explaining the failure of post-Islamist social movements in the Arab spring", *Domes: Digest of Middle East Studies*, 25, 2: 186–209.

Yunus, M. (2010) Wikipedia, https://en.wikipedia.org

Yunus, M. (2017) *A World of Three Zero: Zero Poverty, Zero Unemployment, and Zero Net Carbon*, Public Affairs.

Yunus, M. and Weber, K. (2010) *Building Social Business That Serves Humanities: Most Pressing Needs*, ReadHowYouWant.

INDEX

Note: Page numbers in *italics* indicate a figure and page numbers in **bold** indicate a table on the corresponding page.

Bandaranaike, S. 16, 17, 186

Kolibri 360 GmbH
Ferdinand-Jühlke-Straße 7
99095 Erfurt, Deutschland
produktsicherheit@kolibri360.de